BEER

BEER

MICHAEL JACKSON

DORLING KINDERSLEY
LONDON • NEW YORK • SYDNEY • MOSCOW
www.dk.com

A DORLING KINDERSLEY BOOK
www.dk.com

Senior Editor Sharon Lucas

Senior Art Editor Tim Scott

Editor Anna Milner

Designer Kevin Ryan

Managing Editor Francis Ritter

Managing Art Editor Derek Coombes

DTP Designer Sonia Charbonnier

Picture Researcher Jamie Robinson

Production Controller Ruth Charlton

Research Co-ordinator/Beer Stylist Owen D. L. Barstow

Research Team
Lara Brekenfeld, Casey Clogg, Bryan Harrell,
Andree Hoffmann, Britta Vetter, Silke Wagler

First published in Great Britain in 1998
by Dorling Kindersley Limited,
9 Henrietta Streeet, London WC2E 8PS

2 4 6 8 10 9 7 5 3 1

A CIP catalogue record for this book
is available from the British Library.

ISBN 0-7513-0591-X

Reproduced by Colourscan, Singapore
Printed and bound in England by
Butler & Tanner, Frome, Somerset

CONTENTS

So popular is beer, the world's best-selling alcoholic drink, that it
is often taken for granted. Yet scientific analysis shows that a glass of beer
has within it as many aromas and flavours as a fine wine. Not everyone
understands this, but an increasing number of people do.

In an age when more people work at computers than at coalfaces, the thirst
for beer is changing. There is a trend towards drinking less but tasting more.
This is shown in the choice of beers now available: from the aromatic, original
golden Pilsner lager of Bohemia, in the Czech Republic, to the tart, hazy wheat
beers of Bavaria and Berlin; the rich, orange or chocolate-coloured Trappist brews
of Belgium to the soothing, copper ales of Britain; the dry, black stouts of Dublin
and Cork to the hoppy, amber specialities of Boston and New York – great
flavours from the Sierras and Seattle to Sapporo and Sydney. You might be
surprised at how many of these beers are finding their way into your local
supermarket or speciality drinks store. To track down those that remain elusive,
a beer-hunting vacation might be in order.

Nor every beer tastes best by the pint. Many of the beers in this book
have their own goblets and chalices, saucers and flutes. Never before has such
an array been photographed and described. How should these brews taste?
Why do they taste that way? How, and when, might they best be enjoyed?
I have spent years probing the mysteries of malt, the magic of hops.
Now you can see for yourself, and learn, in the pages that follow. Come with
me, inhale the aromas, taste the flavours. Enjoy the world's greatest beers...
and some of the most unusual.

WHAT MAKES A GREAT BEER?

THE TESTS OF A GOOD BEER ARE AROMA, flavour, and finish. Beer is made principally from malted grains, water, hops, and yeast, but there is no point in using those ingredients if the result tastes like fizzy, alcoholic water. As a great beer is enjoyed, its character seems to develop, so that the drinker notices new flavours and finds constant interest. Nor do the flavours suddenly vanish. The drinker looks forward to the beer; enjoys the experience; and is left with a lingering memory of it. A good beer delivers the style it promises on the label. If it says Pilsner, wheat beer, ale, or stout, it truly has the characteristics of that style. A great beer combines aroma, flavour, finish, and fidelity to style with its own distinctive balance and memorability.

WHERE BEER IS GROWN

JUST AS WINE IS GROWN, so is beer; the first as fruit (usually grapes), the second as grain (most often barley). Both drinks are as old as civilization, and each assumed its present form in central and western Europe. While temperate but warm countries grow grapes and make wine, cooler nations cultivate cereal grains and brew beer. The Czechs, Austrians, Germans, Belgians, Dutch, Danes, British, and Irish shaped modern beer. In the US, the northeast, middle America, and recently the northwest have been especially influential. The principal flavouring in beer, the hop plant, also grows in cool climates. These are the countries and regions with the great, established brewing traditions.

BARLEY-GROWING REGIONS

Just as grapes may be used as a dessert fruit, raisins, or juice, as well as in wine, so barley is the basis for many foods and drinks (*page 12*). Like the wine-maker, the brewer has special requirements. The barley that is used to make beer must have plump, fine-skinned kernels, rich in starch and low in protein.

While grapes are crushed to release their juices, grain is malted to render it soluble. This is a process of soaking, sprouting, and drying. After this, the grain is called malt.

Fine malting barley is cultivated mainly in the northern hemisphere, notably in a band just to the north of latitudes 45 and 55. Famous growing areas include Moravia and Bohemia in the Czech Republic; the Munich Basin of Bavaria, Germany; Denmark; the English regions of Wessex, East Anglia, and the Vale of York; the Scottish Borders and the Moray Firth; the American midwestern states (especially North Dakota) and the northwest; and Saskatchewan and Alberta in Canada.

In the southern hemisphere, similar latitudes cultivate malting barley, although on a lesser scale. Regions include the Australian states of Victoria and South Australia; the southernmost part of New Zealand; Cape Province, South Africa; and a belt across South America, from Uruguay to Peru and Ecuador.

Just as different regions champion their own grapes, so there are debates among brewers as to the merits of "continental" barleys, such as those grown in Bavaria, as against the "maritime" examples of

A field of beer
Not only does barley like temperate, cool, dry climates, it also enjoys well-drained, fertile chalk, loam, or light clay soils. It is vulnerable to wind, and is most easily harvested in flat countryside.

Denmark or the UK. Continental barleys are said to provide a sweet, nutty flavour, while maritime varieties have a clean, "sea-breeze" character. There are also two races of malting barley, distinguished by the number of rows of grain in each ear. Two-row barleys impart a soft, sweet flavour, favoured by lager brewers. Six-row barleys create a firmer, crisper, huskier character, championed by some ale producers. The time of sowing is also a factor. Winter barleys, sown in October or November, tend to be husky. Spring varieties, sown in March, are softer and sweeter.

HOP-GROWING REGIONS

Just as cool, temperate zones favour barley, so it is with hops, though this plant prefers a more clay soil. The most important hop regions are in the Pacific northwest US, Canada, the South of England, the borders of Belgium and France, Bavaria, Bohemia in the Czech Republic, and Slovenia. In Poland, the Lublin region is growing in importance. The Ukraine grows hops around Zitomir, west of Kiev; China in the Xinjiang region. In the southern hemisphere, Tasmania and Nelson, on the South Island of New Zealand, are key hop-growing regions.

THE FIRST BREWERS

Fruit falling from trees and fermenting on the ground introduced humans to wine, but this drink lacks nutrition. When humans ceased to be nomadic hunters and gatherers and began to farm the land, they grew grains. The world's first known recipe, on clay tablets, appears to be a method for making beer. This drink was very nutritious, but it also had the side-effect of making the Mesopotamians feel "exhilarated, wonderful, and blissful". A magical incantation in runic scripts seems to have given us the word *alu*, in the longest-

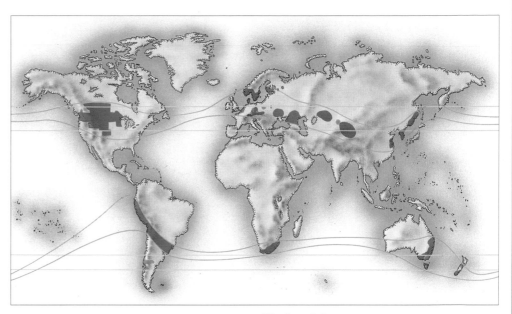

The beer belt
In both the northern and southern hemispheres, the broad belt in which malting barley is cultivated also accommodates the narrower band of hop-growing areas. Cool weather suits both crops.

surviving pagan civilizations in Europe; this is probably the root of the word ale in the English language.

Did the first civilizations live by beer alone, or did they discover the drink while trying to convert grain into edible gruel, porridge, or bread? Beer and bread, both made from grain and water, and fermented with yeast, are companion products. There is a theory that the words bread and brewed have the same origin.

THE SPREAD OF BEER

Recent work on Mesopotamian pictograms shows that this ancient civilization already distinguished between early forms of barley and wheat. As the cultivation of grain radiated from the earliest sites in the Middle East, the Africans in the hotter south began to brew beer from sorghum and millet; the Asian peoples in the wetter east grew rice, leading to the production of sake in China and Japan (sake, being made from a grain, is really a variant on beer, rather than being rice "wine"); the Slavic people to the north cultivated rye, often on poorer soil, making a version of beer called *kvass*; and the Western Europeans stayed with wheat and barley.

Barley's husk acts as a natural filter in brewing. Barley is less easy to work with in baking – barley breads are hard and crumbly. Conversely, wheat makes good bread but is less kind to the brewer. Lacking a full husk, it tends to clog the brewing vessels. As the knowledge of brewing developed, barley gradually became the predominant grain used in beer, while wheat was favoured in the bakery. In Germany, especially, beer is often known as liquid bread.

Until recent years, wheat beers were regarded as being old-fashioned, but in the last two decades they have become newly appreciated for their thirst-quenching qualities and fresh flavours.

The first straw
The golden straw (left) is from Mesopotamia, and is believed to have been used by a high priestess for the consumption of beer. It is in the Museum of the University of Pennsylvania. The Mesopotamian plaque (above) shows beakers of beer taken from an amphora. The gazelle is reminiscent of the goat used today to symbolize Bock beers.

Going with the grain
Stylish symbols survive today, and the image of grain stands high on this tap-handle from the Widmer brewery, of Portland, Oregon. Its fruity Hefeweizen beer is a northwestern favourite.

THE GRAINS

MANY BEERS ARE MADE entirely from grains that have been malted. Because malt provides natural enzymes needed in fermentation, it always accounts for at least 60 per cent of the grain. Even in wheat beers, malted barley usually accounts for at least 40 per cent of the grain. The barley imparts a softness and cleanness, and its husks form a natural filter in the brewhouse. Wheat imparts a quenching fruitiness and can contribute to a good head on the beer. Malted or rolled oatmeal, often used in stouts, makes for silky smoothness. Rye, usually malted, adds a spicy tastiness. Cooked rice lightens the beer, as does corn (maize), which can leave an unpleasant "chicken feed" flavour, typically in cheap lagers.

MALTING

The building in which raw grain is transformed into malt is called a maltings. A number of breweries have their own maltings, but more often the two are separate enterprises.

The process of malting is simple in principle, but control of moisture and temperature is critical if the grain is neither to over-germinate nor die. The soaking of the grains, known as steeping, takes 36–48 hours, with frequent changing of the water. The most traditional method of sprouting is to spread the grains in a layer about 12 cm (5 in) deep on a stone floor for up to a week. During this time, the grains are constantly raked and turned to aereate them and stop them tangling. Floor malting is very labour-intensive, but some brewers feel it produces an especially clean, dry flavour. Other, more widely used techniques employ ventilated, tray-like boxes or rotating drums. The drying of the grains stops the sprouting before it goes too far. It also influences the colour and flavour of the malt, and of the finished beer.

DRYING THE GRAIN

If the grains are dried gently, their appearance will change little and they will make a beer with a naturally golden colour and a cracker-like or cookieish malt flavour. There are many other ways of heating the grains, and several combinations of these treatments. For example, if the grains are stewed, their colour will turn amber-red, and this will be reflected in the colour of the beer, which will have a nutty or toffee flavour. If the grain is toasted, that flavour will emerge in the beer, along with a brown colour. Malts roasted in drums (like those used for coffee beans) produce black brews such as stouts, sometimes with flavours reminiscent of espresso.

Some beers are made with only one style of malt, for a simple clarity of flavour. Other beers contain as many as eight or nine malts or grains, providing a layered complexity of aromas, flavours, and textures.

OTHER SUGARS

Under the German Beer Purity Law, which also applies in Norway, only malted grains are permitted in brewing. This excludes the use of rice, corn, and other sugars. Honey and maple syrup are both old ingredients that have been revived in recent years in the English-speaking world. Traces of their flavours will remain in the beer, but the use of these sugars also changes the natural biochemistry of fermentation; that, too, influences flavour. Lactose, a sugar extracted from milk, is used in some stouts.

Some Belgian beers gain rummy flavours from candy sugar (similar to the crystal sugar sometimes served with coffee). Dark, "luscious" sugars are also used by some British brewers for this purpose. More refined sugars may be used to boost alcohol content, lighten the body of the beer, or reduce costs. Australian lagers sometimes have a cane-sugar flavour and thinness.

Hand-made beer
Malted grains in sacks at a famous regional brewery in England. In small breweries, "hand-made" beer involves a lot of hoisting and carrying. At bigger breweries, malt is less visible: delivered in bulk into silos, and fed through closed systems.

GRAINS AND MALTS, COLOURS AND FLAVOURS

THE MALT OF THE CITY

The ways in which grains are malted are sometimes named after the city where a particular process was first used. These malts in turn give their names to styles of beer. In Britain, beer styles such as mild and pale ale also give their names to types of malt. Terms such as amber malt and black malt are also used. Each represents a slightly different process.

MALTS BY FLAVOUR

Some malts are known by the aromas or flavours they impart. Good examples are aromatic malt, which is toasted; honey malt, made by a long, gentle stewing process; and biscuit malt, which is very lightly roasted. Variations in the way the grains are sprouted, the levels of moisture before kilning, and the sequences of drying or drum-roasting make for endless permutations.

OTHER GRAINS

Originally, brewers used the grains that were most readily available to them. Today, they increasingly choose grains to add distinctiveness to their beers. Rye, traditionally baked into bread, is an example. Rye beers, such as the Slavic *kvass*, are made using bread that has been steeped and fermented. In recent years, though, rye has also begun to feature in variations on wheat beer.

Munich malt
Dark Munich malt has rounded, full flavours with some dryish coffee character. It is an influential ingredient in a dark, Dunkel-style lager.

Vienna malt
The Austrian capital was once known for bronze lagers made with this type of malt. Today, it is typically used in toffeeish Märzen or Oktoberfest lagers.

Pilsner malt
The palest malt originates from Pilsen, in Bohemia. It was floor-malted from Moravian barley. Soft, clean, and sweetish, the style is used in golden lagers.

PILSNER MALT MADE FOR THE WORLD'S FIRST GOLDEN BEER.

Chocolate malt
This style contains no chocolate, but mimics the flavour. Kilned at high temperatures without being burned, it is used in dark beers, such as porters and stouts.

Crystal malt
Used in reddish-brown ales. Stewing creates a crystal-sugar, nutty character. There are many variations, and the term caramel malt is also used.

Smoked malt
Once, all malt was dried by wind, sun, or fire. Beechwood fires are still used in Bamberg, Germany. Several brewers also use malt dried over peat fires.

ALASKAN SMOKED PORTER USES MALT DRIED OVER A FIRE OF ALDER TWIGS.

Rye
As in bread, or some North American whiskeys, rye adds a grainy, bittersweet, subtle spiciness to beer. This flavour can be reminiscent of mint.

Wheat
The refreshing flavours of wheat beers have given them a revival in recent years, especially in Germany and Belgium. The Belgian style is also spiced.

Oats
The notion of oats as a sustaining, nutritious grain led to their use in stouts, especially after World War II. Oats have been used since Neolithic times.

MACLAY OAT MALT STOUT IS A PRESENT-DAY EXAMPLE FROM SCOTLAND.

ROASTED BARLEY... MODEST STRENGTH

Dark it may be, but the bottled Guinness sold in Ireland and the UK has only 4.2abv (3.4w).

COLOUR, BODY, AND STRENGTH

Contrary to popular belief, darker beers are not necessarily fuller in body or stronger in alcohol. There is no connection between colour, fullness, and potency. Colour derives from the malt used. Dark malts do not always create body, and their colour has nothing whatever to do with alcohol.

BIG BEER... PILSNER MALT

An innocent-looking golden beer, but Belzebuth has a devilish 15.0abv (12.0w).

THE HOPS

THE HOP IS A CLIMBING PLANT, most closely related to cannabis, and both plants are members of the botanical order that includes the nettle, mulberry, and elm. Hop shoots were known to the ancients as a salad (similar to bean sprouts), and are still served in this way in growing regions. The part used to aromatize and flavour beer is the resiny cone. Hops may be the plant referred to in relation to "strong drink" in the Jewish Talmud, but firm evidence of their use in beer is much later. The first undisputed reference is from the Benedictine Sister Hildegarde (1098–1179), the abbess of Rupertsberg, in Germany. The hop was to become the dominant flavouring in beer, perhaps because it is also a good preservative.

PROCESSING THE HOP

Once picked, the hop cone will, like a flower, shrivel within hours unless it is dried and pressed. It is dried in a kiln, known as an oast, and, in the most traditional method, pressed into tall sacks called pockets. Some brewers feel that this method causes the least abrasion to the resins and essential oils that impart aroma, flavour, and dryness to beer. They also like to see the leaf shape and quality of their chosen variety. Others prefer the modern technique in which the hop is compacted into a tiny, cylindrical pellet and vacuum-packed in foil, like coffee. This method has the benefit of protecting the hop from oxidation. In addition to whole hops in these two forms, hop extract (like a green jam) and hop oils are also used in beer.

HOP VARIETIES

Those hop varieties with resins high in certain acids are used primarily to give the beer dryness or bitterness, to balance the sweetness of the malt. Varieties high in certain essential oils are employed to impart flavour and, especially, aroma. The latter are known as noble or elegant hops. Just as wine-makers usually champion the grapes of their own region, and may even deride other varieties, so brewers can occasionally be dismissive of other countries' hops.

The hop varieties with international reputations for fine aromas and flavours are mainly grown in Europe and North America. The traditional European hops tend towards a herbal delicacy, while those varieties grown in the US, whether originally imported or locally bred, are more scented, piney, and zesty. In recent years, some brewers have experimented by making beers with only one variety of hop. Most beers employ several, and sometimes as many as eight or nine, for balance and complexity. The hops may be added at several stages of the brewing process, sometimes in different blends at each point, variously for aroma, flavour, and bitterness.

Flowery beer
Sunflowers add colour to this hop garden in the German Hallertau region. The hop shoots begin to grow in early spring; by late August or September the vine will be up to 5 m (20 ft) tall, and heavy with aromatic cones.

Locally farmed
The Harveys brewery, in Sussex, England, takes a pride in using hops from its own county's tiny output, as well as those from across the line in Kent. The name of the farm is chalked on the bin where each pocket is stored.

CLASSIC HOP VARIETIES...AROMAS AND FLAVOURS

CONTINENTAL EUROPE

Poland has its cedary Lublin hops, grown to the west of that town, and Slovenia its Styrians, with a hint of orange skin, but the most famous variety grown in continental Europe is the Saaz, taking its name from the German rendition of Žatec, the famous hop-growing town in the northwest of Bohemia. A wide range of hops are grown in Bavaria and the south of Germany, among which perhaps the most famous is the Hallertau Mittelfrüh.

Hallertau Mittelfrüh
This aroma hop is famously delicate and flowery, perhaps with a suggestion of lemon grass. Hallertau is the region of cultivation, north of Munich, Bavaria.

Saaz
Sometimes known as the Saazer, or Bohemian Red. This most famous of all aroma hops is cleansing and fresh, with suggestions of camomile or gorse.

THE SAAZ AROMA, WITH A TOUCH OF STYRIANS, IS EVIDENT IN BELGIAN DUVEL.

BRITAIN

Britain's hop-growing areas, primarily in East Kent, the Weald, Worcester, and Hereford, are relatively small, but have their own range of distinct hop varieties, from the quinine-like Challenger to the junipery Progress to the geranial Target. A new variety is the dwarf First Gold, which has a suggestion of tangerines. The most famous English hops, both named after the growers who propagated them, are Golding and Fuggle.

Golding
A family of varieties from Canterbury, and dating from 1790. The prized version is the Canterbury, or East Kent, Golding. A lemony, pithy, cedary, earthy aroma hop.

Fuggle
Noticed in 1861, in Horsmonden, Kent. Propagated in 1875, by Richard Fuggle. A bittering and aroma hop. Soft, with complex, resiny, aniseedy, almost tropical notes.

THE FUGGLES AROMA AND FLAVOUR IS VERY EVIDENT IN SUFFOLK STRONG ALE.

NORTH AMERICA

The US is one of the world's largest growers of hops, especially in the Pacific northwest: the Willamette Valley of Oregon, the Yakima Valley of Washington State, and the Snake River Valley of Idaho. Hops are also grown across the Canadian border: in British Columbia around Chilliwack and Kamloops. North America grows European varieties of hops, but also breeds its own, from the piney, flavoursome Chinook to the freshly woody, bitter Nugget.

Mount Hood
Released in 1989, and bred in Oregon from seedlings of the Hallertau-Hersbruck hop. A flowery and herbal aroma hop, with hints of elderberry, apple, sage, oregano, and mint.

Cascade
Widely used example of the floral, leafy piney, zesty, citrussy American aroma hop. Powerfully aromatic and scenty. Released in 1972. Its parents include the Fuggle.

ANCHOR LIBERTY ALE IS SOMETHING OF A TRIBUTE TO THE CASCADE HOP.

HOW THE HOP PROVIDES FLAVOUR

Between 250 and 300 natural chemical compounds in beer arise from the essential oils in the hop. Several influential compounds present in the hop are in a group of liquid hydrocarbons called terpenes. One is called pinene; another is limonene, which also occurs in citrus fruits; a third is selinene, which occurs in celery; a fourth is myrcene, which is found in bay leaves. Some of these compounds are also found in lavender, spearmint, and nutmeg. When a panel of specialists in fragrances and flavours was invited to nose 15 varieties of hop at Oregon State University, they arrived at more than 50 comparisons, ranging from anise, basil, and cedar to tobacco, violets, and wet hay. A study at Coors' brewery used 60 herbs as comparisons, dividing aroma hops into spicy, minty, piney, floral, and citric groups.

ADDITIONAL FLAVOURINGS

IN THE DAYS WHEN MAKERS of drinks did not have the technical knowledge to achieve clean aromas and tastes, they used flavourings to cover defects. Long after techniques improved, the flavourings remained as part of the balance of some drinks. This is true of beers (whether the flavouring is the hop, or the other ingredients shown on these pages), vermouths (which are wines with herbs, spices, and fruits), all liqueurs, gins, flavoured vodkas, some brandies (with nut or fruit essences), and spiced rums. More conventional wines, brandies, whiskies, rums, and tequilas balance the flavours of their raw materials with tannins and vanilla notes from the casks in which they are aged.

HERBS, SPICES, AND FRUITS

The Mesopotamians, the earliest known brewers, used "sweet" materials in their beers, but did not record which. Some experts feel this referred simply to the sweetness of malt, but others believe honey, dates, or figs may have been added. This would have been a very early precedent for today's fruit beers.

Pottery shards 4,000 years old, bearing traces of barley and oats, but also honey, heather, and herbs such as meadowsweet (*Spiraea ulmaria*) and royal fern (*Osmunda regalis*) were found on the Scottish island of Rhum. Home brewing of heather ale has never totally vanished from the Scottish islands, especially Orkney.

There are some suggestions that the Romans knew of northern Europeans using heather and bog myrtle (*Myrica gale*). By the 1100s, Sister Hildegarde was mentioning myrtle berries, ash leaves, and hops. By the 1200s, bog myrtle, wild rosemary (*Ledum palustre*), and the daisy-like yarrow (*Achillea millefolium*) were typical ingredients in Germany. They were used in a pre-mixed blend of flavours known as grug, or gruit.

In the 1300s, the records of the Archbishop of Cologne mentioned those ingredients but also more exotic items, such as aniseed, caraway, and ginger. To protect the trade in these spices, hops were at times banned, but sometimes the opposite was true. The Bavarian Beer Purity Law in the 1500s, for example, insisted upon hops as the only flavouring in beer.

Coriander is a traditional flavouring in Belgian beers. Another is grains of paradise (*Aframomum melegueta*), a peppery-tasting seed native to West Africa, introduced during colonial times. The use of Curaçao oranges may date from the same era. The Spanish are Europe's principal growers of licorice, which historically was often used in stouts by British and American brewers. The custom survived vestigially on both sides of the Atlantic until the 1970s. A decade later, the revival of interest in speciality beers was bringing back such exotic flavourings.

PINE TIPS

Pine tips add hoppy, medicinal flavours to the Scottish ale Alba (*page 38*). Birch beer has been made in the US in soft-drink and alcoholic versions. American root beer fits into the former tradition.

Sweet and dry
The small, dryish cherries that grow around Brussels make a perfect foil for the lambic *beers of the region. The Boston Beer Company* (left) *makes a sweeter interpretation.*

REVIVING THE RANGE OF FLAVOURS

HERBS

The term herb is usually applied to a green plant or leaf. Coriander leaf (sometimes known as *cilantro*, or Chinese parsley) features on the label of the peppery, citric-tasting, Umbel Ale, from the Nethergate brewery of Clare, in Suffolk, England. (An umbel is a flower cluster.) Camomile was used in England in the 1700s, and is employed by several American breweries today. It imparts a flowery, lemon-grass flavour to a Belgian-style white beer, Wits' End, made by the Great Lakes Brewing Company of Cleveland, Ohio. Clover is an unusual ingredient, but gives aroma and herbal sweetness to the Winter Vorst ale from the Grolsch brewery, in The Netherlands.

Coriander leaf
In the same family as fennel and European anise, coriander is usually grown in the east Mediterranean.

Camomile
This daisy-like flower is most commonly used in vermouths and teas, and often as a tonic.

Clover
Its aromas and flavours are also found in whiskies made on the clovery hillsides of Scotland.

WINTER VORST ...A SEASONAL BEER FROM GROLSCH.

SPICES

This term is usually applied to woody plants, barks, or seeds. Grains of paradise are widely used in Belgium, and were extensively employed in Britain in the 1700s and 1800s. They impart a peppery dryness to Southampton Saison, from Long Island. Cinnamon was used in England and Wales as early as the 1300s. It is employed in some porters and widely used in old and winter ales (typically with spices like nutmeg and cloves) in Britain and especially the US. A less common use is in Belgian-style white beers, typically the sherbety Steendonk. The same style of beer almost always uses coriander seeds, along with Curaçao orange peels.

Grains of paradise
This seed, also known as guinea pepper, is also used to give aromatic dryness and assertiveness to some gins.

Cinnamon
This tree bark, grown especially in Sri Lanka, has been used in drinks since ancient Egyptian times.

Coriander seeds
Aromatic, spicy, sweetish, and sometimes orangey, these seeds are also used in gins and vinegars.

HOEGAARDEN IS THE CLASSIC EXAMPLE OF A BELGIAN WHITE BEER.

FRUITS

A drink based on fruit is a wine; a beverage fermented from grain is a beer, even if fruit is added later. In beers of this type, the fruit is primarily a flavouring, even though it contributes sugars that aid fermentation. Technically, a berry is a fruit. Juniper berries are the classic example of such an ingredient in beer, having been used since at least the 1300s. These berries have dry, aromatic flavours, not too much sugar, and good preservative qualities. Damsons and the Belgian type of small cherry are good for colour and flavour, with a stone to add almondy dryness. The American fashion for peach "schnapps" encouraged some brewers of *lambic* beers to use this sweet fruit.

The damson
Of Middle Eastern origin. Like the sloe (as used in gin), it is close to the "frontier" between plums and cherries.

The peach
Originally associated with Persia. Peach "schnapps", like cherry "brandy", is a sweet liqueur, not a spirit.

The cherry
Best for beer are the "sour", or acidic, varieties, like the kriek of Belgium, the morello, and the maraschino.

NEW GLARUS USES CHERRIES FROM BRUSSELS, WISCONSIN.

OTHER FLAVOURS

Many unlikely-sounding ingredients have been used in beer. In the 1700s, cockerels, often soaked in Madeira, were used, perhaps to provide nutrition for the yeast, but also as a flavouring. Some domestic brewers continued to add meat well into the 20th century. In 1996, the Boston Beer Company made a Cock Ale in this way. At the same time, some brewers began to use non-narcotic hemp. By comparison, beers made with chocolate or coffee seem quite conventional. Brewers in the southwest US have in recent years used sagebrush and even chillis, the latter sometimes remaining as a pod in the bottle.

Coffee
The fashions for good espresso and great beer met in the city of Seattle, Washington in the late 1990s.

Chilli
Spice or fruit? It is New Mexico's state vegetable. Chilli beers are hot in more than one sense.

Chocolate
The real thing is sometimes used, but its flavour can be mimicked by "chocolate" malt.

YOUNG'S OF LONDON MAKE A STOUT FOR CHOCOHOLICS.

WATER AND YEAST

JUST AS WATER IS THE BIGGEST constituent of wine (in the form of rainfall that becomes juice in the grape), so it is basic to beer. Grain takes far smaller amounts of water from the soil, so the brewer has to provide some assistance. He (or she) runs water through the malted and milled grains in order to make a solution of their fermentable sugars. This solution is then boiled with hops, and sometimes other flavourings, and fermented by the addition of yeast. It could be argued that neither water nor yeast is an ingredient of beer. Water is a medium; yeast is an agent of fermentation. Yet each has its own influence on the character of the finished product.

"OUR OWN SPRING"

In the days before motorized transport, almost all beer was produced locally, and brewers had to make do with whatever quality of water was available. It was when steam power made it possible to produce beer in far larger volume, and transport it by train to a much wider market, that water became an issue. A brewer planning to expand on an industrial scale would choose a location where there was a guaranteed source of water that was "clean", but also in an inexhaustible, year-round volume of a consistent quality. The best possible source would be a spring or deep well near or inside the premises. The mineral content of the water would be determined by the geological strata from which it rose.

DRAUGHT BASS
BUILDS BODILY STRENGTH
BREWED SOLELY FROM

MALT. That gives you nourishment. Sustains you through a hard day's work.

HOPS. They've tonic powers, they give you energy and vigour, put life into you when you're tired out.

BURTON WATER. Famous for its purity.

GREAT STUFF

HOW TASTE IS AFFECTED

The first golden lager was made in Bohemia, at Pilsen, where the water is low in minerals and the beer soft-tasting. The first pale ales were brewed in England, at Burton, where the water is high in calcium sulphate; calcium reduces haze and sulphate enhances hop flavours. Porters and stouts became famous in London, then Dublin, cities with chloride and carbonate water that made for fuller and grainier flavours respectively. In each instance, the water helped shape the beer.

Pure draught
The internationally-known Bass brewery is in Burton. Malt, hops, and specifically Burton water are the selling points in this 1950s' poster.

Budweis...
This famous brewing city in Bohemia has as its symbol a fountain, in a statue of Samson.

...and its lager
Budvar has a softness enhanced by water from its own wells 300 m (984 ft) deep. The Budweis brewery dates from 1895, though beer has been made in the town since the 1200s.

Burton...
The water-tower is salient in this townscape of the Burton breweries.

...and its ale
A calcium sulphate aroma is typical in Marston's famous Burton ales.

Dublin...
Water from the mountains was once held in a cistern at the gates of the city.

...and its stout
Carbonates favour the dark colours and grainy flavours of dry stouts.

THE MAGIC MICRO-ORGANISM

Yeast is a microscopic plant, a member of the fungus family. It exists in the atmosphere and is invisible to the naked eye. When it encounters sugar, it converts it into alcohol and acid, a process called fermentation.

Early brewers made solutions of grain, water, and flavourings, then witnessed them turn by apparent magic into beer. They were unaware of the existence of yeast. This method of spontaneous fermentation by wild yeasts that are airborne or resident in the brewery is still used by producers of *lambic* beers in Belgium. Beers made in this way usually taste very acidic and winey.

CONTROLLED FERMENTATION

When a brew ferments in an open vessel, it warms and develops a foam head that grows and can overflow. By catching the foam, comprising millions of yeast cells, and adding it to the next batch, medieval brewers learned how to achieve a consistent fermentation. This "top-fermentation" technique is still used to make most wheat beers and all true ales, porters, and stouts. It typically produces complex, fruity flavours.

In summer, the atmosphere was so alive with wild yeasts that beer making became uncontrollable. Brewers would make a final batch of the season in spring, store it in a cool cellar for the summer, and re-start in autumn. Brewers in Bavaria, who stored their beer in icy caves in the Alps, learned that the cold made the yeast "hide" at the bottom of the brew. Bottom-fermented beer is known as lager (meaning "store" in German), and typically has a clean, rounded taste.

Recovering the yeast
The yeasty foam overflows...and is recaptured at the Unertl wheat beer brewery in Bavaria. The equipment is shiningly modern and purpose-built, but the method hardly differs from medieval times.

WILD FERMENTATION (LAMBIC)

Spontaneous fermentation has only survived in a handful of tiny breweries around the town of Lembeek, in Belgium, but these make some of the world's most distinctive beers. A brew is made, then left overnight in an open vessel in the attic of the brewery, with open windows or shutters. The wild yeast settles on the beer and begins the fermentation. In the morning, the brew is decanted into wooden casks, in which further yeasts may be resident. The yeasts include a semi-wild type called Brettanomyces, which can add "hop-sack" aromas.

TOP-FERMENTATION (WHEAT BEERS)

Two distinct types of top-fermentation give emphatic flavours and aromas to German styles of wheat beer. The *Berliner Weisse* type has a blend of conventional yeast and a lactic culture, imparting a sharp acidity. The south German types use their own family of yeasts, which often impart banana, bubble-gum, and clove flavours to the beer. These derive especially from natural compounds called *guaiacols*. Some British and American brewers of wheat beers use more conventional ale or lager yeasts.

TOP FERMENTATION (ALES, PORTERS, STOUTS)

Fermentation originally took place at ambient temperatures, as refrigeration had not been invented. These would have been winter temperatures in the traditional brewing nations. With today's sophisticated temperature controls, top-fermentation is normally kept at 15–30°C (59–86°F), followed by a short maturation period at 10–13°C (50–55°F). This type of fermentation can create restrained orangey, strawberryish, or dessert apple aromas and flavours, and sometimes butterscotch, arising from the compound diacetyl.

BOTTOM FERMENTATION (LAGER)

This technique may have been practised earlier, but lager-brewers did not begin to understand how it worked until the 1830s. Knowledge improved with Pasteur's studies on yeasts in the 1860s, but a pure culture single cell was not finally identified under a microscope until the 1880s, at the Carlsberg brewery. This work, and the development of refrigeration, were essential to methodical brewing. A lager fermentation classically takes place at 5–9°C (41–48°F), followed by maturation close to 0°C (32°F).

Geuze Boon
This classic from Lembeek itself is a blend of lambic *beers. It has a typical rhubarb acidity, imparted by a sequence of wild fermentations for a period of up to three years.*

Schneider Weisse
Among widely available South German wheat beers, Schneider Weisse is a good example of the fruity, bubble-gum, clovey style. The yeast and fermentation are carefully monitored to maintain this.

St-Ambroise Pale Ale
This renowned Canadian ale has an orangey aroma and flavour arising from a famous ale yeast associated with the Ringwood brewery of Hampshire, England. The yeast was earlier used by now-defunct breweries in Yorkshire.

Spaten Oktoberfestbier
Beers from the pioneering lager brewery of Spaten typically have a creamy, "new-mown hay" aroma that is typical of very traditional bottom-fermenting styles.

MAKING BEER

Brewing is an agricultural industry. Whether the brewing takes place in a farmhouse or what appears to be a factory, malted grains are made into an infusion or decoction, boiled with hops, and fermented. For the visitor, these processes are easiest to see, and follow, in breweries with open vessels. Often, these are local or regional breweries built in Victorian times, where even the newer brewing vessels may be more than 50 years old. Some modern breweries have outdoor fermentation and lagering vessels, in clusters known as "tank farms". These can mislead passers-by into thinking that a brewery is a chemical works, but even in the most high-tech of breweries there is no such thing as "chemical beer".

THE MASH

Anyone who has ever made coffee in a filter will find the first stage in the brewhouse familiar. At its simplest, the malted grains are ground in a mill, then put into a vessel with warm water. The grains soak and infuse in the water for an hour or two. Then the false bottom of the vessel is opened so that the infusion can run through a filter-like base. What emerges, like the coffee, is a solution of malt in water; this is known as sweet wort.

As with most stages of beer-making, this process, called mashing, can be varied in many ways to achieve different characteristics in the finished product. These variations are often decided in advance, according to the type of beer being made that day, but they may also be fine-tuned by the brewer on the day if the mash is not developing quite as planned. Despite everyone's best efforts, there might be slight variations in the character of the malt, and the weather may be influencing the water temperature.

TIMES AND TEMPERATURES

The chief variables throughout beer-making are times and temperatures, and the different regimes of mashing are a good example of that. Lower temperatures release sugars that are fermentable, higher ones liberate unfermentable sugars, making for more body in the beer but less alcohol. Temperatures can be increased, often in several steps, by adding more hot water or by using a vessel with a heated jacket.

A more complex system, often used by traditionalist lager brewers in the Czech Republic and Germany, involves moving proportions of the mash to a second vessel, boiling them, then blending them back. This is known as a decoction: single, double, or triple, depending upon how many times it is performed. Decoction-mashed lagers often have a malt character that is especially aromatic, rich, and soft.

VISITING A BREWERY

No one should miss the chance to visit a traditional brewery and enjoy, first-hand, the hot, steamy brewhouse with its heady aromas of sweet wort and infusing hops.

Lid is raised to release heat and steam.

The mash is over
Spent grains lie in this drained mash tun at St Feuillien, a Belgian brewery making malty but spicy, flavoursome, abbey-style beers.

Copper tun
Traditionally, the mash was ready when the steam cleared and the brewer could see his reflection in the wort.

Running off
Watching the run-off enables the brewer to check clarity and the even spread of filtration. Each tap is connected to a different part of the filter bed.

The gift of hops
Hops are added to the brew-kettle. In this instance, pressed "blossom" or "leaf" hops are being used, as opposed to pellets or the jam-like extract.

THE BREW

The simplest brewhouse layout has two principal vessels. One is the mash tun, (this is called the mash tub in the US), where the infusion of grains is made. The other is the brew-kettle, where this infusion is boiled with the hops. The second of these two processes is the actual act of brewing. This usually takes about 90 minutes, though some breweries do it for an hour, and occasional strong beers can demand several hours.

The main function of the boil is to introduce into the sweet wort the aromas and flavours of the hops. It also sterilizes the brew, killing any unwanted micro-organisms in the wort; to some extent concentrates it, by evaporation; and clarifies it, by coagulating proteins. Most brew-kettles are heated by steam coils, but some sit over gas or oil burners. The latter, "direct-flame", system creates hot spots in the kettle, making for some caramelization of the malt sugars and perhaps imparting slightly toffeeish flavours to the beer. This older system is sometimes known as "fire-brewing", and some brewers feel that it makes for a more satisfying flavour.

Even in large breweries, the hops are often added by hand. Because the hop is a condiment, it is used in small amounts, like the salt or pepper in a stew. Very small variations in the quantities of hops greatly affect the aroma, flavour, and bitterness of the beer. Hops are added in kilos, pounds, or even ounces; malt in tonnes.

THE ART OF HOPPING

Some beers are made with only one addition of hops, but most have more. Brewers, especially in Germany, sometimes refer to these additions as "gifts"; the hops are "given" to the beer as though they were a present. Many master brewers have a love affair with hops, and would like to use more, but are afraid of making their beers too assertive for the consumer. Hops do not contribute alcohol to the beer, but they do make for powerful aromas and flavours.

Varieties of hop intended to impart dryness or bitterness are added early in the boil. Some brewers have a second addition in mid-boil, to add flavour. Most have a "gift" around the end of the boil to accentuate aroma. This "late hopping" is done with especially aromatic varieties.

When the brewing is completed, the hop leaves and protein sediment may be removed by centrifugal force. Another method is to run the brewed wort through a strainer, known in Britain as a hop-back, in the US as a hop-jack. Some brewers add more hops to form a bed in the strainer, causing more aromatic hop oils to be added to the filtering wort. Additional aroma hops may even be placed, sometimes in a muslin sack like a bouquet garni, in the maturation vessel. In Britain, especially, this "dry-hopping" may go into the cask that matures in the pub cellar.

FERMENTATION AND MATURATION

Advertisements sometimes talk of beer being "fully brewed" or "slow brewed". All beer is fully brewed, and this does not happen slowly. The ads are really referring to fermentation or maturation, usually the latter. Typically, fermentation takes only three or four days, or at most a week, in the case of wheat beers, ales, porters, and stouts, the styles made with "top" yeasts. In most instances, they also mature in a matter of days or weeks. (A notable exception would be beers that have a living yeast in the bottle, where a slower evolution might continue for some years.)

Scarcely more time is given these days to many lager beers, though the very finest, especially in Germany and the Czech Republic, still have the best part of two weeks' fermentation and several months' maturation. The odd very strong lager might approach a year in the making, but that is unusual. The only style of beer that customarily takes more than a year is the old type of Belgian *lambic*.

The oldest techniques of fermentation and maturation use wooden vessels, and some traditionalist brewers still prefer open fermenters to closed ones (despite the risk of contamination by wild yeasts). Top-fermenting beers develop more of their characteristic fruity flavours in such vessels. Even those brewers who use closed vessels sometimes admit that good flavours can be purged, and maturation be uneven, if their vessels are built too tall.

The meeting of flavours
The green of the dry, herbal-tasting hops mixes into the amber of sweet barley wort.

Open fermenter
The inverted funnel in the middle of this open fermentation vessel is an overflow for the removal of the yeasty head. This is known as "skimming".

Lagering vessels
Lagering means cold storage, or maturation. The traditional wooden lagering vessels have largely been replaced by stainless steel ones, such as these.

TASTING BEER

ALL GOOD BEER TASTES of malted grains and hops, and a truly clean lager of little else. Good ales have both of those elements but also some fruitiness from the use of top-fermenting yeasts. Good porters and stouts have chocolatey or espresso-like flavours from the roasted malts used. Good wheat beers are tart and refreshing. But whatever the profile of the beer, if a brew is offered as a lager or ale, porter, stout, or wheat beer, it should live up to the style. If it is a good beer, the flavours will not only be appropriate but also in an interesting balance and combination. This is the meaning of "complexity". A beer with this quality seems to offer further aromas and flavours every time the glass is raised.

HOW TO APPRECIATE AROMA AND FLAVOUR

LOOK

SWIRL

SNIFF

SIP

The pleasures of all food and drink are experienced with the eyes as well as the nose and palate. Clarity is an issue in most, but not all, types of beer. Colour certainly is, and the greatest beers often have colours that are distinctive, subtle, complex, and appetizingly attractive.

A gentle swirl disturbs the beer enough to help release its aromatic compounds. This level of study might best be pursued at home, as serious swirling might easily be thought pretentious when conducted in a bar or restaurant.

Whether the drinker sniffs or not, much of what we think we taste is actually experienced through our potent and evocative sense of smell. In the finest beers, the appetizing aromas are a hugely significant element of the pleasure they impart.

Let the beer lap over the tongue. Sweet flavours (malt for example) may be more obvious at the front of the tongue; salt (as in the water) at the front sides, fruity acidity farther back at the sides; while hop bitterness is best detected at the back.

JUDGING BEERS

Enjoyment of great beer does not demand some special tasting talent. All it requires is an open mind, an interest in beer, and a keenness to find aromas and flavours without fear of mockery.

TASTING CONDITIONS: Choose a naturally lit room for better evaluation of colour. Music can be a distraction. Avoid cigarette smoke, cooking smells, or perfumes. For judging purposes, the beers should all be sampled in the same type of glass. A large, clear wine-glass is ideal, with some curvature to showcase the aroma.

BEER TEMPERATURE: The serving temperatures indicated for each beer in this book are those at which each may be most enjoyable. They are merely suggestions, and do not always accord with the brewers' own guidelines. If, rather than being enjoyed as a drink, the beer is being judged, the aromas and flavours will express themselves most fully at room temperature.

ORDER OF BEERS: Start with the beers expected to be lightest in intensity of flavour, and work upwards, especially if they are in several styles.

HOW MANY BEERS?: Even five or six beers can confuse the palate, and 10 or a dozen are more than enough. In order fully to taste the beer, the bitterness must be sensed at the back of the mouth. Beer-tasters therefore tend to swallow at least some of the fluid, and are less exhaustive in spitting than wine judges. As alcohol is ingested, the faculties become less acute.

SCORE-SHEETS: In a formal tasting, for a beer or wine club, or class, a score-sheet is a handy aide-mémoire. A simple system is to have scores for: fidelity to style (if it is labelled as a Pilsner, wheat beer, or ale, is it a good example?); appearance (head formation, colour, and perhaps clarity); aroma (pleasant, appetizing, complex, true to style?); palate (the same criteria); and finish (does it develop late flavour, or simply vanish without saying "goodbye"?).

BETWEEN BEERS: Plain bread, crackers, or matzos will clear the palate. Avoid anything with its own flavours, such as salty pretzels, and butter or cheese, because their greasiness will flatten the beer. A neutral-tasting, still, bottled water, generously provided, is the best option.

A LEXICON OF FLAVOURS AND AROMAS

MANY AROMAS AND FLAVOURS in beer have more than one origin. Explanations of some typical flavours are given below. Tasters often express flavours in terms of "aroma metaphors" that refer to other drinks and foods.

ACIDITY: An appetizing acidity, sometimes lemony, comes from hops. A fruity acidity derives from the yeast in fermentation, especially in ales and even more so in *Berliner Weisse*, Belgian *lambic* styles, and Flemish brown and red ales.

APPLES: A fresh, delicate, pleasant, dessert-apple character arises from the fermentation process in some English ales, famously Marston's. A more astringent, green-apple taste can arise from insufficient maturation.

BANANAS: Very appropriate in some South German wheat beers.

BITTERNESS: Sounds negative, but it is positive. "Good" bitterness comes from the hop. It is present to varying degrees in all beers, and especially appropriate in a British bitter. Robust bitterness, as in Anchor Liberty Ale, is appetizing. Astringency is not.

BODY: Not actually a taste, but a sensation of texture or "mouth feel", ranging from thin to firm to syrupy. Thinness may mean a beer has been very fully fermented, perhaps to create a light, quenching character. Firm, textured, or grainy beers may have been mashed at high temperatures to create some unfermentable sugars. Syrupy ones have been made from a high density of malts, possibly with some holding back of fermentation.

BUBBLE-GUM: Very appropriate in some South German wheat beers. Arises from compounds called guaiacols created in fermentation.

BURNT: Pleasant burnt flavours arise from highly-kilned barley or malt in some stouts. Burnt plastic,

deriving from excessive phenol, is a defect caused by yeast problems.

BUTTERSCOTCH: Very appropriate in certain British ales, especially some from the north of England and Scotland. Unpleasant in lagers. This flavour derives from a compound called diacetyl created in fermentation.

CARAMEL: Most often a malt characteristic, though brewers do sometimes also add caramel itself. A malty caramel character is positive in restrained form in many types of beer. Too much can be overwhelming.

CEDARY: A hop character.

CHOCOLATEY: A malt character in some brown ales, porters, and stouts. Typically arising from chocolate malt (*page 13*).

CLOVES: Very appropriate in some South German wheat beers. Arises from phenols created in fermentation.

COFFEEISH: A malt character in some dark lagers, brown ales, porters, and stouts.

COOKIE-LIKE: Typical character of pale malt. Suggests a fresh beer with a good malt character.

EARTHY: Typical character of traditional English hops. Positive characteristic in British ales.

FRESH BREAD: *See* cookie-like.

GRAPEFRUIT: Typical character of American hops, especially the Cascade variety.

GRASS, HAY: Can be a hop characteristic. Fresh, new-mown

hay is typical in some classic European lagers. It arises from a compound called dimethyl sulphide, caused by fermentation with traditional lager yeasts.

HERBAL: Hop characteristic. Examples of herbal flavours are bay leaves, mint, and spearmint.

HOPPY: Herbal, zesty, earthy, cedary, piney, appetizingly bitter.

LICORICE: A characteristic of some dark malts, in German *Schwarzbier*, English old ales, porters, and stouts. In the English-speaking world, licorice itself is sometimes used as an additive.

MADEIRA: Caused by oxidation. In very strong, bottle-conditioned beers that have been aged many years, this will be in a pleasant balance. In another type of beer, it is likely to be unpleasant.

MALTY: *See* cookie-like, fresh bread, nuts, tea, toast, and toffee.

MINTY: Hop characteristic, especially spearmint.

NUTS: Typical malt characteristic in many types of beer, especially northern English brown ales. Arises from crystal malt (*page 13*).

ORANGEY: Typical of several hop varieties. Can also arise from some ale yeasts. Positive if not overwhelming.

PEARS: Yeast characteristic in some ales. If overwhelming, suggests that the beer has lost some balancing hop due to age.

PEPPER: The flavour of alcohol. Suggests a strong beer.

PINEY: Characteristic of some hops, especially American varieties.

PLUMS: Yeast character, found in South German wheat beers.

RAISINY: Typical in beers made with very dark malts and to a high

alcohol content, for example, imperial stouts. This flavour develops in fermentation.

RESINY: Typical hop characteristic.

ROSES: Can arise from hops. Also from yeast development during bottle-conditioning, especially in some Belgian beers.

SHERRY: Dry, fino sherry flavours are typical in Belgian *lambic* beers. Sweet sherry can arise in strong, bottle-conditioned beers that have been aged. *See also* Madeira.

SMOKY: Appropriate in "malt whisky beer", smoked beer, and some dry stouts.

SOUR: Appropriate in *Berliner Weisse*, *lambic*, or Flemish brown or red specialities, but not in other styles of beer.

STRAWBERRIES: In extremely restrained form, and in balance with malt and hop, an appropriate fermentation characteristic in some British ales.

TEA: A strongish tea, of the type made in England (Indian, especially Darjeeling, with milk) is a good aroma metaphor for malt.

TOAST: Malt characteristic in some dark ales, porters, and stouts.

TOBACCO: Fragrant tobacco smoke can be evoked by the Tettnang hop, grown near Lake Constance in Germany and used in many lagers.

TOFFEE: Malt characteristic, especially in Vienna-style, *Märzen*, and *Oktoberfest* amber lagers. Very appetizing if not overwhelming.

VINEGARY: See acidity.

WINEY: Typical of *lambic* and some other Belgian styles aged in wood.

YEAST: The aroma of fresh yeast, like bread rising, is typical of some ales. Can appear as a "bite" in some from Yorkshire, England.

BEERS FOR THE MOMENT

MANY PEOPLE THINK BEER IS MERELY A refresher, but such consumers may not know the world's most quenching, cooling brews...and what about the winter warmers, for a cold night? Others believe that the purpose of beer is to intoxicate, but it is very inefficient in this respect: the average strength of beer, worldwide, is about half that of wine, and about a tenth that of spirits. Some beers are sociable relaxants, others restoratives after work or exercise. Nothing arouses the appetite quite like a really hoppy beer. Other brews especially suit certain foods. After dinner, with a cigar? A single malt Scotch...or a very strong, rich, calming beer. With a book at bedtime? As the following pages will demonstrate, there is a beer for each of these moments, and many more.

WHICH BEER, WHEN?

THE FIRST OBSTACLE to the full enjoyment of beer is the idea that it all tastes the same. The second is the notion that beer is exclusively a thirst-quencher, or an accompaniment to a football game, or may be enjoyed only by the pint in the pub. Just as any wine can be consumed at any time, so can any beer but, like the grape, the grain does have its favoured moods and moments. Brewers sometimes fight shy of this idea, fearing that a "perfect moment" for their product would restrict its sale. This seems unlikely. No true beer-lover would be so bound by rules, but there is much to be said for trying a brew in its ideal setting. It is in this spirit that the beers below and on the following pages are presented.

SOME BEERS, from the golden lagers of Munich to the golden ales of Cologne, from the ales of Antwerp to those of America, are soothing and moreish, and ideally suited to sociable drinking. If a beer is to sustain a few hours' conversation, it must be long and easily drinkable, yet not gassy and bloating – and tasty, not tedious. In England, a bitter ale such as Young's Special (*starting the line-up below*) has the qualifications.

A beer that would work better as a greeting drink at a party or barbecue would

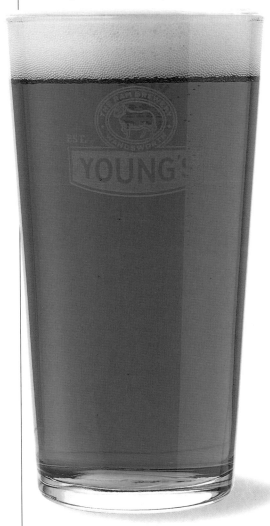

A sociable beer
English bitter is usually modest in alcohol, so that it can be consumed in relatively high volume...pints to pass an evening.

A greeting beer
Save the strong stuff for later...a small flute of Rosé de Gambrinus is a perfect, light-hearted start to the proceedings.

A thirst-quenching beer
Berliner Weisse has a quenching style so acidic that it tends to be sweetened with a herbal or fruit syrup, either green, red, or au naturel.

be a raspberry or cherry brew, especially a dryish one like Cantillon Rosé de Gambrinus, from Belgium. This elegant, winey brew is the beer world's answer to a pink champagne. It is typically served in a champagne flute: a pretty drink, with a flirtatious flourish.

To cool the brow and quench the thirst on a summer's day, there are better choices than a standard lager. A fruity wheat beer from the south of Germany, or a "sweet and sour" Belgian red ale, might suit. Or a light, fresh, sharp *Berliner Weisse* laced with lemon-grassy essence of woodruff. In its

native city, this champagne-like brew is typically served in an over-sized saucer.

Summer or winter, to accompany a road movie on television, or a book during a relaxing, restful evening at home, the peppery, warming Old Knucklehead, from Portland, Oregon, is a perfect choice.

But what about dinner? In the pages that follow, styles of beer are nominated, and examples shown, that might accompany soups, salads, fish, poultry, meats, and a variety of other dishes. The spicy, aniseedy,

aromatic La Choulette, a *bière de garde* from northern France, goes wonderfully well with lamb, perhaps served braised with leeks and carrots. There are beers that go well with cheese and with desserts, whether fruity, creamy, or chocolatey. And for a port-like, brandyish, after-dinner digestif, Belgium's opulent, luxurious, relaxing Kasteel Bière du Chateau is a good example, in its chunky goblet.

Only the dedicated would put beer to all its uses in a single day, but each offers its own pleasure...not necessarily by the pint.

A nightcap beer
Old Knucklehead is typical of the jokingly gnarled names given to barley wines made in the Pacific northwest of the US.

A beer to accompany lamb
La Choulette is a classic example of the spicy bières de garde *made by small breweries in northern France, near the Channel coast.*

An after-dinner beer
Kasteel Bière du Chateau is a rich, malty, Belgian brew with a stomach-calming potency reminiscent of an after-dinner brandy.

SEASONAL BEERS FOR SPRING

THE IDEA OF SPECIAL BEERS for spring is strongest in Germany, especially in the state of Bavaria and its capital, Munich. Spring beers there are usually strong lagers, often dark in colour. German brewers call a very strong product a *Bockbier*. Some even have "Double" Bocks. In Munich, a *Doppelbock* is regarded as a strong warmer to cure the winter blues as spring arrives. A third variation is the May Bock, sometimes paler and drier.

Knight rider
A jousting tournament is held at Kaltenberg castle, near Munich, over three weekends in July.

PAULANER SALVATOR

Germany's most famous spring beer is made by the Paulaner brewery, in the city of Munich. This brewery was founded in 1634 by monks in the order of St Francis of Paula. They brewed an especially malty beer as "liquid bread" to sustain them during Lent. They called it "Salvator", Latin for "The Saviour". The brewery is no longer owned by monks, but its products still include Paulaner Salvator. This extra-strong lager has a head like whipped cream; a rich, deep, amber-brown colour; a buttery-malty aroma; and a toffeeish flavour, drying in a long, moreish finish. In honour of this beer, some other Double Bocks have names ending in *-ator*.

Region of origin
Munich, Upper Bavaria, Germany

Style Double Bock (*Doppelbock*)

Alcohol content 7.5abv (6.0w)

Ideal serving temperature 9°C (48°F)

Small but strong
A suitably small serving for a very strong, dark lager.

A BEER WITH A KICK

A DUKE FROM SAXONY brought strong beer to Bavaria from Einbeck. In the local accent, Einbeck sounded like Einbock. This was shortened to Bock, which also means billy goat, so this animal has become a symbol of the beer style.

AYINGER CELEBRATOR

Munich's best-known "country" beers are made in the nearby village of Aying, comprising little more than a church, maypole, and brewery (with its own restaurant and inn). Locally grown barley is malted at the brewery. The Ayinger brewery's Double Bock, called Celebrator, has a dark brown to ebony colour; soft, rich, coffeeish, malt flavours, and a figgy dryness in the finish.

Region of origin
Upper Bavaria, Germany

Style Double Bock
(*Doppelbock*)

Alcohol content
7.2abv (5.8w)

Ideal serving temperature
9°C (48°F)

Going for the goat
The virile symbol appears twice on the label and the glass, and again round the neck of the bottle.

KALTENBERG RITTERBOCK

Although Bock beer originated in Einbeck, it was popularized by the royal court brewhouse built by Duke Wilhelm V of Bavaria at the end of the 1500s. One of the Duke's descendants, Prince Luitpold, today brews near Munich at the castle of Kaltenberg. Among his beers is his Ritterbock, available during Lent. It is light-bodied for the style, but with a bitter-chocolate praline character.

Region of origin Upper Bavaria, Germany

Style Double Bock
(*Doppelbock*)

Alcohol content
7.7abv (6.2w)

Ideal serving temperature
9°C (48°F)

Fit for a knight
The "Ritter" of "Ritterbock" means rider or knight.

BRAND DUBBELBOCK

The oldest brewery in The Netherlands is Brand's, dating from 1341. The Brand family became involved in 1871, and still are – though for 10 years the company has been owned by Heineken. The Brand's brewery has in its range a well-regarded Pilsner-type and three Bock beers. Its Dubbelbock (Dutch spelling) has the creaminess and fruity "warming" maltiness of a Lowland Scotch whisky.

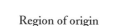

Region of origin
Province of Limburg,
The Netherlands

Style Double Bock
(*Dubbelbock*)

Alcohol content
7.5abv (6.0w)

Ideal serving temperature 9°C (48°F)

Triple Dutch
In addition to its Double, Brand's has different Maytime and year-round versions of Bock.

VICTORY ST. VICTORIOUS

No fewer than seven German malts are used in this aromatic, creamy, complex Double Bock, which has a finish like a nutty port. It is made by the Victory brewery and pub, established in 1995/96, in Downingtown, Pennsylvania. The brewery's founders met when they were 10 years old. Why Victory? "Being near Philadelphia, we wanted to call our brewery Liberty, but that name was already taken."

Region of origin Northeast US

Style Double Bock

Alcohol content 7.4abv (5.9w)

Ideal serving temperature
9°C (48°F)

Victory "V"
A whimsical label, but this full-flavoured brew is one of the best German-style Bocks in the US.

ALFA LENTE BOK

The English word "Lent" probably refers to the lengthening days of spring. In Dutch, "lente" means "spring". This seasonal brew is made by the small, old-established Alfa brewery, north of Maastricht. The brewery is noted for all-malt lagers. This *Bok* has a beautifully retained head and a textured, dryish, fresh, malt character. Strong but light-bodied for the style and very drinkable.

Region of origin Province of Limburg, The Netherlands

Style Spring Bock (*Lente Bok*)

Alcohol content
6.5abv (5.2w)

Ideal serving temperature
9°C (48°F)

A golden Bock
Quenching beers for later spring avoid the darker malts.

HB MAI-BOCK

The initials stand for Hofbräuhaus: the Royal Court brewhouse. The beer-hall, the world's most famous pub, still functions, on a small square called the Platzl in the centre of Munich; the brewery is on the edge of town. The State of Bavaria owns both brewery and beer-hall. The beer claims on its label to be Munich's oldest Bock, though that is not strictly true of this Maytime version. It is a fine beer nonetheless, huge in its malt aromas, nutty flavours, and peppery, warming finish.

Region of origin
Munich, Upper Bavaria, Germany

Style May Bock (*Maibock*)

Alcohol content
7.2abv (5.8w)

Ideal serving temperature
9°C (48°F)

HANSA URBOCK

The company name is an old German word for a guild of merchants. "Ur" means "original". This traditional May Bock is made in the former German Southwest Africa, now known as Namibia. It is surely the most remote example of the style. Hansa Urbock, made according to the German Beer Purity Law, has a bright, tawny colour; a sweet toffee aroma and flavour; a smooth, medium body; and a brandyish finish.

Region of origin
Namibia, Southern Africa

Style May Bock

Alcohol content
6.0abv (4.8w)

Ideal serving temperature
9°C (48°F)

ROGUE MAIERBOCK ALE

The local Rogue river gives its name to this micro-brewery, founded in 1988, in Newport, Oregon, in the beery Pacific Northwest of the US. Rogue is noted for colourful, big-tasting beers. Its brewer's family name is Maier; hence the jokey naming of this product. The beer aims for the smooth yet crisp character of a true May Bock, but is made with an ale yeast. It achieves its objective remarkably well.

Region of origin
Pacific Northwest US

Style May Bock (top-fermenting)

Alcohol content
6.0abv (4.8w)

Ideal serving temperature
9°C (48°F)

Rogue brewer
Brewer John Maier features on his own label, but just for one punning beer in a big range.

SEASONAL BEERS: SPRING

ABITA SPRINGS ANDYGATOR

From New Orleans, the bridge-like causeway across Lake Pontchartrain leads to Abita Springs, where one of the American South's earliest micro-breweries was established in 1986. Abita has a Bock at about 6.0abv (4.5w) for Mardi Gras, but at its pub (72011 Holly St), and occasionally in the bottle, also, offers a stronger golden lager with the -ator ending typical of many Double Bocks. Andygator is firm and very smooth, with a clean, whiskyish, dry maltiness. The brewer who created it is called Andy, and (Alli)'gators abound in swampy Louisiana.

Region of origin Southeast US

Style Pale Double Bock

Alcohol content 8–8.5abv (6.4–6.8w)

Ideal serving temperature 9°C (48°F)

ADLER BRÄU DOPPLE BOCK

The name Adler dates from a German-American brewery of the mid-1800s. The brewery was in the home town of Harry Houdini: Appleton, near Oshkosh, Wisconsin. It closed at Prohibition, and was turned into a shopping centre. In 1989, a new, small brewery was installed, initially to serve two restaurants in the shopping centre. Its oddly spelled Dopple Bock is a tawny brew with a creamy malt aroma; a body that is light for the style, but smooth, with a late development of licorice-like malt flavours.

Region of origin Midwest US

Style Double Bock

Alcohol content 6.5abv (5.2w)

Ideal serving temperature 9°C (48°F)

H.C. BERGER MAIBOCK

Named after Harry Calvin Berger, who was the first paediatrician in Kansas City in pioneering days. Berger, a home brewer, was the grandfather of Sandy Jones, who founded this micro in Fort Collins, Colorado, in 1992. It has since changed ownership and increased its range. Its beers include a deep amber, smooth Maibock that initially seems very light but develops clean, toffeeish, fruity, malt flavours and a late, dry finish.

Region of origin Southwest US

Style May Bock

Alcohol content 6.0abv (4.8w)

Ideal serving temperature 9°C (48°F)

BERLINER BÜRGERBRÄU MAIBOCK

This old-established East Berlin brewery has been given a new life since being acquired by the Bavarian brewing family Häring. It has a golden Maibock as well as a dark Dunkler Bock. The Maibock has a creamy malt aroma; a relatively light body; a faintly buttery, malt character; and a crisp, grassy, herbal, hop finish.

Region of origin Berlin, Northern Germany

Style May Bock (*Maibock*)

Alcohol content 8.5abv (6.8w)

Ideal serving temperature 9°C (48°F)

BUDELS MEI BOCK

Very small, old-established (1870) brewery in the village of Budel, North Brabant, The Netherlands. An interesting range of products includes (in the Dutch spelling of the month) a Mei Bock, with a full golden colour; hop flavours that are distinctively herbal, almost like wintergreen; and a lingering dryness. Budels also has a brandyish dark Bock.

Region of origin Province of North Brabant, The Netherlands

Style May Bock (*Mei Bock*)

Alcohol content 6.5abv (5.2w)

Ideal serving temperature 9°C (48°F)

OLD DOMINION SPRING BREW

The "Old Dominion" is a nickname for Virginia. Old Dominion Brewing, of Ashburn, Virginia, is one of the most successful micro-breweries in the eastern US. Its beers are readily available at the nearby Dulles Airport, Washington DC. The brewery was established in 1989. Its range has included a Spring Bock that combines a very good malt background with a very assertive hop in the finish.

Region of origin Mid Atlantic US

Style Spring Bock

Alcohol content 7.3abv (5.8w)

Ideal serving temperature 9°C (48°F)

EINBECKER MAIBOCK

The town of Einbeck, in Lower Saxony, became famous for strong beers when it was the brewing centre for the Hanseatic League. This beautifully kept, late-Gothic town still has a (mainly modern) brewery, called Einbecker Brauhaus, making no fewer than three Bock beers, in dark, pale, and Maytime styles. The Maibock is notably spritzy, with a slightly fruity spiciness. It is intended to be more refreshing than the more wintry interpretations.

Region of origin Northern Germany

Style May Bock (*Maibock*)

Alcohol content 6.5abv (5.2w)

Ideal serving temperature 9°C (48°F)

GROLSCH LENTEBOK

This brewery takes its name from its birthplace, originally called Grolle (now Groenlo), in The Netherlands. Its principal product is its lightly hoppy Pilsner-style beer, but it also has a range of specialities. These include an assertive, amber Lentebok, with a lot of hop for the style, both in its grassy aroma and its dry finish.

Region of origin Eastern Netherlands

Style Spring Bock (*Lentebok*)

Alcohol content 6.5abv (5.2w)

Serving temperature 9°C (48°F)

HOLSTEN MAIBOCK

This major North German brewing company takes its name from the Duke of Holstein, who granted brewing rights to Hamburg, its home city. Holsten is most widely known for its dryish, Pilsner-style beer, but it also produces several specialities. One is a Maibock, crimson-tinged dark brown in colour, with a licorice-like malt aroma and treacle-toffee flavours, developing to a light, toasty finish.

Region of origin Northern Germany

Style May Bock (*Maibock*)

Alcohol content 7.0abv (5.6w)

Ideal serving temperature 9°C (48°F)

SEASONAL BEERS FOR SUMMER

WARM WEATHER AND BEER go hand in glass, but some brews are much more cooling and refreshing than others. Among the several styles that are particularly quenching, Belgium's traditional *saison* beers were created specifically for the summer season. Most wheat beers are refreshing but some are available only in summer. So are some of the crisp, golden summer ales from brewers of British bitter.

Lazy Sunday
A British summer Sunday means a pint at the pub, with half an eye on the cricket.

HOPBACK SUMMER LIGHTNING

After the hops have been boiled in the brew, the leafy cones have to be removed, using a vessel called a hop back. The Hop Back brewery, in Salisbury, England, dates from 1987. Soon after its foundation, it launched Summer Lightning, initially for a beer festival but then as a regular product. At the time, the colour was unusually sunny for a British ale. The beer may be light, crisp, and dry, but it is full of subtle flavours: the sweetness of Maris Otter barley malt from Wiltshire, the fragrance of East Kent Golding hops, and the very delicate, banana-like fruitiness of the house yeast.

Region of origin Southern England, UK

Style Summer Ale

Alcohol content 5.0abv (4.0w)

Ideal serving temperature
Just above 10°C (50°F)

SINKING THE SAHTI

IN THE NORDIC COUNTRIES, midsummer festivities feature farmhouse brews of rye-and-juniper. The best-known, the Finnish *sahti*, is traditionally served in this two-handled vessel. First a sauna, then a dive into the lake, then a *sahti* or two...and the sun scarcely sinks.

MARSTON'S SUMMER WHEAT BEER

This brewery is famous for its Pedigree pale ale, but makes a growing number of styles. Its Summer Wheat Beer was launched

in 1997. Unlike some wheat beers in the English-speaking world, it uses a Bavarian yeast: hence the pronounced banana-like fruitiness, with dryish vanilla notes and juicy suggestions of bubble-gum. Like a Bavarian *Kristall Weizen*, it is filtered. A bright summer refresher.

Region of origin Trent Valley, England, UK

Style *Kristall Weizen*

Alcohol content 4.2abv (3.4w)

Ideal serving temperature 9°C (48°F)

VAUX HOW'S YOUR FATHER SUMMER ALE

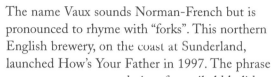

The name Vaux sounds Norman-French but is pronounced to rhyme with "forks". This northern English brewery, on the coast at Sunderland, launched How's Your Father in 1997. The phrase derives from ribald holiday humour. This lemon-tinged wheat ale has a sherbety aroma; a light, firm body; a dryish, crisp palate; and a light finish.

Region of origin
Northeast England, UK

Style Wheat Ale

Alcohol content 4.6abv (3.7w)

Ideal serving temperature
10°C (50°F)

Wish you were here
The jokey image on the label features the fat lady and gawky man of British seaside postcards.

GOLDEN HILL EXMOOR GOLD

At Wiveliscombe, Somerset, a brewery that had been closed for 20 years was brought back to life in 1980. Six years later, the

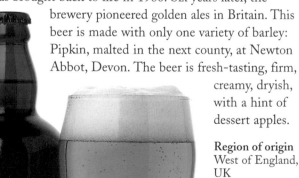

brewery pioneered golden ales in Britain. This beer is made with only one variety of barley: Pipkin, malted in the next county, at Newton Abbot, Devon. The beer is fresh-tasting, firm, creamy, dryish, with a hint of dessert apples.

Region of origin
West of England, UK

Style
Golden Ale

Alcohol content 5.0abv (4.0w)

Ideal serving temperature
10°C (50°F)

Back-label boast
"A Single Malt Beer" is the boast on the back-label.

McMULLEN HAYTIME SUMMER ALE

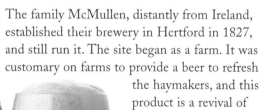

The family McMullen, distantly from Ireland, established their brewery in Hertford in 1827, and still run it. The site began as a farm. It was customary on farms to provide a beer to refresh

the haymakers, and this product is a revival of such a brew. It has more substance than most summer ales, with the spicy, junipery aroma of the hop variety Progress; a smooth, nutty, crystal-malt background; and appetizing bitterness.

Region of origin
Eastern England, UK

Style Summer Ale

Alcohol content 5.0abv (4.0w)

Ideal serving temperature
10–13°C (50–55°F)

SEASONAL BEERS FOR AUTUMN

LAGER WAS "INVENTED" in Bavaria in the days before artificial refrigeration, when the brewing season ended in March or April and did not re-start until September or October. As a provision for summer, quantities of beer were stored in nearby Alpine caves, and the cold maturation made for a smoother style of beer. When summer ended, the last of the March (*Märzen*) beer was consumed at autumn celebrations. This is why the words for March and October sometimes appear on the same label.

A style for celebration
The malt-accented, medium-strong lagers produced for the season are ceremonially served at the Oktoberfest.

STEINER MÄRZEN

Stein is a hamlet where a rocky cliff on the river Traun once formed the frontier between Bavaria and Austria. Caves in the cliff-face are still used for the lagering of beer, and contain the lagering vessels of the Schlossbrauerei ("Castle Brewery") Stein. Its Märzen (March) beer, brewed to be consumed in September, is a good example of the style. It has the reddish bronze colour that was traditional in *Märzen-Oktoberfest* lagers; a richly malty aroma (also with some spicy hop balance); and juicy, almost chewy, barley-sugar flavours.

Region of origin
Upper Bavaria, Germany

Style *Märzen/Oktoberfest*

Alcohol content 5.5abv (4.4w)

Ideal serving temperature 9°C (48°F)

THE OKTOBERFEST

MANY PLACES IN GERMANY have annual festivals centred on beer tents on the village green or town fairground. Some take place after the harvest, or mark summer's end. Munich's *Oktoberfest*, the most famous such celebration, has more formal origins. The first marked the wedding of Crown Prince Ludwig and Queen Theresia, in 1810. The 16-day festival actually starts in late September.

SPATEN OKTOBERFESTBIER

Lager-brewing had its beginnings as a modern technique at the Spaten brewery in Munich, around the end of the 1830s. The brewery dates from 1397. The custom of making reddish-bronze, malt-accented lagers specifically for *Oktoberfest* also began with Spaten, but in recent years the brewery has produced only a golden version. This beer has a creamy aroma and a clean, firm, smooth, light malt accent. It is traditionally the first beer to be tapped at the *Oktoberfest*.

Region of origin
Munich, Upper Bavaria, Germany

Style
Märzen/Oktoberfest

Alcohol content
5.9abv (4.7w)

Ideal serving temperature 9°C (48°F)

HB OKTOBERFESTBIER

HB – the Hofbräuhaus – takes a special interest in a festival that began with the wedding of the Crown Prince. Its label illustrates the horses and drays that take part in the procession to "Queen Theresia's Meadows". Its Oktoberfestbier forms a head of Alpine proportions, and has a creamy, malty spiciness reminiscent of licorice or aniseed.

Region of origin
Munich, Upper Bavaria, Germany

Style *Märzen/ Oktoberfest*

Alcohol content
5.7abv (4.6w)

Ideal serving temperature
9°C (48°F)

Beautiful bloom
One result of all-malt beers is a solid foam, prized as a "beautiful bloom".

AYINGER OKTOBER FEST-MÄRZEN

None of the breweries outside the city limits is permitted to have its beer at the Munich *Oktoberfest*, but many make the seasonal style. Ayinger, in the countryside nearby, has a good example. The beer has a gold-to-bronze colour, very fresh hop and malt aromas, nutty flavours, and a lightly firm body. The Ayinger brewery organizes many smaller festivals in the countryside around Munich.

Region of origin
Upper Bavaria, Germany

Style *Märzen/Oktoberfest*

Alcohol content
5.8abv (4.6w)

Ideal serving temperature
9°C (48°F)

Special claim
Ayinger's label refers to its beers as "specialities". The brewery makes about a dozen styles.

DINKEL ACKER VOLKSFEST BIER

Around the same time as the Munich *Oktoberfest*, the other great southern German capital, Stuttgart, has its own "People's Festival" (*Volksfest*). The city's breweries make special beers for the occasion. The Carl Dinkelacker brewery makes a lively example with a big, malty start and a good hop balance. The city's Schwaben Bräu has a similar *Märzenbier*, with a delicate hop aroma and sweetish malt character.

Region of origin
Baden-Württemberg, Germany

Style *Märzen/Festbier*

Alcohol content
5.5abv (4.4w)

Ideal serving temperature
9°C (48°F)

FRAOCH HEATHER ALE

The purple heather that warms the mountains of Scotland was a flavouring in the local beers long before hops were used. In the early 1990s, brewers Bruce and Scott Williams restored the tradition with their Fraoch ("heather" in Gaelic) ale. The beer has a sunny, amber colour; a flowery bouquet; a slightly oily body; and a spicy, apple-like, faintly winey finish. The heather is picked in July, and the new season's beer is available in August/September.

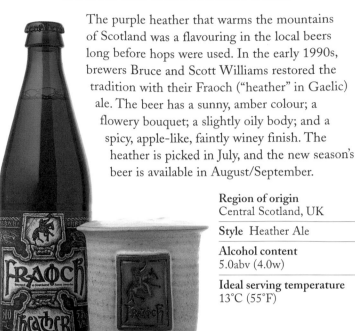

Region of origin
Central Scotland, UK

Style Heather Ale

Alcohol content
5.0abv (4.0w)

Ideal serving temperature
13°C (55°F)

Ceramic chalice
The vessel favoured by the brewers of Fraoch conceals the colour of the beer.

GROZET GOOSEBERRY & WHEAT ALE

The name is Scottish for gooseberry. Literary references to a beer of this name spurred the brewing brothers Williams to re-create the style. Their gooseberry beer is flavoured with bog myrtle and meadowsweet. The beer is perfumy and spritzy, with a tangy suggestion of gooseberry skins. The beer is available in September.

Region of origin
Central Scotland, UK

Style Gooseberry Ale

Alcohol content
5.0abv (4.0w)

Ideal serving temperature
13°C (55°F)

Hide and sink
Leather drinking vessels such as this one were once common.

ALBA SCOTS PINE ALE

Another unusual Scottish brew from the Williams brothers is an ale with no hops at all – just pine sprigs and spruce shoots. This is available earlier in the year, but might best be saved until the cooler weather. It is aromatic, oily, peppery, and medicinal. The brothers produce these beers at Maclay's, in Alloa, but plan their own brewery in a watermill at Strathaven, south of Glasgow.

Region of production
Central Scotland, UK

Style
Pine/Spruce Beer

Alcohol content
7.5abv (6.0w)

Ideal serving temperature
13°C (55°F)

TRAQUAIR JACOBITE ALE

Traquair House is a castle on the Scottish side of the border with England, owned by a branch of the Scottish royal family Stuart. Bonnie Prince Charlie is said to have visited the house during his campaign in the autumn of 1745. The beer, produced in the house's own brewery, was launched in 1995. It is a purple-to-black ale, rich, with a sweetish, spicy, soft, rooty flavour.

Region of origin
Scottish Borders, UK

Style
Spiced Scottish Ale

Alcohol content
8.0abv (6.4w)

Ideal serving temperature
13°C (55°F)

Loyalty to royalty
Jacobite, after King James II, means a supporter of the royal Stuart succession.

USHERS AUTUMN FRENZY

One of the first English brewers to launch an autumn beer was Ushers, which has a speciality for each of the four seasons. When the leaves begin to fall, look out for the autumnal hue of this gently sustaining, dryish brew. Both the colour and the smooth, nutty, spicy palate owe something to the use of rye, a grain once found only in some Baltic and Russian speciality brews.

Region of origin
Southern England, UK

Style Rye Ale

Alcohol content
4.0abv (3.2w)

Ideal serving temperature
10–13°C (50–55°F)

BRECKENRIDGE AUTUMN ALE

The Rocky Mountain ski resort and former gold-mining town of Breckenridge, Colorado, gained its first brewpub in 1990, probably America's highest, at 2,926 m (9,600 ft). Branches have since opened in Denver and other cities. Breckenridge produces a wide range of beers. Its bottled Autumn Ale has a chestnut colour; a firm, toffeeish, textured body; and hints of sweet treacle and cocoa. A delicious beer.

Region of origin
Southwest US

Style Brown Ale/Old Ale

Alcohol content
6.8abv (5.4w)

Ideal serving temperature
10–13°C (50–55°F)

HALE'S HARVEST ALE

Inspired by a brief spell in 1981, working as an "apprentice" at near-namesake Gale's brewery, in Hampshire, England, young American Mike Hale fired his own kettles in Washington State in 1983. He now has an English-accented micro-brewery in Spokane and a brewpub in the Seattle suburb of Fremont. His Harvest Ale has the aroma of fruit gums; a juicy palate; and a clean apple note in a dry, perfumy finish.

Region of origin
Pacific Northwest US

Style Strong Ale

Alcohol content
4.5abv (3.6w)

Ideal serving temperature
10–13°C (50–55°F)

Hale and hearty
"Rich, robust and distinctive...as brisk and refreshing as a fall morning,"
says Hale's publicity material.

LEINENKUGEL'S AUTUMN GOLD

The name means "Linen Bobbin". The German Leinenkugel family established their brewery in Chippewa Falls, Wisconsin, in 1867. The family still run the brewery today, though it is now owned by the national giant Miller. There is now a second Leinenkugel brewery in Milwaukee. The Autumn Gold, slightly fuller in colour than its name suggests, has spicy, malt-loaf aromas and flavours, and a dryish hop balance.

Region of origin
Midwest US

Style Vienna Lager

Alcohol content
4.8abv (3.8w)

Ideal serving temperature
9°C (48°F)

SEASONAL BEERS FOR CHRISTMAS

THE COLDER COUNTRIES, especially in the far north, have a long tradition of comforting themselves with strong beers during the darkest, shortest days of winter. Elsewhere, the new season's barley and hops make for seasonal specials that are released in November. This assumes that the barley has two months' dormancy, to permit the biological changes that will ease germination in malting, and that the beer has also had a reasonable period of maturation. In North America, some brewers make pumpkin ales for Hallowe'en and for Thanksgiving, the beginning of a winter holiday season that stretches through to New Year.

Tankard time
Ale-and-hearty images are part of the folklore of British Christmas past.

SAMICHLAUS BIER

The name is "Santa Claus" in the Swiss-German dialect of Zürich. This immensely rich, darkish lager is brewed there each year on St Nicholas' Day, December 6. The beer matures for the best part of 12 months, gaining strength in the lagering tank, and is released on the same date of the following year, with a vintage date. Samichlaus was first made in 1980, in both dark and pale versions. Because the beer is so dense, there was still plenty of colour in the pale. Eventually, the brewery decided to make only the dark. Of the world's super-strong lagers, Samichlaus is the most complex and satisfying. It has a reddish chestnut colour; a brandyish aroma; a firm, oily body; creamy and cherryish flavours; and a warming, spicy, peppery finish. It is made by the Hürlimann brewery, now owned by Feldschlösschen.

Big beer, tiny serving
With Swiss caution, a stein the size of an espresso cup was issued by the brewery.

Region of origin	Switzerland
Style	Double Bock
Alcohol content	14.0abv (11.2w)
Ideal serving temperature	9°C (48°F)

SANTA'S OFFICE

SANTA CLAUS, Saint Nicholas, Father Christmas...neither his name nor his nationality are certain but a strong claimant works from an office at Rovaniemi, in Finnish Lapland. He answers letters from children all over the world. This Santa has been known to drink the amber seasonal Jouluolout (Christmas beer) from the nearby brewery Lapin Kulta (Lapp Gold).

GORDON XMAS

Scotland may celebrate Christmas less than New Year, but as a cold northern country, it has a use for the rich and warming ales that were introduced to Belgium by British regiments in two World Wars. Scottish Courage brews this beer in Edinburgh for the Belgian market. It is a ruby-to-black ale, pouring with a mountainous head. It has a clean, sweet maltiness, but finishes with a toasty dryness. Much the same brew is made for France under the name Douglas.

Region of origin
Southern Scotland, UK

Style Strong Scottish Ale

Alcohol content
8.8abv (7.0w)

Ideal serving temperature
13°C (55°F)

ABBEY AFFLIGEM NÖEL CHRISTMAS ALE

The Benedictine abbey of Affligem, west of Brussels, was founded in 1074. It ceased to make its own beers during the First World War, but some fine products are created on its behalf by a local brewery. Its Christmas brew is garnet in colour, and hugely complex, with notes of prunes, spiciness, and sappy dryness.

Region of origin
Province of Flemish Brabant, Belgium

Style Strong Spiced Ale

Alcohol content
9.0abv (7.2w)

Ideal serving temperature
13°C (55°F)

Nöel or Noël?
This label has the umlaut (dots) in the wrong place on the French word, Noël.

BUSH DE NOËL

The Dubuisson family brewery, of Pipaix, Belgium, translated its name into the English "Bush" after its premises were liberated by a British battalion in the First World War. In the US, to avoid a conflict with Busch, of St Louis, the beer is known as Scaldis (after the river Schelde). The Christmas beer has an attractive, full amber colour; a delicately leafy, hop aroma; and a beautiful balance of sweet malt and fruitiness.

Region of origin
Province of Hainaut, Belgium

Style
Strong Ale/Barley Wine

Alcohol content
12.0abv (9.6w)

Ideal serving temperature
10–13°C (50–55°F)

KOFF JOULUOLUT

A Russian founded the Sinebrychoff brewery, oldest in the Nordic countries, in 1819. The brewery, often abbreviated to Koff, in 1987 introduced a lager in the amber-red, malt-accented Vienna style, as a Christmas beer. The word *Joulu* has the same origin as "Yule". The Finnish word for beer is *olut*. The word itself shares a root with the English "ale". This example is on the pale side for the style, with a firm, clean, nutty maltiness.

Region of origin Finland

Style Vienna Lager

Alcohol content
4.6abv (3.7w)

Ideal serving temperature
9°C (48°F)

VAUX ST. NICHOLAS'S CHRISTMAS ALE

Vaux is one of many English brewers that produce Christmas beers. These are often darker, stronger versions of a bitter. Although described as a bitter, St. Nicholas is more of a dark ale. It has a rich chestnut colour; a light body for the style; a fruity palate reminiscent of sweet pears; and a dry, toasty finish.

Region of origin
Northeast England, UK

Style Bitter/Dark Ale

Alcohol content
5.0abv (4.0w)

Ideal serving temperature
13°C (55°F)

MOCTEZUMA NOCHE BUENA

The name means "Good Night", referring to Christmas Eve. This is the time when Mexicans have their Christmas dinner. Noche Buena, a strong, dark lager, is one of the tastiest beers from Mexico. It has a deep, amber-brown colour, and is very smooth, with both malty sweetness and hoppy dryness in its long finish. Noche Buena is made by Moctezuma, which also produces the popular Vienna-style Dos Equis.

Region of origin
Province of Vera Cruz, Mexico

Style Munich Dark Lager/Bock

Alcohol content 6.0abv (4.8w)

Ideal serving temperature
9°C (48°F)

Scarlet leaves
The label shows a poinsettia. Because it turns red in midwinter, it is a symbol of Christmas.

ANCHOR "OUR SPECIAL HOLIDAY ALE"

San Francisco's Anchor brewery is famous for its dry, sparkling Steam Beer, but the company has several other specialities. Its Special Holiday Ale is released after Thanksgiving and is available until New Year. It is almost always spiced, but the ingredients change from one year to the next. In various "vintages", tasters think they have detected allspice, cinnamon, cloves, coriander, juniper, licorice, nutmeg, and zest of lemon.

Region of origin
California, US

Style Spiced Ale

Alcohol content
5.5–6.0abv (4.4–4.8w)

Ideal serving temperature
13°C (55°F)

SIERRA NEVADA CELEBRATION ALE

Perhaps the most famous new-generation brewery in the US is near the Sierra Nevada mountains, at Chico, California. The brewery is known for beers full of character and complexity. Its winter holiday Celebration Ale is typically aromatic and lively in flavour, with hints of oily dark chocolate and lots of lemony hop bitterness. The variety of hops varies each year, and experimental growths are sometimes used. The beer is broadly in the style of an India Pale Ale.

Region of origin
California, US

Style Ale/IPA

Alcohol content
6.0abv (4.8w). May vary

Ideal serving temperature
10–13°C (50–55°F)

CELEBRATION BEERS

Beer lovers do not need excuses, but it is always pleasant to celebrate an anniversary. The appropriate beer for the day adds a splash of colour, and the chance to explore new flavours. If you do not have the good fortune to be in the appropriate nation at the time, or cannot find its best beers nearby, try at least to find something from that country. It may even accompany a national dish for dinner.

JANUARY

New Year is still a legitimate moment for a Gordon's Xmas and, at a stretch, that beer could be served to honour the poet Robert "Rabbie" Burns on the 25th. Russian Orthodox Christmas, on the 7th, might be an excuse for a Baltika Porter. Australia Day, on the 26th, calls for a Burragorang Bock.

BALTIKA PORTER

FEBRUARY

Sri Lankan Independence Day, on the 4th, demands a Lion Stout. On the 6th, New Zealand celebrates one of its most important national days, to mark the Waitangi treaty between colonists and Maoris: raise a Mike's Mild or Emerson's 1812. The Independence Day of Estonia, on the 24th, could be celebrated with a Saku Hele.

MARCH

Wales marks St David's Day on the 1st: it's Brain's you'll want. Ireland's celebration of St Patrick's on the 17th tends to prompt Guinness, though several beers may be required. Namibian Independence Day, a more esoteric anniversary, on the 21st, suggests a Hansa Urbock.

HANSA URBOCK

APRIL

England marks St George's Day, once the end of the brewing season, on the 23rd: a case for London Pride. The 25th is Liberation Day in both Italy and Portugal, calling for a Moretti La Rossa or a Sagres Dark respectively. It is also Anzac Day in Australia and New Zealand, to be celebrated with a Toohey's Old or Coopers Sparkling Ale.

MAY

The 1st is a public holiday almost everywhere: settle for any May Bock you can find. The 5th is Liberation Day in The Netherlands, with plenty of Dutch beers on offer: try Het Elfde Gebod. The same date, in the guise of Cinco Mayo, is perhaps Mexico's best-known national day: any Noche Buena left? The 17th is Norwegian Independence Day: celebrate with an Aass Bock.

JUNE

Denmark celebrates Constitution Day on the 1st: an opportunity for a Ceres. Traditionalist Finns like to drink home-brewed, rye-and-juniper *sahti* at Midsummer's Eve. In the absence of such delights, seek out a Koff Porter. If your inclinations are more Swedish, try a Carnegie Porter.

JULY

Salute Canada Day with a Molson Signature or Granite Peculier on the 1st. American Independence on the 4th calls for an Anchor Liberty Ale or a Sam Adams Triple Bock. The Flemish have their national day on the 11th: the moment for a De Koninck. France's Bastille Day, on the 14th, suggests a Sans Culottes.

ANCHOR LIBERTY ALE

AUGUST

In England, the 1st is Yorkshire Day, demanding a Black Sheep or a Samuel Smith's. Swiss Confederation Day, on the 1st, calls for an Ueli Reverenz Spezial. Jamaica begins the month with Emancipation Day, then celebrates Independence on the 6th: either day will do for a Dragon Stout.

SEPTEMBER

The first Monday of the month is Labor Day in the United States: perhaps a Climax ESB? South African Heritage Day on the 24th suggests a Mitchell's Raven Stout. The French-speaking part of Belgium celebrates its National Day on the 27th: a case for Cuvée de l'Ermitage.

OCTOBER

Germany's Day of Unity is the 3rd, calling for a Berliner Bürgerbräu. Japan's National Sports Day, on the 10th, sounds like a good moment for a restorative Csarda Sweet Stout. Austria's National Day is on the 26th: celebrate with an Eggenberg Urbock or something from Baron Bachofen von Echt. The Czechs mark Independence on the 28th: time for Pilsner Urquell or Budweiser Budvar.

CSARDA SWEET STOUT

NOVEMBER

Polish Independence Day is on the 11th, suggesting an Okocim Porter. The United States celebrates Thanksgiving on the fourth Thursday of this month, perhaps calling for a Sierra Nevada Celebration. On the 30th, the Scots honour St Andrew: take the Flying Scotsman, from the Caledonian Brewery, or try for a sighting of Nessie.

DECEMBER

Switzerland's super-strong lager Samichlaus launches on the 6th, beginning the Christmas beer season. It has been another great year for John Barleycorn.

SOCIABLE BEERS: GOLDEN LAGERS

IN THE ORIGINAL HOME OF LAGER, that term is rarely used. A German drinker fancying an everyday lager would order a *Helles*, from the German word for "bright". The term sounds odd to the English speaker, but the word *Helles* has the same origins as "howl" or "yell". A "bright" sound; a "clear" colour. Not so much "yell" as yellow. A *Helles* is a golden lager with a sweetish, malt accent but a delicate balance of spicy hop. *Helles* lagers, originally made in Munich, are less bitter than the famous golden style of Pilsen, and not as firm-bodied as the Dortmund Export type.

Friday picnic, after work
In a Munich beer garden, the food must include salted radishes...and the beer is probably a Helles.

OTARU HELLES

German brewer Johannes Braun created this outstanding *Helles*, albeit an especially far-flung example of the style. He has worked in many countries, but developed this beer at a brewpub in Otaru, a college town and major port on Hokkaido, the northern island of Japan. The pub is decorated with scenes of German village life and photographs of Braun's family. In the centre is a copper-clad brewhouse built in Bamberg, Bavaria. Otaru Helles pours with a huge, rocky head, and has a bright gold colour. It has the flowery aroma and flavour of German Tettnang hops, with a cookie-like maltiness in the middle. The brewpub also produces an orangey-brown dark lager with a firm, smooth, Vienna-malt character, and seasonal specialities such as a smoked beer.

Deep "growler"
Unfiltered beer is filled into litre "growlers" but the yeast sediment drops during storage to reveal a bright brew.

Region of origin Hokkaido, Japan

Style *Helles* Lager

Alcohol content 5.0abv (4.0w)

Ideal serving temperature 9°C (48°F)

UNIONS BRÄU HELL

One of the smallest and most interesting breweries in Munich is Unions, on Einstein Strasse. Once it was larger, formed by the union of four breweries. That incarnation ended in the 1920s, in a merger with Löwenbräu. The Unions premises reopened in 1991, as a brewpub. Its principal product is its

Helles: sweet, malty, smooth, and slightly oily; and served from pitch-lined oak barrels. Organically grown barley and hops are used.

Region of origin
Munich, Upper Bavaria, Germany

Style *Helles* Lager

Alcohol content
4.7abv (3.8w)

Ideal serving temperature 9°C (48°F)

FISCHERSTUBE UELI REVERENZ

One of the first new-generation brewpubs in Europe was established at the Fischer café, in Basel, Switzerland, in 1975. The owner is a doctor of medicine, who playfully calls his brewery Jester *(Ueli)*. Among the beers is a *Helles* rather seriously called Reverenz. It is light and malty in its aroma and palate, with some cookie-like flavours in the middle and a touch of hoppy tartness in a dryish finish.

Region of origin
Switzerland

Style *Helles* Lager

Alcohol content
5.4abv (4.3w)

Ideal serving temperature
9°C (48°F)

SAKU HELE

A German landowner established a brewery on his estate at Saku, near Tallinn, the capital of Estonia, in 1820. The Saku brewery, now owned by a Baltic group, is especially known for its cedary, coffeeish, strong Christmas porter. Its year-round *Hele* (Estonian spelling) pours with a dense, bubbly head and has a very pale colour; a light but firm body; and a very hoppy, appetizing finish. Fairly dry for the style.

Region of origin
Estonia

Style *Helles* Lager

Alcohol content
4.9abv (3.9w)

Ideal serving temperature
9°C (48°F)

HÜBSCH SUDWERK HELLES

Sudwerk is one of the best German-style breweries in the US (Sudwerk is from the German for a brewhouse). Hübsch is a family name of one of the founders. A brewpub and micro in Davis, in northern California, Sudwerk makes a wide range of German styles, including this firm, smooth *Helles*, with a textured, malty start and a clean, crisp smack of hops.

Region of origin
California, US

Style *Helles* Lager

Alcohol content
4.9abv (3.9w)

Ideal serving temperature
9°C (48°F)

Drinking in the study
The Sudwerk beers are made in Davis, home of California's wine university. The subject of beer-making is also studied at the college.

SOCIABLE BEERS: DORTMUNDER EXPORT

DORTMUND BECAME GERMANY'S biggest brewing city in the days when its beers soothed the souls of coalminers and steelworkers in the Ruhr valley. Its style of golden lager, known as Dortmunder Export, is distinctively firm-bodied (from the local water), dryish, and very slightly stronger than the golden lagers of the Munich or Pilsner types. Some Exports are also slightly fuller in colour.

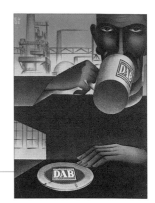

Thirsty work
This 1930s' DAB postcard creates a potent image of the industrial-strength thirst.

Original style
Once, Dortmund's own style was sold far and wide. Hence "Export". Today, the city makes more Pilsner.

DORTMUNDER UNION EXPORT

Dortmunder Union-Brauerei (DUB) is the best-known of the city's brewing companies. Its Export has a firm, mouth-filling body; a restrained, malty sweetness; and a lightly dry, rounded finish. DUB acquired Dortmunder Ritter, which also has an Export in its range. The two Exports are similar, but the Ritter seems smoother and more assertive. DUB's traditional local rival is Dortmunder Actien-Brauerei (DAB), which has a light-tasting Export and a similar brew under the name of Dortmunder Hansa. DAB has in recent years acquired Dortmunder Kronen, with a clean, soft Export.

Region of origin	Dortmund, North Rhine-Westphalia, Germany
Style	Dortmunder Export
Alcohol content	5.3abv (4.2w)
Ideal serving temperature	9°C (48°F)

DORTMUND DRAYMAN

THIS TEN-FOOT BRONZE was given to Dortmund by DAB in 1979 to symbolize the city's major industry. It stands in the Neuer Markt (New Market). To mark ten years of their being twin cities, the same figure was presented to Leeds, England. The bronze there is in Dortmund Square in the city centre. The sculptor was Artur Schulze-Engels.

GREAT LAKES DORTMUNDER GOLD

The most traditional examples of the Dortmunder Export style, in their fuller colour and body, are today found in the US. This one is perhaps even too generous in colour and maltiness, though its grainy dryness and touch of new-mown hay are exemplary. The Great Lakes micro and pub is at 2516 Market St, Cleveland, Ohio. The pub still has original bullet holes from the Prohibition days of Eliot Ness.

Region of origin
Midwest US

Style Dortmunder Export

Alcohol content
5.6abv (4.9w)

Ideal serving temperature
9°C (48°F)

Inspirational study
Great Lakes' co-founder Patrick Conway, a Jungian academic, was inspired by German beers when he studied in Europe.

ST. GALLER KLOSTERBRÄU SCHÜTZENGARTEN NATURTRÜB

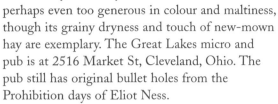

The oldest brewery plans in Europe, dating from the ninth century, are from the abbey of St Gallen, founded in Switzerland by an Irish monk. The town still has a brewery, Schützengarten, albeit a mere 220 years old. Its "naturally turbid" (unfiltered) speciality has the appropriate strength and colour to be deemed an Export. It has an excellent balance of malty sweetness and flowery, herbal, peppery hop.

Region of origin
Switzerland

Style Unfiltered Lager/Export

Alcohol content
5.2abv (4.2w)

Ideal serving temperature
9°C (48°F)

GULPENER DORT

The village of Gulpen is south of Maastricht, in The Netherlands, but close to Belgium and Germany. The Gulpener brewery's products include this Dort, a shorter but darker and stronger echo of the German style. It has a marshmallowy maltiness, balanced by a leafy hop finish. Nearby, Leeuw has a slightly drier Dortmunder; Alfa a creamy Super Dortmunder, even stronger; and De Ridder the well-balanced Maltezer.

Region of origin
Province of Limburg, The Netherlands

Style Dutch Strong Dortmunder Export

Alcohol content
6.5abv (5.2w)

Ideal serving temperature
9°C (48°F)

CERES DANSK DORTMUNDER

The mythological Roman goddess of farming and cereal grains, Ceres, gives her name to this brewery in the Danish city of Aarhus. This brewery has a strong "Danish Dortmunder". The beer has a buttery maltiness and some fruitiness. Ceres' other products include a beer flavoured with rum and lemon essence, named after the navigator Bering (who died of scurvy); and a peppery, phonetic Stowt.

Region of origin
Denmark

Style Danish Strong Dortmunder Export

Alcohol content
7.7abv (6.2w)

Ideal serving temperature
9°C (48°F)

SOCIABLE BEERS: KÖLSCHBIER

AT A GLANCE, they look like Pilsner-style lagers, but the beers of the Cologne area are less assertively bitter and have an ale-like fruitiness, albeit very light. This style of beer, gaining its special character from a top-fermenting yeast, is very delicate, soft, and digestible. More than a dozen breweries in a defined region around Cologne make about 20 examples, almost always serving the beer in its own cylindrical glass. Cologne, a city of neighbourhoods, has a strong culture of taverns, and several make their own *Kölschbier*. For all their similarity of style, each has its own subtle personality.

Cologne cartridges
The city's smartly uniformed waiters are all regarded as being called Jakob, and are known as 'Köbes. The glasses are loaded into perforated trays like cartridges into a six-shooter.

FRÜH KÖLSCH

Opposite the cathedral, on a street called Am Hof (after the Archbishop's Court), the turn-of-the-century tavern of P. J. Früh is the best-known destination for visitors wishing to sample *Kölschbier*. The beer was made on the premises until the 1980s, but is now brewed on a separate site, and is bottled for general sale. P. J. Früh is a classic Cologne pub, with the typical standing area jokingly known as the *Schwemme*. When it is crowded, the Schwemme may seem like a swimming bath, but the reference is actually to a place where horses are watered. Deeper into the pub are scrubbed wooden tables, where the beer is enjoyed with snacks of cheese, blood sausage, and tartare-like pork *Mettwurst*. The beer has a faint strawberry fruitiness of aroma; a creamy malt background; and an elegant balancing dryness of hop.

Region of origin
Cologne, North Rhine-Westphalia, Germany

Style *Kölschbier*

Alcohol content 4.8abv (3.8w)

Ideal serving temperature 9°C (48°F)

KINGS OF THE CITY

THE TAVERNS' OFTEN-BRISK waiters have become symbols of Cologne, as shown in this rendition by Franz Mather, a local writer who has done much to publicize the city's beer. The illustration is from his book, *Waiter, another Kölsch!* This particular waiter seems also to be bringing the classic meal, "Three Kings": knuckles of three different meats.

DOM KÖLSCH

The name means cathedral, and that is the trademark of this medium-sized brewery. Dom is on the corner of Tacitus and Goltstein Streets, just south of the centre of Cologne. Its Tacitus tavern there was dubbed "the best kitchen in town" by the influential French critics Gault and Millau. Local dishes are offered. The beer is fresh, clean, and well balanced, with a smooth maltiness and lemony, hop dryness. Dom, founded in 1894, is now part of the same group as Stern, of Essen.

Region of origin Cologne, North Rhine-Westphalia, Germany

Style *Kölschbier*

Alcohol content 4.8abv (3.8w)

Ideal serving temperature 9°C (48°F)

Slow maturation
Cologne's cathedral was not completed until the 1800s. It is a symbol of the entire city, as well as this beer.

GARDE KÖLSCH

The first golden beer in the region, a heavier parent to today's *Kölsch*, is said to have been brewed by Garde in 1898. Today's Garde Kölsch is very soft and fresh, with a light, clean, dessert-apple fruitiness and a dry finish. It is a very good example of the style, and one of the fuller in flavour. The beer is bottled, but can also be found on draught in Cologne at the Bei d'r Tant in Cäcilienstrasse. Garde Kölsch is popular on the town's north side. The brewery is north of the city, at Dormagen, in the direction of Düsseldorf.

Region of origin Dormagen, North Rhine-Westphalia, Germany

Style *Kölschbier*

Alcohol content 4.8abv (3.8w)

Ideal serving temperature 9°C (48°F)

Guarding the style
Garde, named after the German Imperial Guard, stands at the perimeter of the defined Kölsch-*producing region.*

GILDEN KÖLSCH

Very flowery in aroma – an attribute of a good *Kölsch*. The palate is light, sherbety, and slightly winey. This beer is made by the Bergische Löwen brewery, in Mülheim, across the river from the city centre of Cologne. This brewery is owned by the national group Brau und Brunnen. The brewery also produces Sion Kölsch, which seems maltier, with a pear-brandy fruitiness and a late hop dryness. Sion has a tavern in the city centre, in a street called Unter Taschenmacher.

Region of origin Cologne, North Rhine-Westphalia, Germany

Style *Kölschbier*

Alcohol content 4.8abv (3.8w)

Ideal serving temperature 9°C (48°F)

Gilding the glass
Gilden takes its name from a trade guild. Today's Association of Brewers in Cologne protects the Kölsch *style and its region of production.*

KÜPPERS KÖLSCH

One of the few *Kölsch* beers to be found on occasion in export markets. Gustav Küpper brewed in the city in the 1800s, but the *Kölsch* and the present brewery date from the 1960s. It is a large brewery, on the banks of the Rhine. With a relatively "new" *Kölsch* to promote, Küppers emphasized heritage by establishing at the brewery an excellent museum of beer advertising. The brewery also has a restaurant serving local dishes. The beer is flowery, perfumy, and sweetish.

Region of origin Cologne, North Rhine-Westphalia, Germany

Style *Kölschbier*

Alcohol content 4.8abv (3.8w)

Ideal serving temperature 9°C (48°F)

Coopering the barrel
Like the English word "cooper", Küpper probably means "barrel-maker", but in an old dialect of the Rhine. The modern German word, Küfer, *is more often understood as "cellarman". A barrel-maker is a* Fassbinder *("vat-binder").*

MÜHLEN KÖLSCH

The *Malzmühle* (Malt Mill) is an old-established, unpretentious brewpub making a distinctly malty, almost marshmallow-like *Kölschbier*. Mühlen Kölsch pours with a dense head, has a very fresh aroma, and a balancing spicy dryness. The brewpub is in the centre of Cologne, on the square called the Haymarket (*Heumarkt*). An interesting contrast is offered at the opposite end of the square by Päffgen, a smarter bar-restaurant offering a hop-accented *Kölsch*. Päffgen has a brewpub in Friesenstrasse.

Region of origin Cologne, North Rhine-Westphalia, Germany

Style *Kölschbier*

Alcohol content 4.8abv (3.8w)

Ideal serving temperature 9°C (48°F)

Brewing in the wind
Was the Malt Mill wind-powered? Unlikely, as the brewery dates from only 1858. Perhaps there were windmills by the banks of the Rhine.

REISSDORF KÖLSCH

Heinrich Reissdorf, from an old agricultural family, established this brewery in 1894. After the Second World War, it pioneered the style of *Kölsch* as universally brewed in Cologne today. The company is still privately owned, and said to be very conservative. It is in the St Severin district, in the south part of Cologne's inner city. Its beer has a minty, hop aroma; sweet, vanilla-like, malt flavours; and a crisp, dry, cedary finish. A delicious *Kölsch*, which briefly inspired a very fruity beer called St Severin's Kölsch in California.

Region of origin Cologne, North Rhine-Westphalia, Germany

Style *Kölschbier*

Alcohol content 4.8abv (3.8w)

Ideal serving temperature 9°C (48°F)

RICHMODIS KÖLSCH

A spritzy, lemony, dryish *Kölsch*, with a crisp finish, from a Cologne brewery. The original brewery, built in 1888, was destroyed by Allied bombs in 1944. Richmodis is in Gremberghaven, south of the river. The beer is widely available in Cologne taverns and restaurants. A good outlet is Zum Neuen Treffpunkt (The New Meeting Point), 25 Nussbaumerstrasse. The brewery is owned by Königsbacher, of Coblenz.

Region of origin Cologne, North Rhine-Westphalia, Germany

Style *Kölschbier*

Alcohol content 4.8abv (3.8w)

Ideal serving temperature 9°C (48°F)

Mother country
In Roman times, Cologne was a colonial capital, hence the name. This beer's label remembers "Colonia est Mater". Coeln and Cöln are old spellings, Köln today's German form.

SESTER KÖLSCH

A very fragrant, firm-bodied *Kölsch*, smooth and slightly oily, with an orangey fruitiness. The beer's long-time slogan, *Trink Sester mein Bester*, means "Drink Sester, my friend". The firm of Sester was founded in 1896, but in recent years the beer has been made by the Bergische Löwen brewery. Sester's symbol is a team of dray-horses, called Max and Moritz, after characters in a book by German poet, painter, caricaturist, and satirist Wilhelm Busch (1832–1908). The characters inspired the American strip, the Katzenjammer Kids.

Region of origin Cologne, North Rhine-Westphalia, Germany

Style *Kölschbier*

Alcohol content 4.8abv (3.8w)

Ideal serving temperature 9°C (48°F)

HELLERS WIESS

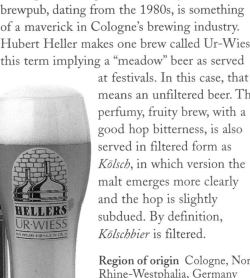

In premises that formerly housed a distillery making a bitter liqueur, this new-generation brewpub, dating from the 1980s, is something of a maverick in Cologne's brewing industry. Hubert Heller makes one brew called Ur-Wiess, this term implying a "meadow" beer as served at festivals. In this case, that means an unfiltered beer. This perfumy, fruity brew, with a good hop bitterness, is also served in filtered form as *Kölsch*, in which version the malt emerges more clearly and the hop is slightly subdued. By definition, *Kölschbier* is filtered.

Region of origin Cologne, North Rhine-Westphalia, Germany

Style *Kölschbier*

Alcohol content 4.5abv (3.6w)

Ideal serving temperature 9°C (48°F)

SÜNNER KÖLSCH

After five generations, Sünner is the oldest family concern still making its own beer in Cologne. Christian Sünner founded the brewery in 1830 and it has been on the same site since 1859. It is across the river from the city centre, in the high street of the Kalk neighbourhood. There is a beer garden at the brewery. Sünner Kölsch has a fresh, creamy aroma; a peachy fruitiness; and a dry, spicy, almost salty, hop tang in its crisp finish. The brewery also makes a rye whiskey.

Region of origin Cologne, North Rhine-Westphalia, Germany

Style *Kölschbier*

Alcohol content 4.8abv (3.8w)

Ideal serving temperature 9°C (48°F)

Winning over wine
This brew can be enjoyed in the city centre at Im Walfisch, a typical Cologne beer tavern on a site that was a brewery in the 1400s. Another of Sünner's outlets, the shellfish restaurant Bieresel, traces its history to 1297.

BUDELS PAREL KÖLSCH

Not made in the region, or even in Germany, and a little stronger than the original, but broadly in the style of a *Kölsch*. This beer is made across the Dutch frontier, beyond even the border province of Limburg, in the Brabant town of Budel. The enterprising Budels brewery launched it in 1985 as a novel speciality. *Parel* is Dutch for "pearl". The beer has a very good, resiny, hop aroma; a firm, smooth body; a dry palate; a faint hint of raspberry and vanilla fruitiness; and a dry, appetizing finish.

Region of origin Province of North Brabant, The Netherlands

Style *Kölsch*-type

Alcohol content 6.0abv (4.8w)

Ideal serving temperature 8–9°C (47–48°F)

FIREHOUSE KÖLSCH LAGER

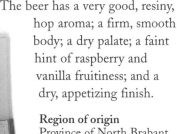

Germany's restrictions on the term *Kölsch* have not yet reached the US, where many breweries try to emulate the style. This example is oddly subtitled a "Kölsch Lager". It is produced in a brewery and pub in a former fire station in Cleveland, Ohio. It has a lightly hoppy aroma; delicate flavours; a firm, slightly oily, creamy body; and a dry, faintly tart finish.

Region of origin Midwest US

Style *Kölsch*-type

Alcohol content 4.7abv (3.8w)

Ideal serving temperature 9°C (48°F)

Hot beer
The horses on this label are, on closer inspection, pulling a fire engine. Several new-generation American breweries are in former fire stations.

SOCIABLE BEERS: ALTBIER

THERE ARE STRONG SIMILARITIES between the ales of England and Belgium and the *Altbier* made in Düsseldorf and other north-western German cities – not only in typical colour, but also in method of production, These copper-coloured German beers are really ales, in that they are made with top-fermenting yeasts. *Alt* is German for "old", and these are beers still loyal to the "old" style that was common before lager brewing spread from south-easterly cities such as Munich and Pilsen. Today, Düsseldorf is one of Germany's most cosmopolitan cities, and its lively bars take a pride in their *Altbier*, a style widely emulated in the US and Japan. Perhaps the Japanese acquired the taste in Düsseldorf. The city has the European headquarters of many Japanese companies.

Over a barrel
Altbier *blends the generations at Düsseldorf's Zum Uerige.*

A tasty drop...
...is the meaning of "dat leckere Dröppke". "Obergärige" *is "top-fermenting". Germans are expected to understand the significance.*

UERIGE ALT

Fashion icons, rock stars, punks, men in suits, old ladies with big hats...everyone in Düsseldorf drinks at Zum Uerige by the river in the Old Town (the Altstadt). Zum Uerige has its own sausage butchery, and its specialities are brawn and a smelly Mainzer cheese marinated in beer. The beer at this rambling old brewpub, the classic example of *Alt*, is also bottled for general sale. It has a fresh hop aroma; a firm, smooth, almost slippery, clean maltiness; and a robust punch of bitterness. The name Uerige refers to a past cranky proprietor. A slightly stronger, "secret" version, given extra aroma with a hop tea, is brewed once or twice a year under the name *Sticke Bier*, a Düsseldorf tradition. Uerige Alt inspired the excellent Ur Alt of the Widmer brewery, in Portland, Oregon.

Region of origin
Düsseldorf, North Rhine-Westphalia, Germany

Style *Altbier*

Alcohol content 4.5abv (3.6w)

Ideal serving temperature 9°C (48°F)

BARD OF BEER

THE HOUSE OF the German lyric poet Heinrich Heine (1797–1856) is near the *Altbier* brewpub Zum Schlüssel. He noted that "Germans have a thousand words for beer". On travels in Bavaria, he criticized the "best beer" there, preferring English Porter.

IM FÜCHSCHEN ALT

The name means "The Fox Cub". This is another rightly renowned brewery and pub in the Old Town of Düsseldorf. Its *Alt*, also a favourite among lovers of the style, is a well-balanced but hoppy interpretation. It has a creamy malt character; a restrained, pear-like fruitiness; and a hoppy acidity in the dry finish. The brewery, a classic of its type, stands like a miniature industrial building behind the tavern. Inside, customers share scrubbed tables, and the beer accompanies a hearty menu. The house speciality is *Eisbein*: boiled knuckle of pork.

Region of origin Düsseldorf, North Rhine-Westphalia, Germany

Style *Altbier*

Alcohol content 4.5abv (3.6w)

Ideal serving temperature 9°C (48°F)

SCHUMACHER ALT

A family-owned brewery and pub in the modern centre of the city. The Schumacher family were beer-makers even before they owned their first brewery, in 1838, and the present premises date from the 1870s. This is a quieter, more café-like brewpub, with a beer garden. Its beer is one of the paler examples in colour; sweetish, malt-accented, and softly, nuttily fruity; but with a good balance. Typical dishes include *Sauerbraten*, the marinaded beef dish of the Rhineland.

Region of origin Düsseldorf, North Rhine-Westphalia, Germany

Style *Altbier*

Alcohol content 4.6abv (3.7w)

Ideal serving temperature 9°C (48°F)

Symbols of brewing
The malt shovel and mashing fork on the label are symbols of the brewer's art. The mini-barrel is used like a ladle. The big vessel is a mash-tun.

FRANKENHEIM ALT

This light, dry, peppery, spicy *Altbier* is from a major privately-owned brewery in Düsseldorf. The brewery dates from the 1870s, and is still in the Frankenheim family. Another family-owned brewery, Diebels, of Issum, produces the biggest-selling *Altbier* nationally: a smooth, firm, malty example. Other privately-owned breweries include Rhenania (making a sweetish, slightly thick-tasting *Altbier*) and Gatzweiler (very fruity).

Region of origin Düsseldorf, North Rhine-Westphalia, Germany

Style *Altbier*

Alcohol content 4.8abv (3.8w)

Ideal serving temperature 9°C (48°F)

Private pride
"Privatbrauerei" on German beer labels implies that private owners can indulge their pride in making great beer rather than filling the pockets of their shareholders.

SCHLÖSSER ALT

The name derives from the word for "lock". The Schlösser family founded the enterprise as a brewpub in the Old Town in 1873. Between the two World Wars, a series of mergers and expansions began, and Schlösser is now the biggest *Altbier* brewery within Düsseldorf, and is part of the national Brau und Brunnen group. Its beer is on the light side in both body and taste. It has a syrupy start, with flavours like brown sugar, becoming nuttier, firmer, and drier in the finish.

Region of origin Düsseldorf, North Rhine-Westphalia, Germany

Style *Altbier*

Alcohol content 4.8abv (3.8w)

Ideal serving temperature 9°C (48°F)

The true tradition
Schlösser's short, cylindrical glass is the most traditional shape used for Altbier. Some brewers have moved to taller, slimmer vessels more reminiscent of Kölschbier.

BOLTEN UR-ALT

A truly "old" brewery, tracing its history to 1266, in Korschenbroich, west of Düsseldorf. Since the 1600s, the brewery, inn, and farm have been owned by the Bolten family. Early beers of the region used peat-smoked malt, were spiced, and were fermented with wild yeast. The term *Altbier* was introduced in the 1890s. The beers had a low carbonation until the post-war period. Bolten Alt has deep, complex, dry, malty flavours. The version called Ur-Alt is unfiltered, more textured, and juicier-tasting.

Region of origin
Korschenbroich,
North Rhine-
Westphalia, Germany

Style *Altbier*

Alcohol content
4.7abv (3.8w)

Ideal serving temperature
9°C (48°F)

PINKUS MÜLLER ALT

This golden, wheat-tinged interpretation, very dry, crisp, and quenching but with some buttery maltiness, is a quite different style of "old" beer. It evolved in the university city of Münster, capital of North Rhine-Westphalia. This version is made only at a famous brewery and pub called Pinkus Müller. This establishment began in 1816 as a bakery and brewery in the Old Town, and has expanded over the years through nine houses. In summer, the beer is offered laced with soft fruits.

Region of origin
Münster, North Rhine-
Westphalia, Germany

Style Münster *Altbier*

Alcohol content 5.0abv (4.0w)

Ideal serving temperature
9°C (48°F)

NUSSDORFER ST. THOMAS BRÄU

Thomas, the patron saint of the village of Nussdorf, on the edge of Vienna, Austria, gives his name to this *Altbier*, produced there by Baron Bachofen von Echt. A Nussdorfer brewery established in 1819, and run by the Baron's family for five generations, closed in the 1950s, but he revived the tradition in 1984. His *Altbier* has robust malt flavours – sweet, creamy, nutty, and juicy – with a good hop balance.

Region of origin Austria

Style *Altbier*

Alcohol content
4.8abv (3.8w)

Ideal serving temperature 9°C (48°F)

Pure by law
The top line of the label makes clear that this Austrian beer is brewed according to the German Purity Law.

WARTECK ALT

A director of the Warteck brewery developed a love of *Altbier* from his wife, who came from the Lower Rhine. From such chance origins, this brewery in Basel, Switzerland gained its own *Altbier* in the late 1970s. The beer has a malty aroma; a lightly toffeeish start, developing to cinnamon spiciness and perfumy fruitiness; and a balancing touch of hoppy dryness. Warteck was acquired by a local rival, and the beer is now produced in the cathedral-like brewhouse of Feldschlösschen.

Region of origin
Switzerland

Style *Altbier*

Alcohol content
4.7abv (3.8w)

Ideal serving temperature
9°C (48°F)

BUDELS ALT

Few European breweries are as eclectic in their beer styles as Budels, of North Brabant in The Netherlands. Its range includes not only a *Kölsch* type but also this *Altbier*, albeit at an alcohol content that is higher than typical. This interpretation has a pale colour for the style; fresh spicy hop and fudgy malt in the aroma; lively flavour development, with hints of ginger; and a firm, very dry finish.

Region of origin
Province of North Brabant, The Netherlands

Style *Altbier*

Alcohol content 6.0abv (4.8w)

Ideal serving temperature
9°C (48°F)

Toasting Alt
On this label, the crowned head of Brabant, Jan Primus, is shown as the mythical King of Beer, Gambrinus, alleged inventor of the toast.

ALASKAN AMBER

A beer that sounds in style to have been an *Alt* was produced by a German immigrant brewer in Alaska around the turn of the century. This was discovered by Geoff and Marcy Larson when they established their micro-brewery in the state capital, Juneau, in 1986. They decided to brew an *Alt*, which they called Alaskan Amber.

This has become their principal product. It is a very complex beer, with a malty aroma; a slightly oily, clean, malty palate; and a spicy dryness in the finish.

Region of origin
Pacific Northwest US

Style *Altbier*

Alcohol content
5.2abv (4.2w)

Ideal serving temperature
9°C (48°F)

SOUTHAMPTON SECRET

Modelled on a *Sticke*. Made with imported German ingredients: no fewer than five malts (pale, Vienna, Munich, black, and wheat) and three varieties of hops (Northern Brewer, Hallertau Tradition, and Spalt) and an *Altbier* yeast. Very fresh in aroma and palate, with a sweetish, slightly chocolatey, smoothly malty start but a good balance of late dryness. It is from the Southampton Publick House, on Long Island, New York.

Region of origin
Northeast US

Style *Altbier*

Alcohol content
5.2abv (4.2w)

Ideal serving temperature
9°C (48F°)

First resort
The seaside pavilions and sail-boarding of Southampton seem a far cry from the cosiness of Old Town taverns by the Rhine in Düsseldorf.

SCHMALTZ'S ALT

The jocular-sounding alliteration derives from a local nickname in the largely German-American town of New Ulm, Minnesota. In this instance, it applied to the late father of the brewery's principal. The August Schell brewery, founded in 1860, is one of the few old-established region breweries left in the US. It is also the prettiest, set in woodland with its own deer park. Schmaltz's Alt is a very dark, roasty, vanilla-tinged, dry interpretation of the style.

Region of origin Midwest US

Style *Altbier*

Alcohol content 5.9abv (4.7w)

Ideal serving temperature
9°C (48°F)

Frontier spirit
The brewery's owning family survived a Sioux uprising in the early pioneering days – their hospitality had apparently been appreciated by the Native Americans.

SOCIABLE BEERS: BELGIAN ALES

THE WORD "ALE" IS USED IN BELGIUM to describe bronze or amber-red brews for everyday drinking. While English ale is often more fruity or bitter, and German *Altbier* notably rounded and smooth, the Belgian members of this family can have an appetizing spiciness, usually deriving from the character of the local top-fermenting yeasts. These softly teasing brews perfectly suit the pace of café life in a country where neither food nor drink is consumed in a hurry.

Symbolic sculpture
A Brabant draught horse, shown here sculptured in bronze, is the symbol of Palm ale, appearing on both bottle and glass.

DE KONINCK

The name of this beer means "king", but it was the surname of a man who owned a beer garden in Antwerp, capital of Flanders and second city of Belgium. The beer garden has long gone, but its brewery survives. Its principal product is known simply as De Koninck. This is the much-loved local beer of Antwerp. It is not described on the tap handle or label as an ale, but it certainly is one. As a bottled brew, De Koninck is good, but its fresh, yeasty, dusty, cinnamon-like spiciness is at its best when the beer is served on draught. It has a dense head that leaves lacework with every swallow. It is subtle, dryish, but beautifully balanced, toasty, soothing, and drinkable. A stronger (8.0abv/6.4w), spicier, brandyish version is called Cuvée De Koninck.

Region of origin Province of Antwerp, Belgium

Style Belgian Ale

Alcohol content 5.0abv (4.0w)

Ideal serving temperature The brewery suggests 7°C (45°F), but the flavours are more evident at a less severe temperature, around 12°C (54°F)

Vulgar fractions
De Koninck's curved goblet is ordered as a bolleke *(little ball) in Antwerp. The word sounds vulgar to the British drinker. The "women's" alternative, a flute (*fluitje, *in Flemish), has phallic connotations locally.*

DE KONINCK YEAST

OPPOSITE THE DE KONINCK brewery is the Pilgrim café, where the brewery's surplus yeast is traditionally offered to customers by the shot-glass, as a tonic. Some chase it down with a glass of De Koninck, while others add it to their beer. In recent years, the practice has spread to other De Koninck cafés in the city.

PALM SPECIALE

This ale was introduced in the 1920s. It became Belgium's biggest-selling ale, and the brewery is now also known as Palm. The beer is made in Steenhuffel, north-west of Brussels. Palm Speciale has a malty accent, with a rounded, orangey, yeasty finish. The brewery also has a stronger (7.5abv/ 6.0w), drier, hoppier ale called Aerts 1900.

Region of origin
Province of Flemish Brabant, Belgium

Style Belgian Ale

Alcohol content
5.0abv (4.0w)

Ideal serving temperature
12°C (54°F)

Uncommon style
The term "Speciale" is sometimes used on labels in Belgium to indicate an ale rather than a more common lager style.

OP-ALE

In Flemish, *op* means "up", as in "drink up" – an apt abbreviation for Opwijk, the town where this ale is made. Op-Ale has a refreshing, sweet-apple fruitiness; a light, clean, dry, crisply malty palate; and a citric spritziness in the finish. It is made by the De Smedt brewery, which also produces beers for the abbey of Affligem.

Region of origin Province of Flemish Brabant, Belgium

Style Belgian Ale

Alcohol content 5.0abv (4.0w)

Ideal serving temperature
The brewery suggests 7°C (45°F), but the flavours are more evident at around 10°C (50°F)

Pride of the province
Not only the local breweries but also the province adopts the Brabant horse as a symbol.

GINDER ALE

Not "ginger": the man who created this beer was called Van Ginderachter. It is a lively, appetizing beer with apple-brandy flavours deriving from a distinct yeast. Ginder Ale is made by the same company as Stella Artois, in the brewing city of Leuven. The same company, Interbrew, also makes the smooth, anise-tinged Horse Ale and the sherbety, faintly smoky Vieux Temps.

Region of origin
Province of Flemish Brabant, Belgium

Style Belgian Ale

Alcohol content
5.1abv (4.1w)

Ideal serving temperature
10°C (50°F)

PETRUS SPECIALE

The name Petrus sounds like a famous Bordeaux wine but is intended simply to signify St Peter, known as "holder of the keys to heaven". The Petrus range is made by the De Brabandere brewery, of Bavikhove, West Flanders. Its Speciale is an assertive ale, with an earthy aroma; a textured malt background; coriander in the palate (this spice is added); and a rooty, hoppy finish.

Region of origin Province of West Flanders, Belgium

Style Belgian Ale

Alcohol content 5.5abv (4.4w)

Ideal serving temperature
10°C (50°F)

Hop happy
Hops feature on many beer labels. In this case, the illustration is justified. Petrus Speciale is one of the hoppier Belgian ales.

SOCIABLE BEERS: ENGLISH BITTERS

ALL BREWS BALANCE the sweetness of the malt with the bitterness ("dryness" might be a better term) of the hop. The English term for an ale that is well hopped is a "bitter". Some are only very slightly bitter, others have a real smack of hops. The best examples gain a teasing complexity of flavour as they mature in the cellar of the pub.

Pulling power
In Britain, a high proportion of beer is consumed on draught.

Bottled strength
The bottled version of London Pride is slightly stronger than the draught. Pints in the pub are often of modest strength.

FULLER'S LONDON PRIDE

In some parts of the world, Fuller's ales are gaining a cult following. Within Britain, much of the beer is sold very locally, in the suburbs around the brewery. Fuller's has three examples of bitter. The low-strength Chiswick Bitter (named after the brewery's neighbourhood), is refreshingly flowery in its hop character. This is a typically English approach: a beer that is full of flavour but light in body and alcohol, so that several pints can be consumed in an evening. In the middle comes London Pride, with beautifully combined flavours of light, smoothly nutty malt; crisply bitter hop; and faintly honeyish yeast. This is a more satisfying, soothing bitter. Drinkers wanting a little more punch, and perhaps only one pint, opt for the bigger Extra Special Bitter, with its robust hits of malt and hop.

Region of origin London, England, UK

Style Bitter Ale

Alcohol content In bottle: 4.7abv (3.8w)
On draught: 4.1abv (3.3w)

Ideal serving temperature 10–13°C (50–55°F)

HAND-RAISED ALE

GENUINE HAND-PUMPS are more than a decoration in a British pub. They pull beer from the cellar without the use of nitrogen or carbon dioxide pressure. The gentle carbonation in the beer is caused by a secondary fermentation in the cask at cellar temperature. During this "conditioning", the yeast in the cask precipitates.

ENGLISH BITTERS

CHILTERN JOHN HAMPDEN'S ALE

Just north of the Chiltern Hills, in Aylesbury, historic county town of Buckinghamshire. The brewery, established in 1980, revived Aylesbury's beer-making tradition after a gap of 40-odd years. The farm-based Chiltern brewery also sells beer-flavoured condiments and cheeses, and even hop-based toiletries. John Hampden's Ale is straw-coloured, with the aroma of lemons and ginger and a very dry, cracker-like maltiness.

Region of origin
Southeast England, UK

Style Bitter Ale

Alcohol content 4.8abv (3.8w)

Ideal serving temperature
10–13°C (50–55°F)

EVERARDS' TIGER

This brew was once produced in Britain's beer capital, Burton upon Trent, but is today made elsewhere in the Midlands, at the Everard family's modern brewery near Leicester. Everards' Tiger is named after a local regiment that spent a great deal of time in India. The beer, as in a classic Burton ale, has a hint of sulphur on the nose. Its palate is rounded, nutty, and oily, with some orangey flavours and a dry finish.

Region of origin
Central England, UK

Style Bitter Ale

Alcohol content 4.5abv (3.6w)

Ideal serving temperature
10–13°C (50–55°F)

MORDUE'S WORKIE TICKET

Judged "Champion Beer of Britain" two years after this new-generation brewery was established. Founders Matthew and Gary Fawson were inspired to their profession when they discovered that their house near Newcastle had been a brewery called Mordue in the 1800s. "Workie Ticket" is a Geordie (Newcastle) expression for a troublemaker. This full-coloured beer has a robust maltiness, balanced by a surge of nutty dryness in the finish.

Region of origin
Northeast England, UK

Style Bitter Ale

Alcohol content 4.5abv (3.6w)

Ideal serving temperature
10–13°C (50–55°F)

MORLAND "OLD SPECKLED HEN"

Georgian landscape painter George Morland was a member of the family. The brewing company dates from 1711. It bought its present premises, at Abingdon, Oxfordshire, in 1863. The town has a history of malting and brewing, but MG cars were also a local industry. The Old Speckled Hen was a locally famous MG. The beer is malt-accented, but with a distinctly yeasty dryness and appetizingly lively, long finish.

Region of origin
Southern England, UK

Style Bitter Ale

Alcohol content 5.2abv (4.2w)

Ideal serving temperature
10–13°C (50–55°F)

RINGWOOD OLD THUMPER

New-generation beer makers all over the world took their initial advice from veteran brewer Peter Austin. He started his own first brewery here in the New Forest, at Ringwood, Hampshire. His Old Thumper is a bronze ale, with a sherbety aroma; clean, syrupy flavours; a smooth body; and a gentle hop balance. A good interpretation of Old Thumper is made in the US, by the Shipyard brewery, of Portland, Maine.

Region of origin
Southern England, UK

Style Strong Ale/Bitter

Alcohol content 5.6abv (4.5w)

Ideal serving temperature
10–13°C (50–55°F)

WADWORTH 6X

An open copper kettle is still used, and wooden casks are supplied to local pubs, by the traditionally-minded Wadworth brewery in the market town of Devizes, Wiltshire. The classic tower brewery was built in 1885, though earlier premises from at least the 1830s still stand. Wadworth's 6X is modest in alcohol but big in flavour and texture: an oaky aroma, with hints of Cognac; a toasted-nut maltiness; and a sappy, slightly tart dryness in the finish.

Region of origin
Southern England, UK

Style Bitter Ale

Alcohol content 4.3abv (3.4w)

Ideal serving temperature
10–13°C (50–55°F)

CHARLES WELLS BOMBARDIER

Sizable regional brewery, old-established, and still family-run, in Bedford. Its best-known beer evokes the memory of boxer Bombardier Billy Wells, British heavyweight champion from 1911 to 1919. This satisfying, smooth, malt-accented beer has a slightly sulphury, rooty aroma; fruity, cherry-pie flavours; and a cookie-like dryness in the finish. A firmer, drier, stronger ale is neatly named Wells Fargo.

Region of origin
Eastern England, UK

Style Bitter Ale

Alcohol content 4.3abv (3.4w)

Ideal serving temperature
10–13°C (50–55°F)

WOODFORDE'S NORFOLK WHERRY

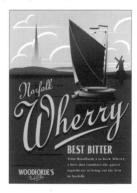

New-generation farmhouse brewery near Norwich. Some of the buildings are thatched with reeds from the nearby system of waterways known as the Norfolk Broads. A wherry is a type of shallow boat typically used in the area. The beer named after the boat is hoppy, with a leafy, sharp, fresh-lime aroma and flavour; a crisp, cookie-like, malt background; and a dry, candied-peel finish.

Region of origin
Eastern England, UK

Style Bitter Ale

Alcohol content 3.8abv (3.0w)

Ideal serving temperature
10–13°C (50–55°F)

SOCIABLE BEERS: SCOTTISH ALES

SCOTLAND CULTIVATES BARLEY for malting, but its climate is too cool for hops. Scottish ales emphasize the malt, typically having a soothing maltiness and roundness. In the days before refrigeration, Scotland's weather made for relatively low temperatures of fermentation and maturation, and this helped to round the beers. The examples shown here are substantial, without being too strong for sociable drinking.

Cross-border café
Scotland's capital, Edinburgh, has ornate pubs, such as the Café Royal.

Towering trademark
The trademark on the glass depicts the kiln in which grain is dried at the end of malting. Some whisky distilleries use a similar symbol.

CALEDONIAN FLYING SCOTSMAN

The small Caledonian brewery, in Edinburgh, produces Scotland's maltiest beers. The brewery dates from 1869, and still boils its kettles by direct flame (as opposed to the more usual steam). This "fire-brewing" creates hot spots, and a caramelization that can heighten the malty flavours. Since 1987, the brewery has been run by a malt expert who formerly worked in the whisky industry. The brewery stands near the Edinburgh-London railway, and the beer Flying Scotsman is named after a famous train on that route. The ruby-coloured brew contains a tiny amount of rye. It is profoundly malty in its aroma and flavours, but very well rounded, with hints of raisiny spiciness and toasty dryness. There is a yet greater maltiness, but not as much balancing dryness, in the marginally less strong Merman and the more potent Edinburgh Strong Ale.

Region of origin Southern Scotland, UK

Style Scottish Ale

Alcohol content 5.1abv (4.1w)

Ideal serving temperature 10–13°C (50–55°F)

SHILLING FOR ALE

SCOTTISH ALES ARE OFTEN LABELLED 60/-, 70/-, 80/-, or 90/-. The symbol represents the shilling, a long-gone currency. These century-old ratings represented tax bands. Today they indicate ascending strength, but in general terms. There is no specific link between the shillings and the alcohol.

MACLAY EIGHTY SHILLING EXPORT ALE

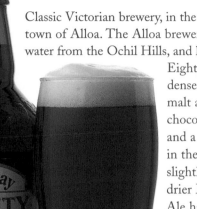

Classic Victorian brewery, in the old beer-making town of Alloa. The Alloa breweries had hard water from the Ochil Hills, and local coal. Maclay Eighty Shilling has a dense head; a perfumy malt aroma; a hint of chocolatey sweetness; and a creamy dryness in the finish. The slightly stronger, paler, drier Maclay Scotch Ale has more of a fresh-bread maltiness.

Region of origin
Central Scotland, UK

Style Scottish Ale

Alcohol content
4.0abv (3.2w)

Ideal serving temperature
10–13°C (50–55°F)

BROUGHTON BLACK DOUGLAS

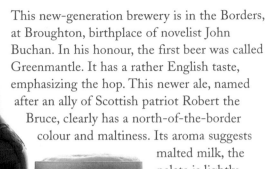

This new-generation brewery is in the Borders, at Broughton, birthplace of novelist John Buchan. In his honour, the first beer was called Greenmantle. It has a rather English taste, emphasizing the hop. This newer ale, named after an ally of Scottish patriot Robert the Bruce, clearly has a north-of-the-border colour and maltiness. Its aroma suggests malted milk, the palate is lightly treacly, and the finish has the bitterness of black chocolate.

Region of origin
Scottish Borders, UK

Style Scottish Ale

Alcohol content
5.2abv (4.2w)

Ideal serving temperature
10–13°C (50–55°F)

BELHAVEN 80/- EXPORT ALE

A Benedictine monastery on a nearby island gave rise to this brewery at Belhaven, near Dunbar, between the border and Edinburgh. The brewery traces its commercial origins to 1719. Its 80/- (labelled with the shilling symbol rather than the full spelling) has a tawny colour; a smooth, firm, toasty palate; and a good flavour development, with a faint, jammy, pineapple note from the house yeast.

Region of origin
Scottish Borders, UK

Style Scottish Ale

Alcohol content
3.9abv (3.1w)

Ideal serving temperature
10–13°C (50–55°F)

McEWAN'S 80/-

Scotland's biggest beer maker, which merged with Younger's, then acquired Newcastle Breweries and later Courage. The resultant company, Scottish Courage, is the biggest brewer in Britain. In Edinburgh, McEwan's products include this 80/-, very slightly lighter in body than its competitors, on the dry side, with a touch of burnt toast. The label emphasizes the use of roasted barley, suggesting that this is a "classic" ingredient.

Region of origin
Southern Scotland, UK

Style Scottish Ale

Alcohol content
4.5abv (3.6w)

Ideal serving temperature
10–13°C (50–55°F)

BERT GRANT'S SCOTTISH ALE

Dundee-born beer maker Bert Grant was a brewpub pioneer in the hop town of Yakima, Washington, in 1982. He is still associated with the Grant's brewery, though it is now owned by a local winery. His Scottish Ale is inspired by his origins as much as the classic style, though it does have a lot of malt in both aroma and palate, as well as the hop character appropriate to the region.

Region of origin
Pacific Northwest US

Style Scottish/
Northwestern Ale

Alcohol content
4.7abv (3.8w)

**Ideal serving
temperature**
10–13°C (50–55°F)

*"Brand" name
Can an ale made in
the US be Scottish?
The US authorities
oblige Grant's to add
the explanatory word
"brand" to the label.*

ODELL'S 90 SHILLING

Doug Odell is an American of Welsh extraction who visited Scotland on vacation, enjoyed the beers, went home to Colorado, gave up his landscaping business, and in 1989 established a micro-brewery in Fort Collins. One of his first beers was his 90 Shilling. It is appropriately malty in both its fresh aroma and satisfying balance of light, smooth syrupiness and nuttiness, finishing with a restrained, moreish dryness.

Region of origin
Southwest US

Style Scottish Ale

Alcohol content
5.6abv (4.5w)

**Ideal serving
temperature**
10–13°C (50–55°F)

PORTLAND BREWING
MACTARNAHAN'S GOLD MEDAL

Portland, Oregon, has 20-odd breweries, more than any other city in the world. The boom began in the mid-1980s, and Portland Brewing dates from that time. In 1992, the brewery won a gold medal at the Great American Beer Festival for its MacTarnahan's. The product is named after a friend of the brewery. It has a touch of butterscotch maltiness in the aroma, rounding out to a fruity, hoppy dryness.

Region of origin
Pacific Northwest US

Style
Scottish/Northwestern Ale

Alcohol content
4.2abv (3.4w)

Ideal serving temperature
13°C (55°F)

*Read the small print
The small print on the label
describes MacTarnahan's as
a Scottish-style amber ale.*

FLATLANDER'S EIGHTY
SHILLING ALE

People from the Plains states of the US sometimes self-mockingly call themselves flatlanders. This brewery is in a large, Prairie-style restaurant in Illinois. The town is called Lincolnshire but, despite that English name, the brewery's most noteworthy product is a very authentic Scottish ale: typically full in colour and textured in body, with a dryish, very faintly peaty maltiness. Scottish malt is used.

Region of origin
Midwest US

Style Scottish Ale

Alcohol content
3.7abv (3.0w)

Ideal serving temperature
10–13°C (50–55°F)

Scottish Ales

Boulder Creek Highlands Amber

In the Redwood Hills, in the old logging town of Boulder Creek, north of Santa Cruz, California. This rather remote brewpub specializes in British styles. Its Highlands Amber is made with pale and brown malts and roasted barley, all from Scotland. The beer has a dense, bubbly head, leaving good lace; a tawny colour; and a delicious interplay of fruity, chocolatey maltiness and crisp, dry toastiness. It is a fine example of a really quaffable Scottish ale.

Region of origin West US

Style Scottish Ale

Alcohol content 4.6abv (3.7w)

Ideal serving temperature 10–13°C (50–55°F)

Flying Dog Scottish Ale

The owner of a ranch called the Flying Dog is a partner in this cellar brewpub in the fashionable ski resort of Aspen, Colorado – hence its unusual name. Flying Dog's beers are also produced, for bottling, in the associated Broadway brewery, in Denver. The Scottish ale, sub-titled Road Dog, is notably smooth, with flavours suggesting cocoa, raisins, and rum, and a balancing dryness of lively yoghurty acidity.

Region of origin Southwest US

Style Scottish Ale

Alcohol content 5.8abv (4.6w)

Ideal serving temperature 10–13°C (50–55°F)

Harviestoun Montrose Ale

A 200-year-old stone cowshed was the original home of this brewery, not far from Alloa. Harviestoun's brews have ranged from a crisp wheat ale to an unfiltered lager. Its more traditional ales have a Scottish maltiness that leans to the dry, nutty side, sometimes with touches of vanilla, and are quite fruity. The brew named after the town of Montrose is a full-flavoured 80/-, with a suggestion of blackcurrant.

Region of origin Central Scotland, UK

Style Scottish Ale

Alcohol content 4.2abv (3.4w)

Ideal serving temperature 10–13°C (50–55°F)

Molson Dave's Scotch Ale

Canada's other national giant was founded in Quebec in 1786 by John Molson, from Lincolnshire, England. It is the oldest brewing company in North America, though it is now partly owned by Foster's, of Australia. Molson is better known for golden ales and lagers, but its specialities include a deep amber Scotch Ale: firm, malty, dry, and faintly peaty. This tasty brew is part of a range created for supermarket principal Dave Nichol.

Region of origin Province of Ontario, Canada

Style Scottish Ale

Alcohol content 5.6abv (4.5w)

Ideal serving temperature 10–13°C (50–55°F)

Moulin Ale of Atholl

The Moulin Hotel is in the Perthshire town of Pitlochry (known for its theatre festival), near the Duke of Atholl's castle. The hotel had a brewery when it opened in 1695, and the idea was revived for its 300th anniversary. Among its several beers is the bottle-conditioned Ale of Atholl: tawny and toffeeish, with some fruit in the finish.

Region of origin Central Scotland, UK

Style Scottish Ale

Alcohol content 4.5abv (3.6w)

Ideal serving temperature 10–13°C (50–55°F)

Orkney Dark Island

Off the northern tip of the Scottish mainland are the Orkney Islands, where the winters are long and dark. On the main island, known simply as Orkney, is this new-generation brewery in an 1870s' school building. The brewery was established in 1988 by a former publican and his schoolteacher wife. Its products have become widely known. Among them, Dark Island is a mahogany ale: peaty, chocolatey, creamy, and juicy.

Region of origin Orkney Islands, Northern Scotland, UK

Style Scottish Ale

Alcohol content 4.6abv (3.7w)

Ideal serving temperature 10–13°C (50–55°F)

Sherlock's Home Piper's Pride

This punning pub, in a suburb of Minneapolis, Minnesota, produces a classic Scottish ale, using malted oats and, in addition to hops, an earlier bittering ingredient called quassia (an extract from a tree that grows in Central and South America). Even the brewer is a Scot, who on occasion plays the bagpipes. The ale is tawny and malt-accented, with a touch of butterscotch and a spicy-herbal balancing dryness.

Region of origin Midwest US

Style Scottish Ale

Alcohol content 4.6abv (3.7w)

Ideal serving temperature 10–13°C (50–55°F)

Tomintoul Wild Cat

The last syllable rhymes with owl. Tomintoul is a village at 355 m (1,164 ft) in the Grampian mountains of northern Scotland. It is known for snow-blocked roads and a malt whisky made near the River Livet. The local brewery is in a 1700s' grain mill, once driven by water. Its Wild Cat ale has a full amber colour; a whiskyish aroma; a light, firm, cookie-like maltiness; and a dryish finish.

Region of origin Highlands, Northern Scotland, UK

Style Scottish Ale

Alcohol content 5.1abv (4.1w)

Ideal serving temperature 10–13°C (50–55°F)

SOCIABLE BEERS: NORTH AMERICAN ALES

THE NEW GENERATION of micro-breweries in the US and Canada makes more ales than any other type of beer. Many of these brews are fresh-tasting, drinkable, and moreish. They usually combine the appetizingly fruity, piney aromas of American hops with a light maltiness and dry finish. For sociable drinking, try a lightish cream ale, a drier pale ale, or a rounder extra special bitter.

Badge drinking
Designer labels belong to beers when they are worn at the annual Great American Beer Festival, in Denver, Colorado.

OLIVER ESB

A family called Oliver from Kent, England, by way of Canada, brews this ESB in Baltimore, Maryland. The Olivers' brewery and Wharf Rat pub opened in 1993. The ESB is served on hand-pumps at the pub, and in half-gallon "growlers" to go. It has an attractive, reddish-amber colour and fine bead; pours with a pillowy head, leaving a good lace; has a peppery hop-and-malt aroma; a nutty palate; a quenchingly tart finish; and a late, typically moreish dryness.

Region of origin Northeast US

Style
American Ale/Extra Special Bitter

Alcohol content 5.6abv (4.5w)

Ideal serving temperature
10–13°C (50–55°F)

JOHNS' BRONZE

BALLANTINE'S WAS ONE of a handful of ales widely known in the US before the micro-brewery movement. This golden, hoppy brew was such a legend as to be cast in bronze by artist Jasper Johns.

CLIMAX ESB

"The name represents the point of greatest excitement", according to one of the principals of this outstanding ale brewery. Climax, one of the first new-generation breweries in the state, was established in Roselle Park, New Jersey, in 1996. Its products range from a dryish, perfumy cream ale to an India pale ale with a rooty, almost artichoke-like bitterness. Between these two extremes is a fruitier, maltier, clean, soft ESB full of moreish flavours.

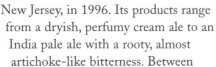

Region of origin
Northeast US

Style American Ale/
Extra Special Bitter

Alcohol content
5.5abv (4.4w)

**Ideal serving
temperature**
10–13°C (50–55°F)

REDHOOK ESB

A name that suggests fishing, for a brewery in the maritime towns of Seattle, Washington State, and Portsmouth, New Hampshire. Established in 1982, Redhook was one of the first new-generation ale breweries. A winter ale was also introduced in 1987 and later dubbed ESB, pioneering that term in the US. The beer is pale for the style; hop-accented in its big bouquet and appetizing dryness; but with a firm malt balance.

Region of origin
Pacific Northwest US

Style
American Ale/ESB

Alcohol content
5.4abv (4.3w)

**Ideal serving
temperature**
10–13°C (50–55°F)

Traditional brew
The small print on the label emphasizes the use of a traditional, top-fermenting ale yeast.

OASIS CAPSTONE ESB

Every good watering hole is an oasis, but this pub and micro-brewery pushes the point with its Egyptian-style interior. The brewpub is in the college town of Boulder, Colorado. Its bottled Capstone ESB has a full reddish-amber colour and fine bead; a dense head, creamy aroma, and malt accent; and satisfying flavour development. It is silky smooth, with toast and marmalade notes, and a cedary finish.

Region of origin
Southwest US

Style American Ale/
Extra Special Bitter

Alcohol content
5.6abv (4.5w)

**Ideal serving
temperature**
10–13°C (50–55°F)

Watchful eye
The thirst-making Egyptian sun god peers out from the label.

BRIDGEPORT ESB

The bridges of Portland, Oregon, unite a city framed by the Columbia and Willamette rivers, both flowing from hop regions. BridgePort, founded in 1984 as Columbia River Brewing, is the oldest micro-pub in this great city of small beers. Its ESB is perfumy and fruity, rounded off by an appetizingly dry, hoppy acidity.

Region of origin
Pacific Northwest US

Style
American Ale/ESB

Alcohol content
5.8abv (4.6w)

**Ideal serving
temperature**
10–13°C (50–55°F)

MOLSON SIGNATURE CREAM ALE

The Canadian giant Molson introduced its Signature range in 1993 as a rival to the tasty products being made by new-generation micros. Its Signature Cream Ale became a local speciality in British Columbia. Cream ales are traditionally pale, light in body and palate, and fruity. This ale has a perfumy aroma; a light, soft body; and flavours reminiscent of lemon jelly, drying in a "fruit gums" finish.

Region of origin Province of British Columbia, Canada

Style Cream Ale

Alcohol content 5.1abv (4.1w)

Ideal serving temperature 10°C (50°F)

Form and character
The tall, slender, waisted glass is perhaps intended to convey a light–but–tasty character.

WALNUT BIG HORN BITTER

America's lively home-brewing scene traces much of its growth and sophistication to an association in Boulder, a college town in the mountains of Colorado. The town's first brewpub was established on Walnut Street in 1990 and now bottles its beers. The Western-sounding Big Horn is, true to its designation, a very English-tasting bitter. It is refreshingly drinkable, with a lightly textured maltiness; restrained, clean fruitiness; rounded with a really appetizing hop-bitterness in the finish.

Region of origin Southwest US

Style English Bitter

Alcohol content 5.2abv (4.2w)

Ideal serving temperature 10–13°C (50–55°F)

HALE'S SPECIAL BITTER

Apart from some well-regarded seasonal brews, Mike Hale makes a solid range of regulars at his micro-breweries in Seattle and Spokane, Washington State. Hale's Special Bitter has a big, rocky head and is dark reddish-amber. It is full of flavour: malty and rounded, with fruity notes reminiscent of glacé cherries and candied peel. It has a spritzy, dry finish. Its initials, HSB, are shared with a similar beer made by Hale's inspiration, Gale's, in Horndean, near Portsmouth, England.

Region of origin Pacific Northwest US

Style English Bitter

Alcohol content 4.7abv (3.8w)

Ideal serving temperature 10–13°C (50–55°F)

Hale's and Gale's
The stylized tankard forms a letter "H". Is the initial in HSB for Hale's or Horndean?

DESCHUTES BACHELOR BITTER

The Deschutes river, in Oregon, shoots over rapids and curves sharply at the town of Bend, near the ski resort of Mount Bachelor. A pub and micro-brewery at Bend produce a wide range of flavoursome beers with alliterative names, and distribute them bottle-conditioned. Bachelor Bitter is big-tasting, firm and assertive, with a fresh dryness of American hop flavours and clean, orangey fruitiness. The beer is also quite bitter, particularly in its lingering finish.

Region of origin Pacific Northwest US

Style American Ale/Bitter

Alcohol content 5.2abv (4.2w)

Ideal serving temperature 10–13°C (50–55°F)

NORTH AMERICAN ALES

ELYSIAN THE WISE ESB

The Greek word for blissful, might, for the beer lover, describe the city of Seattle, Washington State. The city has a good dozen small breweries and invented the notion of an "ale-house". Elysian is a pub and brewery that makes extremely assertive ales with names alluding to mythical qualities. Its ESB, named The Wise, has a deep amber colour; a leafy aroma; and a thick, malty palate, sweet at first, developing to an intense orange-skin bitterness.

Region of origin Pacific Northwest US

Style American Ale/ESB

Alcohol content 5.8abv (4.6w)

Ideal serving temperature
10–13°C (50–55°F)

GOOSE ISLAND HONKER'S ALE

The "island" is a neck of land near Chicago's Halsted nightlife area. In a competitive city where many breweries have been short-lived, Goose Island is the success of the new generation. It is both a pub and brewery, producing a wide and changing range of beers, some available in the bottle. Its principal regular brew is Honker's Ale: orangey-coloured with an appetizing aroma of the hop variety Styrian Goldings; a firm, crisp body; and lively, dry, lightly fruity flavours.

Region of origin Midwest US

Style American Ale

Alcohol content 3.8abv (3.0w)

Ideal serving temperature
10–13°C (50–55°F)

GRITTY MCDUFF'S BEST BITTER

The founder of this brewery had a friend called Sandy, who was nicknamed Gritty. McDuff somehow followed. Gritty McDuff's began as a British-style pub and brewery in an old harbour warehouse in Portland, Maine. Now the beer is also bottled. The dry-tasting Best Bitter has a bright amber-tan colour; a light, spritzy body; some spicy, fruity notes; and a good balance of malt and hop.

Region of origin Northeast US

Style English Bitter

Alcohol content 5.0abv (4.0w)

Ideal serving temperature
10–13°C (50–55°F)

LANG CREEK TRIMOTOR AMBER

The remote Lang Creek brewery is in a former aircraft hangar in Marion, near Kalispell, in western Montana. The brewery's founder, a hobby pilot and aviation enthusiast, honours the pioneering, three-engined, 1930s' passenger plane with this beer. Trimotor Amber is a deep amber ale, broadly in the style of an ESB. It is smooth, tasty, malty, and nutty, with late flavours of chocolate and leafy hop.

Region of origin Pacific Northwest US

Style American Ale/ESB

Alcohol content 5.3abv (4.2w)

Ideal serving temperature
10–13°C (50–55°F)

OTTO BROTHERS' TETON ALE

Brothers Charlie and Ernie Otto and their partner Don Frank run their brewery in a pine cabin at Wilson, in Jackson Hole, between the Teton and Gros Ventre ranges of the Rockies, in Wyoming. Here, in the Snake River valley, the super-rich visit their weekend ranches and enjoy Teton Ale: a deep, reddish-amber brew; malty, light but textured, with suggestions of caramel, well-done toast, and apple-like tannin in the finish.

Region of origin Pacific Northwest US

Style English Bitter

Alcohol content 4.8abv (3.8w)

Ideal serving temperature
10–13°C (50–55°F)

OXFORD CLASS ALE

A British diplomat's son founded this brewery in a suburb of Baltimore in 1988. It was originally called British Brewing but that name proved too colonial-sounding. It is now Oxford Brewing, and American-owned. Oxford Class Ale is in the style of an English Bitter. It has a bright, full, amber colour and is light-bodied but firm, with a hoppy aroma, malty-grainy palate, and dry finish. A cask-conditioned version is available locally as Oxford's Real Ale. There has also been a maltier Special Old Bitter.

Region of origin Northeast US

Style English Bitter

Alcohol content 5.0abv (4.0w)

Ideal serving temperature
10–13°C (50–55°F)

RIVERSIDE PULLMAN PALE ALE

The river is the often-dry Santa Ana, east of Los Angeles. The town of Riverside is in orange-growing country and its pub and brewery are in the former Fruit Exchange. In more leisurely days, Riverside was an inland resort, hence names like Pullman. This Pale Ale is intended to be English in style. It has a sunny, mid-amber colour; a lemony hop aroma; a firm, rounded, lightly malty body; and a very dry finish.

Region of origin California, US

Style English Pale Ale/Bitter

Alcohol content 5.6abv (4.5w)

Ideal serving temperature
10–13°C (50–55°F)

WATERLOO BREWING ED'S BEST BITTER

The famous battle was honoured in the names of several American towns. This particular Waterloo, in Texas, was soon re-named Austin, after a family that settled there. It is now the state capital and known for its many small breweries. The Waterloo pub and brewery, a meeting place for beer enthusiasts, has touches of a 1950s' café. Its Ed's Best Bitter is a superb, subtle brew with a minty hop aroma; soft, sweet maltiness; and a fresh, grassy finish.

Region of origin Southwest US

Style English Bitter

Alcohol content 4.4abv (3.5w)

Ideal serving temperature
10–13°C (50–55°F)

SOCIABLE BEERS: PLAIN PORTERS AND DRY STOUTS

THERE IS NO EXPERIENCE more sociable than lingering in an Irish pub over a pint of the country's famous black brew: soft, creamy, and dry as Irish humour. When the Irish writer Flann O'Brien said: "A pint of plain is your only man", he was referring to a porter of modest strength. After a few decades' absence, "plain porter" has returned to Ireland to stand alongside its stouts. Despite the term "stout", these beers are not especially full in body, or alcohol.

Literary liquid
The black stuff seems to lubricate the wit in every Irishman, especially in the pubs of Dublin.

BURTON BRIDGE PORTER

Britain's brewing capital, the Midlands town of Burton, has, on Bridge Street, one of its livelier new-generation micro-breweries with its own pub. Small enterprises like the Burton Bridge Brewery, established in 1982, reintroduced porter decades after the country's bigger brewers had dropped the style. The Burton Bridge range includes a fine porter at an easily drinkable strength. Burton Bridge Porter has a ruby-to-black colour and a pillowy head. There are hints of crystal sugar in the aroma; smoky, fruity notes; and a sappy dryness in the finish.

Region of origin	Trent Valley, England, UK
Style	Plain Porter
Alcohol content	4.5abv (3.6w)
Ideal serving temperature	13°C (55°F)

THE STUFF OF DREAMS

PORTER WAS ORIGINALLY a London brew, and was hugely popular in England in the mid- and late-1700s. A porter brewery was "not a parcel of boilers and vats but the potentiality of growing rich beyond the dreams of avarice", commented the contemporary lexicographer, essayist, and critic, Dr. Samuel Johnson (*left*). He nursed a jealous passion for Hester Thrale, wife of a gentleman brewer. Johnson's extravagant phrase was intended to help the Thrales sell their porter brewery, in Southwark, London.

CARNEGIE STARK PORTER

A Scot called Carnegie first brewed this beer in the 1830s, in Gothenburg, Sweden (the two countries historically have strong trading links). Doctors traditionally prescribed the porter, enriched with an egg yolk, for nursing mothers. There are two strengths, the lower of which makes more of a "session" beer. The stronger version leans towards being an imperial stout. Carnegie Stark Porter is creamy and licorice-tasting with a long, dry finish. A top-fermenting yeast is used.

Region of origin Sweden

Style Baltic Porter

Alcohol content 3.5abv (2.8w) and 5.5abv (4.4w)

Ideal serving temperature 10–13°C (50–55°F)

Vintage porter
Carnegie is year-dated.
Each "vintage" seems
slightly different, though
the flavours meld with age.

SHEPHERD NEAME ORIGINAL PORTER

This brewery, in the county of Kent, is not far from London, the traditional home of porter. Shepherd Neame reintroduced porter in the early 1990s. Its soothing and very tasty example has hoppy and oaky, sherryish notes in its aroma; a hint of dry, rooty licorice (an ingredient); and a good malt background reminiscent of barley-sugar sweets.

Region of origin Southeast England, UK

Style Porter/Stout

Alcohol content 5.2abv (4.2w)

Ideal serving temperature 10–13°C (50–55°F)

HARVEYS 1859 PORTER

A traditional brewery in the old river port of Lewes, East Sussex. The business dates from the 1700s, and the timbered brewery from the following century. Reintroduced in 1993, this porter is based on an 1859 recipe and uses traditional brown malt. The beer has hop-sack and cedar in the aroma; medicinal, bitter chocolate notes in the palate; and a powerful, roasty dryness in the finish.

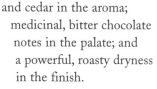

Region of origin Southeast England, UK

Style Porter/Stout

Alcohol content 4.8abv (3.8w)

Ideal serving temperature 10–13°C (50–55°F)

Best bottlings
Harveys Porter occasionally
appears in bottle-conditioned
form. This is less stable but
can develop great complexity.

OKHOTSK MILD STOUT

Close to the Okhotsk Sea, at the small town of Kitami near the east coast of Hokkaido, Japan, a pub and brewery make some delicious beers – flavoursome interpretations of classic styles. This mildly dry, very drinkable stout has a purply-black colour; pours with a dense, rocky head; has an earthy hop aroma; roasted chestnuts in the palate; a creamy body; and a yoghurty tartness in the finish.

Region of origin Hokkaido, Japan

Style Dry Stout

Alcohol content 5.0abv (4.0w)

Ideal serving temperature 10–13°C (50–55°F)

Mild mannered
The word mild usually
implies a sweetish ale. This
brew is certainly mild in
flavour, but a stout in style.

BERT GRANT'S PERFECT PORTER

Bert Grant is one of the personalities of the American brewing industry. He is an expert on hops, was a pioneer of both brewpubs and micro-breweries in the US, and once used advertising seeming to take credit for human happiness. His brand-name Perfect Porter is hardly modest, but the alcohol content is; despite this, the beer is astonishingly well rounded in both body and flavour, with subtle suggestions of cocoa powder, toasted nuts, and a touch of peat.

Region of origin
Northwest US

Style Plain Porter

Alcohol content
4.0abv (3.2w)

Ideal serving temperature
10–13°C (50–55°F)

Looking glass
Bert Grant sees himself every time he raises a glass of his own beer.

CATAMOUNT PORTER

The name celebrates the mountain lion, the state animal of Vermont. The Catamount micro-brewery began in White River Junction, Vermont, in 1987. It now has a second brewery a few miles downriver in Windsor. Catamount Porter is among the best American examples of the style. It has a fragrant, clean fruitiness of aroma; a remarkably smooth, creamy body; and a chocolatey, fruity dryness, with perhaps a hint of blackcurrant.

Region of origin
Northeast US

Style Porter/Stout

Alcohol content
5.3abv (4.2w)

Ideal serving temperature
10–13°C (50–55°F)

FISH TALE MUD SHARK PORTER

Coastal name for a brewery founded in Olympia, capital city of Washington State, in 1993. Founder Crayne Horton also offers that his star sign is Pisces and that he once kept fish. The brewery's beers are big and robust. Mud Shark Porter has a peppery aroma, with hints of pears in cream and rich, dark chocolate that are carried through in the palate. The finish is toasty, roasty, and dry.

Region of origin
Northwest US

Style Porter/Stout

Alcohol content
5.5abv (4.4w)

Ideal serving temperature
10–13°C (50–55°F)

The beer that got away
The small print above the illustration on the label brings the fisherman's boast to the beer-drinker.

BLACKSTONE ST CHARLES PORTER

New-generation brewery and restaurant established in the mid-1990s in Nashville, Tennessee. The beers were created by star brewer Dave Miller. "Saint" Charles is the son of one of the owners. The porter that takes his name has a firm body and offers the sensation of biting into a praline filled with cream. The richness rounds into bitter chocolate. The beer is smooth, sociable, and dry enough in the finish to demand another round.

Region of origin
South US

Style Porter

Alcohol content
5.0abv (4.0w)

Ideal serving temperature
10–13°C
(50–55°F)

PLAIN PORTERS AND DRY STOUTS

EMERSON'S LONDON PORTER

Some outstanding beers are made by the Emerson's new-generation brewery, established in 1993 in Dunedin, New Zealand. The company's London Porter is black with purply highlights, forming a dense head with good lace. It has a perfumy aroma reminiscent of a dessert with pistachio nuts and cream. The flavours start coffeeish and become rummy, with a big, rounded, dry finish. Both soothing and satisfying.

Region of origin
South Island, New Zealand

Style Porter/Stout

Alcohol content 4.9abv (3.9w)

Ideal serving temperature
10–13°C (50–55°F)

GREAT DIVIDE SAINT BRIGID'S PORTER

The continental divide is not far from Denver, Colorado, home of this brewery, but the company was conceived in the union of Brian and Tara Dunn. They married on a Saturday and started their first brew on the Sunday. Their porter is named after the 6th-century Irish saint, who allegedly could turn her bathwater into beer. Saint Brigid's Porter has an earthy, sappy, rooty aroma; is light but very smooth; and has well combined flavours of licorice and toffee. It finishes lightly creamy but dryish.

Region of origin Southwest US

Style Porter/Stout

Alcohol content 5.6abv (4.5w)

Ideal serving temperature
10–13°C (50–55°F)

HOEPFNER PORTER

The only porters made in Germany within living memory seem to have been from the now-defunct Dressler brewery of Bremen and the very active Hoepfner of Karlsruhe. After a gap of nearly two decades, Hoepfner revived its porter in 1998. The beer has a mahogany-to-black colour; a smooth, toffeeish palate; and a powerful burnt character in a rounded finish. The tower of Hoepfner's 1898 brewery is replicated in a lidded stein 43 cm (17 in) tall.

Region of origin
Baden-Württemberg, Germany

Style Porter/Stout

Alcohol content 5.8abv (4.6w)

Ideal serving temperature
10–13°C (50–55°F)

KALAMAZOO BREWING BELL'S PORTER

The Michigan town of Kalamazoo has a local reputation for its eccentrics. There is a café called The Eccentric at this colourful brewery, founded in 1985 by former baker and jazz disc-jockey Larry Bell. The brewery makes something of a speciality of porters and stouts. Bell's Porter is full of whiskyish, grainy flavours, with a long finish.

Region of origin Midwest US

Style Plain Porter

Alcohol content 5.7abv (4.6w)

Ideal serving temperature
10–13°C (50–55°F)

KING AND BARNES OLD PORTER

Bottle-conditioned beers have in recent years become the speciality of this family brewery, in Horsham, just across the Surrey-Sussex border, south of London. The brewery's Old Porter pours with a huge, rocky head; has a ruby-tinged, black colour; a fresh, creamy aroma; a light but smooth palate; and a distinctly dry finish. When young it is cocoa-ish, but it develops more peppery, spicy, bitter notes with bottle age.

Region of origin
Southeast England, UK

Style Porter/Stout

Alcohol content 5.5abv (4.4w)

Ideal serving temperature
10–13°C (50–55°F)

MITCHELL'S RAVEN STOUT

Lex Mitchell, who previously worked for South African Brewery, founded Africa's first micro-brewery in 1984, in Knysna, Western Cape. He has since opened Mitchell's pubs in Johannesburg and Cape Town. His smooth, firm, malty beers are unfiltered and unpasteurized. Raven Stout has a slatey black colour; a creamy aroma; a rummy middle; and a hop-sack, hessian-like dryness in the finish.

Region of origin
Western Cape, South Africa

Style Strong Dry Stout

Alcohol content 6.0abv (4.8w)

Ideal serving temperature
10–13°C (50–55°F)

NUSSDORF SIR HENRY'S DRY STOUT

Nussdorf is on the edge of the Vienna Woods. The name means "nut village", referring not to its inhabitants but to the local walnuts. In the wine cellars of his château at Nussdorf, Baron Henrik Bachofen von Echt makes Sir Henry's Stout. With its chocolatey flavours, this stout could be over-rich, but there is a moreish dryness in the fruity finish.

Region of origin Vienna, Austria

Style Dry Stout

Alcohol content 5.6abv (4.5w)

Ideal serving temperature
10–13°C (50–55°F)

PORTERHOUSE PLAIN PORTER

Porter as a beer style was once especially associated with Dublin. In 1996, it was restored in a brewpub called The Porterhouse, by Oliver Hughes and his cousin Liam LaHart. The Porterhouse is at the corner of Parliament Street and Temple Bar. Its Plain Porter is light but textured in body, with a fruity dryness. The brewery also makes two outstanding stouts.

Region of origin
Dublin, Republic of Ireland

Style Plain Porter

Alcohol content 4.3abv (3.4w)

Ideal serving temperature
10–13°C (50–55°F)

YELLOW ROSE VIGILANTE PORTER

The state's symbol lends a name to the Yellow Rose micro-brewery, in San Antonio, Texas. The brewery was established in 1994. The local sheriff seems to have awarded a star to Vigilante Porter. The beer pours with a dense head; has a light but smooth body; with dark chocolate and bitter orange flavours; and a dry, spritzy finish.

Region of origin Southwest US

Style Plain Porter

Alcohol content 4.4abv (3.5w)

Ideal serving temperature 10°C (50°F)

PARTY GREETINGS: FRUIT LAMBICS

A GLASS OF PINK CHAMPAGNE, a Buck's Fizz or Mimosa, a sangria, punch, or cocktail? The welcoming drink at the barbecue, cook-out, or party should look stylish and perhaps sparkling, be both refreshing and appetizing, and not be too filling. Ideally, it should also be novel. The drier style of Belgian fruit beer does the job perfectly...especially the spritzy, tart type based on a *lambic* (a style of wheat beer fermented and matured with wild yeasts in the area around the town of Lembeek, near Brussels). The fruits are added to the maturing beer, creating both a distinctive flavour and the sparkle and life of a further fermentation.

Wild website
Cobwebs can house wild yeasts, a unique feature of lambic-making. Brewers elsewhere would be astonished.

FRAMBOISE BOON

The French *framboise* (raspberry) is preferred on this label to the Flemish *frambozen*. The brewer, though, is Flemish, and he makes his *lambic* beers in Lembeek itself. A brewery dating from the 1600s was due to close in 1977 when young revivalist Frank Boon acquired the business. He now produces a range of *lambic* beers at a brewery on the banks of the Zenne, the river whose valley helps define the region. The wild yeasts of the valley impart a perfumy, flowery, Chardonnay-like dryness, and oak-ageing offers a touch of vanilla, to balance the raspberry-jam sweetness of this fresh, delicate brew. Although the beer is lightly sweetened, a lemony acidity emerges to dry the finish. For every litre (1.76 pints) of beer, 200g (7 oz) of raspberries are used, and a small proportion of cherries. If this *lambic* is not sufficiently dry, look out for Boon's Mariage Parfait range, which contains a higher proportion of long-matured *lambics*, typically 18 months to two years old.

Party dress
Champagne bottles, dressed with foil, offer an elegant presentation for many Belgian beers, especially lambics. Belgian brewers like their beers to please the eye as well as the nose and palate.

Region of origin
Province of Flemish Brabant, Belgium

Style *Framboise/Frambozen-Lambic*

Alcohol content 6.2abv (5.0w)

Ideal serving temperature Store at 10–13°C (50–55°F). Lightly refrigerate for two or three hours before serving. Serve at 8°C (47°F)

KRIEK MORT SUBITE

The small, dark, dry-tasting cherry typically used in Belgian fruit beers is in Flemish called a *kriek*. *Mort Subite*, meaning "sudden death" is a version of a dice game that was played in a famous café in Brussels. Mort Subite eventually became the name of the café and its house beer, made in the Zenne Valley. Mort Subite contracts orchards to grow specific cherries for its beer. It is a beautifully balanced beer, with a creamy, almondy, cherry-stone note, and a lightly tart finish. Look out, also, for the drier Mort Subite Fond Gueuze, an unfiltered blend of young and old *lambics*.

Region of origin
Province of Flemish Brabant, Belgium

Style *Kriek-Lambic*

Alcohol content
4.3abv (3.4w)

Ideal serving temperature
8–9°C (47–48°F)

BELLE-VUE KRIEK

The Zenne Valley inspired the landscapes of Brueghel, but the Belle-Vue *lambic* brewery, in Molenbeek, is on the urban edge of Brussels. Its *kriek* has an oaky, irony note, as well as some blackcurrant-like fruitiness. A richer, sweeter, cherry character is usually found in Belle-Vue's Kriek Primeur, which is a different blend each year. A batch of Kriek Primeur is launched each April, using the cherries from the previous year's harvest.

Region of origin
Province of Flemish Brabant, Belgium

Style *Kriek-Lambic*

Alcohol content
5.2abv (4.2w)

Ideal serving temperature
8–9°C (47–48°F)

Stellar view?
Belle-Vue is owned by the Belgian national group Interbrew, producer of Stella Artois.

TIMMERMANS KRIEK

The Timmermans brewery dates from 1888, though there may have been a brewery on the site, in Itterbeek, since 1650. The founding family still has a share in the company, though control is in the hands of John Martin's, better known for pale ale. Among the widely available examples of *kriek*, Timmermans' has a more obvious *lambic* character than its competitors – a delicate, fino sherry acidity – before the cherry flavours emerge. An unfiltered *gueuze* called Caveau is yet drier.

Region of origin
Province of Flemish Brabant, Belgium

Style *Kriek-Lambic*

Alcohol content
5.0abv (4.0w)

Ideal serving temperature
8–9°C (47–48°F)

CANTILLON GUEUZE VIGNERONNE

The Cantillon brewery is near Brussels South station, where the Anderlecht district is a gateway to the Zenne Valley. Cantillon's very traditional *gueuze* has an addition of Muscat grapes during maturation. It is very light on the tongue, and very dry indeed. A hint of grape skins in the aroma, and a touch of tannin in the finish, round the lemony flavours that are typical of the Cantillon beers. If this is just too dry, try the brewery's *framboise*, Rosé de Gambrinus.

Region of origin Province of Flemish Brabant, Belgium

Style Fruit *Lambic*

Alcohol content 5.0abv (4.0w)

Ideal serving temperature
8–9°C (47–48°F)

PARTY GREETINGS: FRUIT BEERS

NOT ALL FRUIT BEERS ARE BASED on the winey, *lambic*-style brews. There is a wide variety of non-*lambic* fruit beers, and several of these are dry enough to serve as a welcoming brew. They vary from Belgian cherry beers based on brown ales to French *bières de garde* with raspberries, English ales with damsons, and American ales with grapes. Many American breweries make raspberry wheat beers. Among the more unusual fruit brews is Rogue-N-Berry. This is made with the marion berry, a hybrid of raspberry, blackberry, and loganberry. The Rogue brewery, in Newport, Oregon, devised this beer to satirize the controversial Washington mayor, Marion Berry.

The real thing
The Echte ("Real") Kriek of the Verhaege family's brewery in Vichte, West Flanders, uses morello cherries. Its brandyish Kriek and its hoppy-tasting Vera Pils are a better tonic than a visit from the district nurse, according to this 1950s' poster.

LIEFMANS KRIEKBIER

This cherry beer is based on a classic brown ale in the local sweet-and-sour style of Oudenaarde, in East Flanders, Belgium. Liefmans' brewery was founded in 1625, but its kettles were retired in 1991. The brown ale is now brewed in nearby Dentergem, but fermented and matured in Oudenaarde. This stage of production, using a semi-wild yeast, is essential to the acidic character of the beer. The classic Liefmans' brown ale is called Goudenband (Gold Riband). In the fruit variation, the beer lies with a blend of Danish cherries and the smaller, drier, Belgian *kriek* variety for at least six months. About 13 kilograms (30 pounds) of cherries is used per 100 litres (180 pints) of the fruit – roughly 60 grams per half-litre (two ounces per pint). The beer has an excellent fruit aroma, brandyish flavours, and a balancing, tannic dryness.

Region of origin
Province of East Flanders, Belgium

Style Oudenaarde Brown Ale, with fruit

Alcohol content 6.5abv (5.2w)

Ideal serving temperature 10°C (50°F)

Wrapped with pride
At any one time, four people are engaged in wrapping the beers, each handling between three and five thousand bottles a day. The tissue announces a triumph in a British tasting.

LA CHOULETTE FRAMBOISE

The name refers to a northern French game that was an antecedent of lacrosse. La Choulette is a farmhouse brewery, founded in 1885, at Hordain, south of Valenciennes. The basic La Choulette is a strong, amber brew in the local style known as *bière de garde*. It is the basis for the *framboise*, which is made with natural raspberry extract. This ruby-coloured brew has an almost blackberryish aroma and a hint of cherry brandy in a smooth, cleanly nutty, dryish palate.

Region of origin
Northern France

Style *Bière de Garde*, with fruit

Alcohol content 7.0abv (5.6w)

Ideal serving temperature
10°C (50°F)

Towering brew
This beer is brewed in Ostrevant, a small region centred on Valenciennes. The landmark tower of Ostrevant is a 12th-century fortification.

STRAWBERRY BANK DAMSON BEER

The fruit, the "Damascus plum", perhaps brought to the UK by the Crusaders, has for centuries been cultivated in the Lyth Valley, near Kendal, in the Lake District of England: first to make a dye, then for jam and home-made gin, and now for a beer. With a view to utilizing the neglected damson crop, the beer was created at a nearby pub, the Masons' Arms, Cartmel Fell, Windermere. The beer has a winey bouquet, an intense fruitiness, and a dryish finish.

Region of origin
Northwest England, UK

Style
English Ale, with fruit

Alcohol content
7.0abv (5.6w)

Ideal serving temperature
10°C (50°F)

NEW BELGIUM OLD CHERRY ALE

This pioneering Belgian-style brewery in Fort Collins, Colorado makes an elegant fruit beer from locally grown Montmorency "sour" pie cherries. The beer has a pale, orange-pink colour; a very lightly fruity, dryish aroma; a slightly oily, barley-sugar, malt background; and a very lightly acidic, balancing dryness in the finish. The brew is based on a lightly hopped amber ale, and the cherries are intended to add the tart edge.

Region of origin
Southwest US

Style American/Belgian Ale, with fruit

Alcohol content
5.0abv (4.0w)

Ideal serving temperature
10°C (50°F)

From Paris to Fort Collins
Montmorency cherries are named after their place of origin, near Paris, France. They are known for their bright colour and sourness.

PECONIC COUNTY RESERVE ALE

The name refers to a region that wishes to secede from Suffolk County, on Long Island, New York. The Southampton Publick House there makes a lightly hopped wheat beer, using both raw and malted versions of the grain, and adds Chardonnay grapes grown at the nearby Sag Pond winery by native Bavarian Roman Roth. The beer is matured in white wine casks. It emerges with a raisiny, brandyish aroma; a crisp attack; a restrained fresh-apple and maple palate; and a big, woody, dry finish.

Region of origin
Northeast US

Style Wheat Beer, with fruit

Alcohol content
6.2abv (5.0w)

Ideal serving temperature
10°C (50°F)

THIRST QUENCHERS:
BELGIAN-STYLE WHEAT BEERS

BEERS MADE WITH A SUBSTANTIAL PROPORTION of wheat, in addition to the usual barley malt, are especially refreshing and quenching. Wheat can give a tartness reminiscent of plum or apple. In the Belgian style of wheat beer, there is usually also a fruitiness from the use of Curaçao orange peels, as well as citric, minty, peppery flavours from coriander seeds, and other spices. These ingredients are used in addition to the normal hops.

Pierre Celis
Wheat beer revivalist…
see also page 80.

HOEGAARDEN SPECIALE

The country town of Hoegaarden, east of Brussels, in the heart of wheat-growing country, once had more than 30 breweries making the local wheat beer. The last closed in the 1950s, when traditional brews were being driven out by lagers, but in the 1960s enthusiast Pierre Celis revived the style. In the 1980s, his brewery was acquired by Interbrew. The regular Hoegaarden is perfumy and spicy in aroma, with a fruity palate and a honeyish background. A newer Hoegaarden Speciale, for winter, is slightly firmer and nuttier. Hoegaarden Grand Cru has the same spices, but is stronger in alcohol, and has no wheat. Hoegaarden recently revived a spiced amber ale, DAS.

Region of origin
Province of Flemish Brabant, Belgium

Style Belgian Wheat Beer

Alcohol content 5.0abv (4.0w)

Ideal serving temperature 9–10°C (48–50°F)

Why "white"?
The term "White"
(wit, Flemish;
blanche French;
Weiss or Weisse,
German) implies
a wheat beer.

CURAÇAO ORANGES

THE ISLAND OF CURAÇAO, formerly a colony of The Netherlands, is known for a sour style of orange, used by Dutch liqueurists and gin-distillers, and Belgian brewers. During the colonial period, The Netherlands and Belgium were one country.

DOMUS LEUVENDIGE WITTE

The city of Leuven is the home of Stella Artois, and the biggest brewing centre in Belgium. It is east of Brussels, and close to the wheat-growing area. Leuven has its own tradition of wheat beers, upheld by the Domus brewery and pub. Within the Domus range is Leuvendige Witte, with a fresh, orange-cream aroma; a palate surging with lemon-soda flavours; and a spicy, balancing dryness. Leuven is a university city, known for its many student bars, among which Domus is a classic.

Region of origin Province of Flemish Brabant, Belgium

Style Belgian Wheat Beer

Alcohol content 5.0abv (4.0w)

Ideal serving temperature 9–10°C (48–50°F)

L'ABBAYE DES ROCS BLANCHE DES HONNELLES

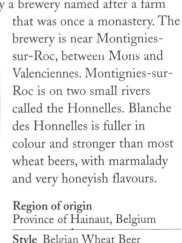

In the French-speaking part of Belgium, "white" wheat beers are identified by the word *blanche*. This example is made by a brewery named after a farm that was once a monastery. The brewery is near Montignies-sur-Roc, between Mons and Valenciennes. Montignies-sur-Roc is on two small rivers called the Honnelles. Blanche des Honnelles is fuller in colour and stronger than most wheat beers, with marmalady and very honeyish flavours.

Region of origin Province of Hainaut, Belgium

Style Belgian Wheat Beer

Alcohol content 6.0abv (4.8w)

Ideal serving temperature 9–10°C (48–50°F)

HAECHT WITBIER

The older spelling of the village of Haacht, between Brussels, Leuven, and Mechelen. This company began as a dairy in the 1800s, and later added a brewery. It uses a magnificently restored 1930s' brewhouse. The company is best known for its Pilsner-style beer. It also produces this dry, grainy, Belgian white, which in aroma and flavour emphasizes the wheat rather than the fruit and spices.

Region of origin Province of Flemish Brabant, Belgium

Style Belgian Wheat Beer

Alcohol content 4.8abv (3.8w)

Ideal serving temperature 9–10°C (48–50°F)

MATER WIT BIER

The ancient Romans probably established the oddly named village of Mater, near Oudenaarde, on the old route from Cologne to the sea. A family named Roman has for 14 generations run this beautifully kept brewery. Like the three neighbouring breweries in the Oudenaarde area, it is best known for its brown beer. It also has this enjoyable white, with the fresh flavours of home-made lemonade, sherbet, and a balancing, dry spiciness.

Region of origin Province of East Flanders, Belgium

Style Belgian Wheat Beer

Alcohol content 5.0abv (4.0w)

Ideal serving temperature 9–10°C (48–50°F)

CELIS WHITE

Having established and sold the Hoegaarden brewery, Pierre Celis moved to the United States. He went to Austin, Texas, where he had Belgian friends, and started a beautifully-appointed brewery there. His Celis White is very similar to the beer he made in Belgium but perhaps softer, less flowery, and with more fruity acidity. The Austin brewery is operated by the Celis family under the ownership of Miller. Celis White is also produced in Belgium, under licence, by De Smedt.

Region of origin
Southwest US

Style Belgian-style Wheat Beer

Alcohol content
4.9abv (3.9w)

Ideal serving temperature
9–10°C (48–50°F)

DE RIDDER WIECKSE WITTE

The "wick" is the neighbourhood where the De Ridder brewery stands, on the Left Bank of the River Meuse (in Dutch, Maas), in the heart of Maastricht, the historic city in Dutch Limburg. The city, surrounded by small breweries, is known for its many cafés. In the centre, De Ridder is a local landmark, dating from 1852. Its wheat beer has melony fruit aromas and flavours, and a dry, gingery, rooty finish. De Ridder is owned by Heineken.

Region of origin Province of Limburg, The Netherlands

Style
Belgian-style Wheat Beer

Alcohol content
5.0abv (4.0w)

Ideal serving temperature
9–10°C (48–50°F)

A cool beer
The back-label suggests a serving temperature of 6–8°C (43–46°F), and some brewers of this style might agree, but such cold kills flavour.

UNIBROUE BLANCHE DE CHAMBLY

The French language is in this instance not from Belgium but from Canada. In the Montreal suburb of Chambly, the Unibroue micro-brewery produces Belgian-style beers of great character. The brewery's founders include Canadian rock singer Robert Charlebois. It received some initial consultancy from the Belgian brewery Riva. Blanche de Chambly is mouth-fillingly spritzy, with big, perfumy, orange and lemon notes.

Region of origin
Province of Quebec, Canada

Style
Belgian-style Wheat Beer

Alcohol content 5.0abv (4.0w)

Ideal serving temperature
9–10°C (48–50°F)

MOKU MOKU BISUCUIT WEIZEN

The phrase *Moku Moku* refers to smoke screens historically used by Ninja warriors, practitioners of martial arts in the local mountains. The brewery is near Ueno, east of Kyoto and Osaka, Japan. The beer's name alludes to biscuit malt, though this Belgian term sits oddly with the German *Weizen*. The beer has an orangey colour; starts with a nutty maltiness; and finishes perfumy, fragrant, and slightly smoky. An interesting hybrid from Japan.

Region of origin
Honshu, Japan

Style
Belgian-German Wheat Beer

Alcohol content
4.5abv (3.6w)

Ideal serving temperature
9–10°C (48–50°F)

BELGIAN-STYLE WHEAT BEERS

COORS BLUE MOON BELGIAN WHITE

The world's biggest brewery is that belonging to Coors, at Golden, Colorado. This company is best known for very light-bodied American lagers, but it also makes several specialities, including a range under the Blue Moon rubric. These include a good example of a Belgian white, made with a proportion of oats. This beer, with a full colour for the style, has a creamy, oily, orange-skin character, moving to a dry, light finish.

Region of origin Southwest US

Style Belgian-style Wheat Beer

Alcohol content 5.0abv (4.0w)

Ideal serving temperature 9–10°C (48–50°F)

VAN EECKE WATOU'S WIT

A statue of an unnamed brewer stands in one of the main squares of Watou, West Flanders, celebrating the town's preoccupation. This little town has no fewer than three breweries. Among them, Van Eecke is known for a golden ale dedicated to the nearby hop-growing town of Poperinge. A stronger (5.8abv, 4.6w) Winter Wit is bigger, with a suggestion of fruit pancakes. The brewery also produces a notably foamy, pale, dry, herbal, flowery *wit*.

Region of origin Province of West Flanders, Belgium

Style Belgian Wheat Beer

Alcohol content 5.0abv (4.0w)

Ideal serving temperature 9–10°C (48–50°F)

GRAND-PLACE BLANCHE

It is possible to have a beer at a pavement café in what appears to be the Grand' Place of Brussels, while actually being inside a former sake warehouse in Nagoya, Japan. The square has been recreated with astonishing credibility by a designer of movie sets. This version of the Grand' Place is actually a brewpub, offering a flowery golden ale, a toffeeish brown ale, and a perfumy, sweetish, very fruity *blanche*, with excellent flavour development. Grand-Place is owned by the Shirayuki sake company.

Region of origin Honshu, Japan

Style Belgian-style Wheat Beer

Alcohol content 5.0abv (4.0w)

Ideal serving temperature 9–10°C (48–50°F)

GULPENER KORENWOLF

A "corn wolf" is a hamster, a creature that gathers grain in summer and stores it for the winter. The Dutch, living in a tiny and physically vulnerable country, have an affection for all that is small, industrious, and prudent. Korenwolf is a Belgian-style wheat beer with an earthy perfume and a big, fruity attack. It is full of flavour: refreshing, satisfying, and appetizing. The beer is made by the respected Gulpener brewery, near the city of Maastricht.

Region of origin Province of Limburg, The Netherlands

Style Belgian-style Wheat Beer

DE LEEUW VALKENBURGS WIT

The name De Leeuw (as in "Leo") means The Lion, a popular heraldic name for breweries. This old-established Lion Brewery is in Valkenburg, east of Maastricht, in Dutch Limburg. The brewery, in one of the few hilly parts of The Netherlands, is particularly proud of its spring water. The *wit* named after the town is soft, malty, and gently fruity, with a dryish finish. The winter *wit* is bigger, with a suggestion of fruit pancakes.

Region of origin Province of Limburg, The Netherlands

Style Belgian-style Wheat Beer

Alcohol content 4.8abv (3.8w)

Ideal serving temperature 9–10°C (48–50°F)

RIVA DENTERGEMS WIT

A river's source originally provided the water for, and inspired the name of, this old-established, family-owned brewery in Dentergem, on the borders of West and East Flanders. Riva makes a wide variety of beers, but is well known for its Belgian white. In some countries, the brew is known as Wittekop, a reference to its big, white head. The beer is dry and cleansing, with a complex spice and fruit character, developing towards a refreshing surge of sweet lemon in the finish.

Region of origin Province of West Flanders, Belgium

Style Belgian Wheat Beer

Alcohol content 5.0abv (4.0w)

Ideal serving temperature 9–10°C (48–50°F)

STEENDONK BRABANTS WITBIER

A Belgian white made by the renowned Palm brewery, in Steenhuffel, to the northwest of Brussels, and marketed jointly by the people who produce the famous, strong, golden Duvel, in nearby Breendonk. The name is a marriage of the two villages. The beer is pale and milky, spicy and dry, with cinnamon in its spicing and a melony fruit character.

Region of origin Province of Flemish Brabant, Belgium

Style Belgian Wheat Beer

Alcohol content 4.5abv (3.6w)

Ideal serving temperature 9–10°C (48–50°F)

TIMMERMANS LAMBIC WIT

The typical spicing of a Belgian wheat, but applied to a *lambic*: the style of beer given a winey taste by the use of wild yeasts. The flavours are reminiscent of light toast with lemon, orange, and ginger marmalade notes (though no ginger is used). Very crisp and refreshing. The beer is made by the *lambic* brewers Timmermans, in the traditional region of that style.

Region of origin Province of Flemish Brabant, Belgium

Style White *Lambic*

Alcohol content 4.5abv (3.6w)

Ideal serving temperature 9–10°C (48–50°F)

THIRST QUENCHERS: BERLIN-STYLE WHEAT BEERS

THE LIGHTEST AND FRESHEST-tasting thirst quenchers are the local wheat beers of Berlin, which have an intentionally sharp, sourish finish derived from the use of a lactic culture as well as a more conventional yeast. *Berliner Weisse* beer is typically sweetened with essences of fruits or herbs and often served with candy-striped straws. The beer is seen especially in the summer on the terrace cafés by the lakes of Berlin.

The beer greener
Woodruff adds colour and flavour to Berlin's brew (page 83).

BERLINER BÜRGERBRÄU WEISSBIER

This brewery, restaurant, and beer garden is on one of the most beautiful lakes and favoured picnic spots, the Müggelsee, in Köpenick, on the edge of Berlin, in the former Eastern sector of the city. It dates from 1869 and is still in the original premises, which are now listed buildings. During the communist period it produced a Pilsner-style beer. At that time, a very intense-tasting *Berliner Weisse* for the East was made at a brewery, now closed, in the Pankow district. After reunification, the Köpenick brewery was acquired by the beer-making Häring family of Bavaria. They have greatly restored the brewery, introducing a wide range of beers, including the first new *Weissbier* in Berlin for many decades. (The city now has three *Weissbiers*, but once had 700). This beer has a crisp, toasty aroma with a hint of hop sack; a light, smooth, firm body; and a late, lemony tartness. It is a very restrained interpretation of the style, a little stronger than the usual low-alcohol *Berliner Weissbier*.

Region of origin	Berlin, Northern Germany
Style	*Berliner Weisse*
Alcohol content	4.8abv (3.8w)
Ideal serving temperature	9–12°C (48–54°F)

The meaning of Weisse
As in Belgium (page 78), so in Germany, the term "white" (Weisse) is sometimes used to describe wheat beers. South German brewers also use the term Weizen ("wheat").

BERLINER KINDL WEISSE

One of the two principal brewing companies in Berlin is Kindl, founded in 1872 and now part of a national group with Binding, of Frankfurt. The brewery is in Neukölln, a blue-collar, residential district. Entered via a monastic-looking arch, it has a handsome, 1950s' copper brewhouse set into marble tiles. The *Weisse*, most readily available in the summer, is firm, carbonic, and fruity, with a cutting hit of sourness. It is at the low strength that is usually associated with this refreshing style of beer.

Region of origin
Berlin, Northern Germany

Style *Berliner Weisse*

Alcohol content
2.5abv (2.0w)

Ideal serving temperature
9–12°C (48–54°F)

SCHULTHEISS BERLINER WEISSE

The city's other big brewer, established in 1842 and now part of the national group Brau und Brunnen. Since the reunification of Germany, Schultheiss has closed its breweries in Kreuzberg and Spandau and moved production to a brewery dating from 1902, at Hohenschönhausen, in the former East. Its *Berliner Weisse* has a secondary fermentation in the bottle, resulting in a more complex character. It is flowery, pollen-like, with hints of celery, and a lemony finish.

Region of origin
Berlin, Northern Germany

Style *Berliner Weisse*

Alcohol content
3.7abv (3.0w)

Ideal serving temperature
9–12°C (48–54°F)

BERLINER WEISSE & WALDMEISTER

Woodruff, the "master of the woods", is a small herb, *Galium odoratum*, which flourishes in moist soil and temperate climates. It grows extensively in the beech forests of northern Germany and is used there in stuffed pillows, and to flavour wines, soft drinks, or beers such as *Berliner Weisse*. Woodruff has notes reminiscent of lemon-grass, hay, and vanilla. Due to concerns about artificial ingredients, woodruff has recently lost ground to *Himbeer* (raspberry) syrup as a flavouring for *Berliner Weisse*.

Green party
The woodruff itself is natural, but additives to enhance the aroma and colouring worry some consumers.

BERLINER WEISSE & HIMBEER

"Beer" in this instance means "berry". The addition of raspberry syrup to *Berliner Weisse* is reminiscent of the way in which Münster *Altbier* is laced with soft fruits. Other fruits, wine, or liqueurs such as *Kümmel* are also sometimes added in Berlin. Mixtures like this may be made by the drinker or bartender, but not by the brewer, under the German Beer Purity Law. A brewer who adds such ingredients is not permitted to call the end result beer. If brewed in Germany, a Belgian raspberry or cherry brew would have to be called a flavoured alcoholic drink.

More than saucer size
The king-sized champagne saucer has long been established as the most typical glass for Berliner Weisse.

THIRST QUENCHERS: SOUTH GERMAN WHEAT BEERS

THE MOST WIDELY AVAILABLE summer refreshers from Germany are the wheat beers associated with the area around Munich, but also made throughout Bavaria, the "rival" southern state Baden-Württemberg, and throughout the country as a whole. As well as a quenching tartness, these beers often have flavours reminiscent of apples, plums, bananas, bubble-gum, and cloves, a result of the wheat's interaction with the region's local yeasts. The examples shown on these two pages are of filtered wheat beers, known as *Kristall Weizen*.

WEIHENSTEPHANER KRISTALL WEISSBIER

The world's oldest brewery is widely believed to be at Weihenstephan (Sacred Stephen), on a hillside near Freising, 25 km (15 miles) north of Munich. Benedictine monks established a community on this hillside in at least 725 AD and were growing hops there by 768 AD. The first specific reference to brewing on the site is from 1040. Today's brewery and beer restaurant share former monastery buildings with the world's best-known university faculty of brewing. The beer is also bottled for general sale. The Weihenstephan brewery makes a wide range of products but is especially known for its wheat beers. Its *Kristall Weissbier* pours with a huge head; has a very fresh aroma; and rich, very fruity, juicy flavours. Some tasters have found suggestions of mango; there are certainly banana flavours and perhaps blackcurrant. A rival local brewery, Hofbräuhaus Freising, dating from at least the 1100s, also makes very fruity wheat beers.

Region of origin	Upper Bavaria, Germany
Style	*Kristall Weisse/Weizen*
Alcohol content	5.4abv (4.3w)
Ideal serving temperature	9–12°C (48–54°F)

The white vase
The vase-shaped glass is traditional for the style. The terms Weissbier *(white beer) and* Weizenbier *(wheat beer) are used interchangeably. There is no difference.*

CUTTING THE THIRST

THE REFRESHING character of south German wheat beers is sometimes heightened by a lemon-slice garnish. In Germany, this is more likely with the filtered type of wheat beer than the sedimented version. This custom has declined in Germany in recent years but has become popular in the US.

FRANZISKANER KRISTALLKLAR WEISSBIER

A Franciscan monastery brewery founded in Munich in 1363, subsequently acquired by the famous Bavarian beer-making family Sedlmayr, and subsumed into their company, Spaten. Founded in 1397, Spaten uses the Franziskaner name for its wheat beers. This "crystal clear" version is very aromatic, with hay and apples in the bouquet; quenchingly fruity, with hints of sherbet lemon sweets, and developing banana flavours.

Region of origin
Upper Bavaria, Germany

Style *Kristall Weisse/Weizen*

Alcohol content 5.0abv (4.0w)

Ideal serving temperature
9–12°C (48–54°F)

MAISEL'S WEISSE KRISTALLKLAR

This Bayreuth brewery, one of several in Bavaria owned by families named Maisel, is known to some beer lovers for an ale-like speciality called *Dampfbier* (steam beer), but has in recent years given more emphasis to its wheat beers. Its *Kristall Weisse* has a very fresh fruitiness of aroma; flavours of lemon pith or zest; and an extremely refreshing, crisp finish, like biting into an ice-cream wafer sandwich.

Region of origin
Franconia, Bavaria, Germany

Style *Kristall Weisse/Weizen*

Alcohol content 5.2abv (4.2w)

Ideal serving temperature
9–12°C (48–54°F)

Star brewery
Traditionally, brewers displayed a star on the label of a new beer. This symbol of brewing is universal, but especially used in Franconia.

LAMMSBRÄU KRISTALL WEIZEN

Organic beers are the speciality of this brewery, which dates from at least 1628. The brewery is in the pencil-producing town of Neumarkt, in a valley 40 km (25 miles) southeast of Nuremberg. Lammsbräu gets organic barley and hops from local farmers. Its wide range of beers includes a distinctive *Kristall Weizen*, which has a very fresh hop character, a creamy malt accent, and a cherryish fruitiness.

Region of origin
Franconia, Bavaria, Germany

Style *Kristall Weisse/Weizen*

Alcohol content 5.1abv (4.1w)

Ideal serving temperature
9–12°C (48–54°F)

SCHÖFFERHOFER KRISTALLWEIZEN

In Kassel, in the state of Hesse, this brewery makes a wheat beer for its parent company, the national group Binding, of Frankfurt. The original brewery site was the home of Peter Schöffer, a pioneering printer from the same enterprise as Johann Gutenberg. The Schöfferhofer *Kristall Weizen* is very dry with a plummy, damson-like fruitiness and a suggestion of grapefruit zest in the finish. Schöfferhofer is one of the more widely available examples outside Germany.

Region of origin Hesse, Germany

Style *Kristall Weisse/Weizen*

Alcohol content 5.0abv (4.0w)

Ideal serving temperature
9–12°C (48–54°F)

THIRST QUENCHERS: GERMAN-STYLE HEFEWEIZEN

THE MOST FASHIONABLE BREW with the youth in Germany in recent years has been the unfiltered, cloudy, yeast-sedimented version of the southern wheat beer. This is sometime labelled as being *mit Hefe* (with yeast). The same style is indicated by the terms *Hefe-Weisse* or, more often, *Hefeweizen*, either hyphenated or as one word. This type of beer is often served with a morning snack of bread and veal sausages. Bavarians call it a "breakfast beer", because it is light, cleansing, and digestible.

SCHNEIDER WEISSE

This brewery is thought to have specialized continuously in wheat beer since 1607. The present owners, the Schneider family, have been making wheat beer in their own right since 1872. They had a brewery on the street known as the Tal, in the centre of Munich, and after the Second World War, they moved into their current historic brewery, north of the city at Kelheim on the Danube. The Schneider wheat beers are among the best examples of the clove-tasting, spicy, full-flavoured style. The principal version, Schneider Weisse, is a darkish interpretation of the *Hefeweizen* style. It is lively, with fruity complexity, maltiness, almondy nuttiness, and clovey notes.

Region of origin	Upper Bavaria, Germany
Style	*Hefeweizen*
Alcohol content	5.5abv (4.4w)
Ideal serving temperature	9–12°C (48–54°F)

Still foaming in Munich
The building depicted on the label is the premises of the Munich beer restaurant. Specialities include offal dishes such as lung.

WEISSE: THE BEER AND THE SAUSAGE

IN MUNICH, THE SEDIMENTED STYLE of wheat beer is often served with coddled veal sausages (*Weisswurst*) and sweet Bavarian mustard. The sausages may contain tiny amounts of beef and bacon, parsley, chives, and onion or lemon. This dish is never served after noon.

UNERTL WEISSBIER

A flavoursome, traditionally made range of wheat beers is produced by the brewery of the Unertl family, in the town of Haag, about 40 km (30 miles) east of Munich. The principal beer is in the *Hefeweizen* style, turbid and full in colour, but not identified as being dark. It has a juicy, toffee-apple character and a smoky, appetizing dryness. It is offered at the brewery's beer garden with bread and pork dripping (*Griebenschmalz*).

Region of origin
Upper Bavaria, Germany

Style *Hefeweizen*

Alcohol content 4.8abv (3.8w)

Ideal serving temperature
9–12°C (48–54°F)

OBERDORFER WEISSBIER

One of the more widely available examples of the style in export markets. The brewery derives its name from its home town, Marktoberdorf (The Market of the Upper Village), which is situated in green, rolling countryside about halfway between Munich and Lake Constance. It traces its history to a tavern in the 1500s. Oberdorfer Weissbier is lively and very light, with a perfumy, bubble-gum character.

Region of origin
Swabia, Bavaria, Germany

Style *Hefeweizen*

Alcohol content 4.9abv (3.9w)

Ideal serving temperature
9–12°C (48–54°F)

TUCHER HELLES HEFE WEIZEN

Founded as a wheat-beer brewery in 1672, and for a time owned by Bavaria's royal family. The Tucher family took over in 1855, and the brewery has had several owners since. This Nuremberg brewery again became a family business in 1994, when Inselkammer, the Bavarian brewing dynasty, took an interest. Its *Hefeweizen* has a firm background with sweet apple flavours, moving to a spicy, dry, crisp finish.

Region of origin
Franconia, Bavaria, Germany

Style *Hefeweizen*

Alcohol content 5.3abv (4.2w)

Ideal serving temperature
9–12°C (48–54°F)

SCHEIDMANTEL HEFE WEISSE

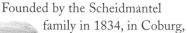

Founded by the Scheidmantel family in 1834, in Coburg, seat of the family that produced many of Europe's royals. The town's fortress provides a dramatic backdrop to the brewery. Today's brewery dates from the turn of the century and still has the lakes that provided ice for lagering until the 1950s. Scheidmantel Hefe Weisse is smooth, orangey, and lemony.

Region of origin
Franconia, Bavaria, Germany

Style *Hefeweizen*

Alcohol content
5.1abv (4.1w)

Ideal serving temperature
9–12°C (48–54°F)

PINKUS MÜLLER HEFE WEIZEN

Such has been the success of south German wheat beers that many northern breweries have devised their own examples of this style. In Münster, the Pinkus Müller pub and brewery has a *Weizen* that is distinctly its own. The beer has a typical southern balance of wheat to barley malt, but a northern yeast character: flowery, dry, and slightly acidic. A smooth, delicate, and appetizing beer.

Region of origin
Münster, North Rhine-Westphalia, Germany

Style *Hefeweizen*

Alcohol content 5.2abv (4.2w)

Ideal serving temperature
9–12°C (48–54°F)

SÜNNER HEFEWEIZEN

The northern brewery Sünner is better known for the *Kölschbier* it makes in its home town of Cologne, but it also has a *Hefeweizen*. This brew has a flowery, perfumy aroma; a smooth, soft, melony body; a light bubble-gum character; and a leafy finish. The label shows the smart brewery with its battlemented gables. In the central window, the brew-kettle is clearly visible.

Region of origin
Cologne, North Rhine-Westphalia, Germany

Style *Hefeweizen*

Alcohol content 4.9abv (3.9w)

Ideal serving temperature
9–12°C (48–54°F)

HERRENHÄUSER WEIZEN BIER

This Hanover brewery, established in 1868, is much better known for its Pilsner-style beer, including a kosher version. Its home state of Lower Saxony may in the distant past have produced sourer, more northern styles of wheat beer, but this recent example is broadly in the southern style. It has a sweetish, spicy aroma; a smooth, faintly syrupy palate; and a lightly tart finish. A field of wheat is vividly depicted on the label.

Region of origin Hanover, Lower Saxony, Germany

Style *Hefeweizen*

Alcohol content 5.5abv (4.4w)

Ideal serving temperature
9–12°C (48–54°F)

UERIGES WEIZEN

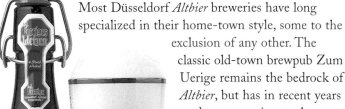

Most Düsseldorf *Altbier* breweries have long specialized in their home-town style, some to the exclusion of any other. The classic old-town brewpub Zum Uerige remains the bedrock of *Altbier*, but has in recent years made a concession to the fashion for wheat beers with its Ueriges Weizen. Made with the *Altbier* yeast, and thus rather northern in style, it has a good, clean, malt background, and is light, flowery, gingery, and very crisp, with a minerally dryness in the finish.

Region of origin
Düsseldorf, North Rhine-Westphalia, Germany

Style *Hefeweizen*

Alcohol content 4.5abv (3.6w)

Ideal serving temperature
9–12°C (48–54°F)

GAMBRINUS BÍLÉ

The name Gambrinus is probably a corruption of Jan Primus, the first duke of Flanders and legendary king of beer. The reference crops up all over the beer world, but Jan Primus did marry into Bohemian royalty, and this Gambrinus brewery is in Pilsen in the Czech Republic. It occupies a site adjoining the Urquell brewery. Like its neighbour, Gambrinus is known for a beer in the Pilsner style. In recent years it has also added this perfumy, peachy, tart, light wheat beer.

Region of origin Pilsen, Bohemia, Czech Republic

Style *Hefeweizen*

Alcohol content 5.1abv (4.1w)

Ideal serving temperature 9–12°C (48–54°F)

SISSONS WISE GUY WEISSBIER

Resting actors are often to be found tending the bar; Hugh Sisson was able to do so in his family's tavern in Baltimore, Maryland. In 1989 a brewery was added, initially making ales and more recently this punning ("Wise") *Weisse*. The beer has a lemony fruitiness. It begins with hints of lemon curd; moves to a pith-like character; and finishes with a suggestion of cloves, nuts, smokiness, and a more grainy note. A Weihenstephan yeast is used.

Region of origin Mid Atlantic US

Style *Hefeweizen*

Alcohol content 4.1abv (3.3w)

Ideal serving temperature 9–12°C (48–54°F)

MICHELOB HEFEWEIZEN

The world's biggest brewing company, and producer of American Budweiser, has in recent years experimented with a wide range of specialities, including dark lagers, bock beers, very hoppy ales, porters, and several wheat beers. In the last category, the one that seems to have become established is under the "super-premium" brand Michelob. This *Hefeweizen* is quite full in colour; freshly aromatic; fruity and sherbety; with a suggestion of banana-toffee.

Region of origin Midwest US

Style *Hefeweizen*

Alcohol content 5.0abv (4.0w)

Ideal serving temperature 9–12°C (48–54°F)

TABERNASH WEISSE

There is a town of Tabernash west of Denver, Colorado, named after a Native American Ute chief. This mystical name also attaches to a micro-brewery in Denver itself, specializing in German beers. One of its founders studied brewing at Weihenstephan, and later wrote a book on wheat beers. Tabernash has a good nutmeg, clovey spiciness in the aroma; is quite sweet; and develops very good fruit flavours, especially banana.

Region of origin Southwest US

Style *Hefeweizen*

Alcohol content 5.5abv (4.4w)

Ideal serving temperature 9–12°C (48–54°F)

White mountains
The snow-capped mountains on the label of this "white" beer are the Rockies. They dominate this part of Colorado, which is dense with small breweries.

THIRST QUENCHERS: GERMAN DARK WHEAT BEERS

ONE OF THE LESSER-KNOWN but most flavoursome brew styles is the dark version of the South German wheat beer. This type of beer combines the toffeeish lusciousness of dark malts with the fruity sharpness of wheat and the spiciness of Bavarian top-fermenting yeasts. These beers are as toothsome as liquid toffee apples. Served cool, they are a quencher for late spring or early autumn. They are also delicious as dessert beers, with fruity or toffeeish dishes. The beers are sometimes identified as black (*Schwarze*) or, more traditionally, dark (either *Dunkel, Dunkle,* or *Dunkles,* depending upon the grammar) wheat (*Weizen*). Often, they are served with a sediment of yeast (*Hefe*).

Weeping Radish...
...is a brewery in Manteo, North Carolina, that in autumn produces an apple-ish, strong, dark wheat beer, at 6.0abv (4.8w).

MÖNCHSHOF KAPUZINER SCHWARZE HEFEWEIZEN

The "Monks' Courtyard" range of beers date from a Capuchin friary that was already brewing in the 1300s, in Kulmbach, in the north of Bavaria. Today, Kulmbach has two major breweries, Reichelbräu and EKU, under the same ownership, and the latter produces the Mönchshof beers. The Schwarze Hefeweizen is a very flavoursome beer, with vanilla aromas and flavours, and some banana notes, drying into treacle toffee and a hint of cloves. Kulmbach is known both for dark and strong brews, and makes a greater volume of beer per head of population than any other town in Germany. It has 30,000 people and produces 1.6 million hectolitres (281,690,141 pints) of beer per year, that is, 5,300 litres (9,390 pints) per person.

Region of origin	Franconia, Bavaria, Germany
Style	Dark Wheat Beer
Alcohol content	5.4abv (4.3w)
Ideal serving temperature	9–12°C (48–54°F)

Black is beautiful
"Black" lagers became fashionable in Germany when examples from the East were rediscovered after the Berlin Wall tumbled. Mönchshof had long made a black lager, and now has this almost ebony wheat beer.

FRANZISKANER DUNKEL HEFE-WEISSBIER

The Franciscan strand in the heritage of the Spaten brewing company is celebrated by a range of light but tasty wheat beers, including this version. Like several other brewers, Spaten-Franziskaner uses the contradictory conjunction of "dark" and "white" in its name for this style. This brew has a toffeeish malt aroma, and a creamy, grainy palate. It finishes with some spiciness, suggesting cinnamon and pepper.

Region of origin Munich, Upper Bavaria, Germany

Style Dark Wheat Beer

Alcohol content 5.0abv (4.0w)

Ideal serving temperature 9–12°C (48–54°F)

HB SCHWARZE WEISSE

The royal family of Bavaria maintained a monopoly on the brewing of wheat beers from the 1600s to the early 1800s. The *Hofbräuhaus* (Royal Court Brewery) of Munich once specialized in the style. It has promoted its own examples since the revival of interest in wheat beers in the late 1970s. This one is very lively, with spicy (licorice-like), chewy malt flavours; treacle toffee in the middle; and a grainy, slightly tannic (green apple) finish.

Region of origin Munich, Upper Bavaria, Germany

Style Dark Wheat Beer

Alcohol content 5.1abv (4.1w)

Ideal serving temperature 9–12°C (48–54°F)

HOPF DUNKLE WEISSE

Hans Hopf, owner of this brewery, almost certainly owes his surname to the hop plant. As chance would have it, he specializes in wheat beer, a style that is usually only lightly hopped. His Dunkle Weisse has a hint of hop in the bouquet, along with some fresh pear and banana. It is a lively beer, firm and smooth, with a restrained dryness, and a quenching, refreshing finish. The brewery is in Miesbach, approximately 56 km (35 miles) south of the city of Munich.

Region of origin Upper Bavaria, Germany

Style Dark Wheat Beer

Alcohol content 5.0abv (4.0w)

Ideal serving temperature 9–12°C (48–54°F)

HERRNBRÄU HEFE-WEISSBIER DUNKEL

The German Beer Purity Law was first announced by Duke Wilhelm IV, in 1516, in Ingolstadt, now the home of the Herrnbräu brewery. At one stage it was an offence for a brewer in the town to fail to meet his quotas. Despite this, Beer Street was built to fetch supplies from nearby Kelheim. Today's dark wheat beer has a nutty sweetness, chocolatey flavours, and a flowery, "violets" dryness.

Region of origin Upper Bavaria, Germany

Style Dark Wheat Beer

Alcohol content 5.3abv (4.2w)

Ideal serving temperature 9–12°C (48–54°F)

THIRST QUENCHERS: WHEAT ALES

WHEAT GIVES A HINT of quenching tartness, and a definite crispness, even to beers made with conventional ale yeasts. Wheat ales are a new style, introduced primarily in Britain and the US in recent years. They are intended as a summery refresher that is easily drinkable but has some character. Most have a pale, gold, or bronze colour and a modest alcohol content. They are often appreciated by the consumer wishing to find a more interesting step up from a light or "premium" lager.

Pigs and pints...
...personify the Loaded Hog chain of brewpubs in New Zealand.

KING & BARNES WHEAT MASH

Once a purely local brewery, in Horsham, Sussex. King & Barnes, which traces its origins to 1800, has in recent years won a far wider reputation by developing a range of bottle-conditioned speciality brews. Some are seasonal, others produced year-round. Several employ unusual grains (one of the best containing rye), others feature specific hop varieties (notably one with Liberty), or use herbs. Wheat Mash is usually available in April. The term "mash" refers to the blending of the grains with the brewing water. This beer contains 40 per cent wheat (the remainder being barley malt), is hopped with the Goldings variety, and fermented with the brewery's clean, dry, two-strain ale yeast. The result is a firm, grainy brew, as crisp as a cracker; with a late, wheaty, lemony, perfumy tartness. Other beers include an outstanding pale ale, called Festive, and a Christmas brew.

Region of origin Southeast England, UK

Style Wheat Ale

Alcohol content 4.5abv (3.6w)

Ideal serving temperature 10–14°C (50–58°F)

Handle with care
The beer should be stored for a day or two before use, to let the yeast settle, and handled gently when the beer is to be served. The neck-label makes this point.

HOPBACK THUNDERSTORM

Having been very successful with a seasonal beer called Summer Lightning, this Salisbury brewery in 1997 paid its further respects to the unpredictability of British weather by adding a wheat ale identified as Thunderstorm. This bottle-conditioned beer is made with 50 per cent wheat and hopped entirely with the variety Progress. It has a light but firm, juicy malt background; the faintest hint of banana yeastiness; long, very dry, lemon-zest and juniper hop flavours; and a crisp finish.

Region of origin
Southern England, UK

Style Wheat Ale

Alcohol content
5.0abv (4.0w)

Ideal serving temperature
Store at 10–14°C (50–58°F)
Serve at 10°C (50°F)

Nectar of the Gods
The ancient Roman god of drink, Bacchus, appears on all of this brewer's labels.

ANDERSON VALLEY HIGH ROLLERS WHEAT BEER

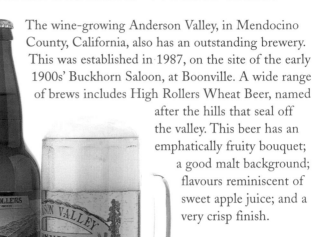

The wine-growing Anderson Valley, in Mendocino County, California, also has an outstanding brewery. This was established in 1987, on the site of the early 1900s' Buckhorn Saloon, at Boonville. A wide range of brews includes High Rollers Wheat Beer, named after the hills that seal off the valley. This beer has an emphatically fruity bouquet; a good malt background; flavours reminiscent of sweet apple juice; and a very crisp finish.

Region of origin
California, US

Style Wheat Ale

Alcohol content
5.3abv (4.2w)

Ideal serving temperature
10°C (50°F)

PYRAMID WHEATEN ALE

The name alludes to a pyramid-shaped peak in the Cascade Mountains. Pyramid and its brother brewery Thomas Kemper now share premises in Seattle, with an additional brewpub at Berkeley, California. The brewery began in Kalama, Washington, in 1984, and pioneered the idea of a wheat brew made with an ale yeast. This unusual approach was signalled in the odd name Wheaten Ale.

The beer is perfumy, with a hint of honey; clean, grainy, and lightly refreshing; with a very slight tartness in the finish.

Region of origin
Pacific Northwest US

Style Wheat Ale

Alcohol content
5.1abv (4.1w)

Ideal serving temperature
10°C (50°F)

SAINT ARNOLD KRISTALL WEIZEN

Two different saints called Arnold are patrons of Belgian and French beer-makers, and either sits oddly with the German term

Kristall Weizen. What the Saint Arnold brewery offers under this name is, in fact, a Wheat Ale. It is a light, perfumy beer; firm and smooth; with hints of vanilla; a very slight, sweet-orange fruitiness; and a crisp finish. Saint Arnold, a well-regarded micro, was founded in 1994, in Houston, Texas. The brewery also makes amber and brown ales.

Region of origin Southwest US

Style Wheat Ale

Alcohol content 4.9abv (3.9w)

Ideal serving temperature
10°C (50°F)

THIRST QUENCHERS: FLEMISH "SWEET AND SOUR" RED ALES

THE MOST REFRESHING of all beers are the curiously sharp, reddish-brown Belgian ales most typically produced in the province of West Flanders. They can shock at the first encounter, but once enjoyed they are forever appreciated by the lover of characterful beer. The classic of the style, Rodenbach, has a growing following in Britain, the US, and Japan. The best of these beers contain sweet, reddish, Vienna-style barley malts, but also gain colour, lactic acidity, and vinegary fruitiness from long periods in magnificent ceiling-high oak tuns.

It's wine!...
...announced this 1930s' poster. A tannic, acidic Barbera, perhaps?

RODENBACH

During Austrian rule in Belgium, the first Rodenbach arrived from the Rhineland as a military doctor, and later married into a Flemish family. In 1820, a Rodenbach bought a brewery, and the family has been involved in the present one, in Roeselare, since 1836. With nearly 300 fixed wooden vessels, it is one of the world's most unusual breweries. The basic Rodenbach is a blend of 75 per cent "young" beer (matured in metal tanks for four to five weeks) and 25 per cent aged brew (more than two years in wood). It emerges with a fruity perfume; passion fruit, iron, and oakiness in the palate; and a late, puckering tartness. Grand Cru, a bottling of the aged version only, is clean and sharp, with a sour-cream acidity. A version sweetened with cherry essence is called Rodenbach Alexander.

Region of origin
Province of West Flanders, Belgium

Style Flemish Red/Brown

Alcohol content 5.0abv (4.0w)

Ideal serving temperature 9–13°C (48–55°F)

THE RODENBACH DYNASTY

THIS STATUE IN ROESELARE commemorates author Albrecht Rodenbach, who wrote in Flemish. Another author in the family, Georges, preferred French. Politician Alexander was active in Belgium's independence movement. Constantine, ambassador to Greece, is buried in front of the Parthenon.

PETRUS OUD BRUIN

In the Petrus range, this reddish-brown brew in the Flemish style is the one that at least superficially resembles the world-famous Pétrus wine. It is a complex brew: it has a tannic aroma and a very smooth palate, with a clean, toffee-like maltiness, and hints of chocolate and cinnamon-dusted pears. This is from the De Brabandere brewery, of Bavikhove, near Kortrijk (in French, Courtrai).

Region of origin Province of West Flanders, Belgium

Style Flemish Red/Brown

Alcohol content 5.5abv (4.4w)

Ideal serving temperature 9–13°C (48–55°F)

Vintage Petrus
The wooden vessels in which this beer ages are laid horizontally. They held white wine and Calvados before being installed at the De Brabandere brewery.

VAN HONSEBROUCK BACCHUS

The orgiastic name is one of several extrovert brands from the Van Honsebrouck brewery, of Ingelmunster, West Flanders. The beer has a vinegary bouquet; a touch of caramel; an oaky, woody palate; and a late, light, spritzy acidity. Wood ageing is used. An East Flanders brewery, Van Steenberge, of Ertevelde, has an entrant called Bios, from the Greek word for life. This has a slightly syrupy start and a late, lactic dryness.

Region of origin Province of West Flanders, Belgium

Style Flemish Red/Brown

Alcohol content 4.5abv (3.6w)

Ideal serving temperature 9–13°C (48–55°F)

Leonine label
The black lion on the label is the symbol of Flanders. The brewery's home town was once the seat of the Count of Flanders.

VERHAEGHE VICHTENAAR

The Verhaeghe family, of Vichte, near Kortrijk, have been brewing since the 1500s, originally in a château farmhouse brewery. Their entrant in the local style pours with a huge, rocky head. It is one of the sweeter examples, but lively and layered, with notes of Madeira, vanilla, oak, iron, and the acidity of a fresh apple. A stronger companion brew called Duchesse de Bourgogne has a similar character but with distinct chocolate and cream flavours.

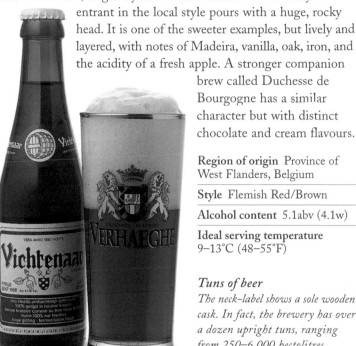

Region of origin Province of West Flanders, Belgium

Style Flemish Red/Brown

Alcohol content 5.1abv (4.1w)

Ideal serving temperature 9–13°C (48–55°F)

Tuns of beer
The neck-label shows a sole wooden cask. In fact, the brewery has over a dozen upright tuns, ranging from 250–6,000 hectolitres (5,500–132,000 gallons).

ALKEN-MAES ZULTE

This beer was originally produced at a brewery founded in 1891, called Anglo-Belge, at Zulte, in East Flanders. Anglo-Belge originally also made vinegar and distilled spirits, and was known for its stout. It closed in 1989, and the beer is now made at the Alken-Maes brewery in Jumet, near Charleroi. The uprooted Zulte is the most caramelly example of the style, grainy, with a fruity dryness and sharpness.

Region of origin
Province of Hainaut, Belgium

Style Flemish Red/Brown

Alcohol content 4.7abv (3.8w)

Ideal serving temperature 9–13°C (48–55°F)

The Zulte uprooting
In 1977, the brewery in Zulte was acquired by Kronenbourg. In 1982 the French company bought Alken and in 1988 Maes, which had owned the Union brewery in Jumet since 1978.

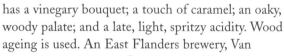

RESTORATIVES: BLACK BEERS

THE MOST RECENT BEER FASHION in Germany has been for brews described as black (*schwarze*), a style once thought especially suitable for nursing mothers. Black beers have been rediscovered in Germany since reunification and are particularly associated with the old eastern states, especially Thuringia. The traditions of black beers and very dark lagers merged in northern Bavarian towns such as Kulmbach and Erlangen. Originally, black beers were very dark ales, and they retained their colour after lager yeasts were introduced. German brewers introduced black beers to Japan more than 100 years ago, and the tradition flourishes there more strongly than ever. Typically, these beers have a bitter-chocolate character.

SAPPORO BLACK BEER

In Japan, sake (really a rice beer rather than a wine) was joined by locally made western-style brews in the late 1800s. These beers were a result of American, Dutch, and German influence. At that time, German lagers were dark. The brewery in Sapporo opened in 1876, before registered brands existed. This national brewer has a wide range of products, including an interesting black beer, which received its first definite mention in 1892. Today's neck-label boasts "Japan's oldest brand". The beer smells like a box of chocolates; has complex, long flavours reminiscent of roasting coffee and figs; and finishes with a licorice note. Sapporo's national rivals Asahi and Kirin both have black beers, and so do many of the small, new-generation breweries in Japan.

Region of origin Hokkaido, Japan

Style Black Beer

Alcohol content 5.0abv (4.0w)

Ideal serving temperature 9°C (48°F)

DIET OF WORDS

GERMANY'S GREATEST writer, Johann Wolfgang von Goethe (1749–1832), took an interest in beer from his student days. He sustained himself on black beer from Köstritz (*right*) when he was unable to eat during a period of illness.

BRAND OUD BRUIN

A smooth and malty interpretation, with a finish reminiscent of saccharine-sweetened coffee, from this brewery in Wijlre, east of Maastricht. An antique-style beer seems very appropriate at The Netherlands' oldest brewery. A spiced beer, fermented with wild yeast, was made in the days when the brewery was a brewpub on the Lord of the Manor's estate. When the local clergyman complained that peasants preferred the pub to the pulpit, the brewery was sold to the Brand family.

Region of origin Province of Limburg, The Netherlands

Style Old Brown Lager

Alcohol content 3.5abv (2.8w)

Ideal serving temperature 8–9°C (46–48°F)

The Lord's beer
When the Lord of the Manor owned the Wijlre brewery, he proclaimed a local monopoly on beer. This is remembered in the text on the neck-label.

BUDELS OUD BRUIN

A hint of fruit and a creamy, grainy palate, with a toffeeish finish in this example from the brewery at Budel, near the Belgian border. Promotional literature from a dozen years ago describes the beer as "tasty, toothsome, soft, mild, gentle, kind, friendly, and suitable for a cosy, sociable drink". The English word "cosy" fails to do justice to the untranslatable Dutch *gezellig*. Comfort and safety, with a beer and friends, are important in a country so vulnerable to the sea.

Region of origin Province of North Brabant, The Netherlands

Style Old Brown Lager

Alcohol content 3.5abv (2.8w)

Ideal serving temperature 8–9°C (46–48°F)

Hope and anchor
Like several other breweries, the one at Budel has an anchor as its emblem. This is not a maritime reference, but a biblical allusion to optimism: "Hope...anchor of the soul" (Hebrews 6: 19).

ALFA OUD BRUIN

Why Alfa? "Because we are the first – the best", said great-grandfather Meens, an enthusiast for ancient Greek. The Meens family date from the 1600s, their farm from the 1750s, and its monastery-like brewery from 1870. Its sandstone spring produces glacial water said to be 6,000 years old. Most of the beers are all-malt, but Old Bruin is sweetened, perhaps less overtly than some: clean, very nutty, and toffeeish, with a treacly malt finish.

Region of origin Province of Limburg, The Netherlands

Style Old Brown Lager

Alcohol content 2.5abv (2.0w)

Ideal serving temperature 8–9°C (46–48°F)

Animal farm
The neck-label shows the three lions of Limburg. The crest on the main label, showing three ducks, represents the Meens family. Four generations of this family have worked in the brewery.

RIDDER DONKER

This brewery's parish church in Maastricht is St Martin's, named after one of the Knights Templar (the order that protected pilgrims). *Ridder* means rider, or knight; *Donker* means dark. A suit of armour can be seen in the conference room of the brewery. The Ridder brewery was founded in 1857 by the van Aubel brothers. When there was no successor, in 1982, it was acquired by Heineken. Ridder Donker is a typical *oud bruin*, with its own soft, fluffy, licorice-like maltiness.

Region of origin Province of Limburg, The Netherlands

Style Old Brown Lager

Alcohol content 3.5abv (2.8w)

Ideal serving temperature 8–9°C (46–48°F)

Donker blend
The back-label on this beer suggests that it be used to make a sjoes, *comprising half-and-half of old brown and Pilsner-style lager.*

RESTORATIVES: MILD ALES

A "MILD" IS AN ENGLISH TERM FOR AN ALE that is only lightly hopped, and therefore lacks any obvious bitterness. The style is usually low in alcohol and inexpensive. A mild is often dark, due to the use of luscious, treacly malts. Initially it was a restorative for farm labourers, and later for industrial workers. It has survived best in the forge towns of England's West Midlands, where castings are made for the car industry. Elsewhere, mild has been half-forgotten in the post-industrial age, but some breweries are rediscovering it.

Mild Thing

Mild can be wild
A Pittsburgh brewpub, The Strip, archly dubs its nutty mild ale, Mild Thing!

Under the volcano
The label shows Mount Taranaki. The volcanic peak last erupted 350 years ago, so drinkers feel reasonably secure as they restore themselves after hiking the local nature trails.

MIKE'S MILD ALE

A rare New World mild. The beer might be mild-tasting, but there is a boldness to its proclamation of style. Mike Johnson, a brewer with 12 years' experience, set up on his own in 1989. His White Cliffs brewery is on the coast at Urenui, on New Zealand's North Island. Behind the coast and to the west lies Mount Taranaki (2,500 m/18,200 ft high). From the start, Mike Johnson's flagship product has been his Mild Ale. This has a fresh, earthy aroma; a smooth body; appetizing and pronounced cookie, milk-chocolate, and malt flavours; and a very lightly roasty dryness in the finish. It shows an outstanding balance of mild malt characteristics, though it lacks somewhat in ale fruitiness.

Region of origin
North Island, New Zealand

Style Mild Ale

Alcohol content 4.0abv (3.2w)

Ideal serving temperature
10°C (50°F)

TREACLY TETLEY

TETLEY, IN LEEDS, Yorkshire, is Britain's biggest cask ale brewery. Tetley Mild is distinctively rummy, lightly treacly, and a typically modest 3.3 abv (2.6w). It contains a small amount of Demerara sugar.

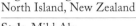

HULL MILD

A claim to fame among beer lovers, especially in North America: the original Hull brewery, based in the Yorkshire fishing and port city of Hull, employed Peter Austin, who later used its distinctively fruity yeast in new-generation breweries throughout the US and Canada. The brewery closed in the 1970s, but the name was resurrected by a micro-brewery in 1989. The micro uses the same yeast to make this smooth, toasty, chocolatey, fruity, winey mild.

Region of origin
Northeast England, UK

Style Mild Ale

Alcohol content
3.3abv (2.6w)

Ideal serving temperature
10–13°C (50–55°F)

WARD'S CLASSIC YORKSHIRE ALE

A great beer-making city, much diminished, Sheffield should be proud of Ward's, a classic Victorian brewery. When the Yorkshire city was also famous for coal and steel, Ward's strong mild was a much-needed restorative. It is a characterful, rummy, dryish interpretation of the style, available only on draught. Ward's Classic Yorkshire Ale is a bottled big-brother brew. It has a very lively interplay of flavours, balancing a perfumy, peachy fruitiness with distinctly nutty maltiness: satisfying, smooth, and drinkable.

Region of origin
Northern England, UK

Style Strong Mild/ Yorkshire Ale

Alcohol content
5.0abv (4.0w)

Ideal serving temperature
10–13°C (50–55°F)

BANKS'S

One of the most famous brewers of mild is Banks's, in the West Midlands city of Wolverhampton. The brewery's renown derives from the quality of its mild, and the high volume of its sales. Nonetheless, fearing that the industrial image of the Midlands might be unfashionable, a marketing genius has in recent years added the meaningless description "uniquely balanced beer", and an exhortation that the brew be served chilled. If the instruction is followed, it will flatten the creamy, oily, nut-toffee maltiness of this delicious, flavoursome brew.

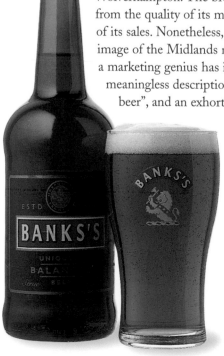

Region of origin
Central England, UK

Style Mild Ale

Alcohol content
3.5abv (2.8w)

Ideal serving temperature
10–13°C (50–55°F)

MANNS ORIGINAL BROWN ALE

This style of dark, malty, sweetish, low-strength brown ale was once made by every English brewery as a bottled version of its draught mild. Few have such a product today, but this minor classic survives. Originally brewed in London, this ale is now made by Ushers in the town of Trowbridge, Wiltshire. It is light, but smooth and creamy, with flavours of chocolate-coated raisins.

Region of origin
Southern England, UK

Style Brown Ale/Mild

Alcohol content
2.8abv (2.2w)

Ideal serving temperature
10–13°C (50–55°F)

RESTORATIVES: SWEET STOUTS

WITHIN THE FAMILY OF STOUTS, the distinctly sweet style has long been regarded as what today might be called an energy drink. Some of these stouts are sweet simply because they emphasize maltiness rather than hop bitterness. Others are given sweetness and body by the use of various types of sugar – often lactose, which is extracted from milk. Having also the coffeeish and chocolatey flavours of toasted or roasted malt, they are the beer world's counterpart to cream liqueurs. In recent years, several Japanese and American breweries have introduced new examples of this old style of beer.

Stout from the sea
The Roman god of the sea, Neptune, arises like a strong man from a garland of malt and hops on Lacto's label.

FARSONS LACTO TRADITIONAL STOUT

As its name suggests, this stout contains lactose. It is a classic example of a beer marketed as a restorative. Lacto Traditional Stout also has added vitamin B. It is made in a palm-fringed, 1950s' brewery by Farrugia and Sons ("Farsons"), on the Mediterranean island of Malta, where it is popular among nursing mothers. The stout is also traditionally used there as an ingredient in Christmas puddings, and its sales soar in November. An important malt in this brew is the dark, sweetish style typically used to make mild ales. Crystal malt is also employed, perhaps contributing to the nutty, polished oak aroma. The beer is light-bodied, but creamy and smooth, with rich flavours suggesting ginger, dark chocolate, and currants. It has a slightly yoghurty finish.

Region of origin Malta

Style Sweet Stout

Alcohol content 3.4abv (2.7w)

Ideal serving temperature 13°C (55°F)

STOUT PUNCH

THE USE OF SUGAR in some beers derives from colonial times. Cane grown in the former British Caribbean has left people there with a sweet tooth. A local drink is made with stout, rum, condensed milk, and an egg. Jamaica's Dragon Stout (7.0abv/5.6w) is sweetish, creamy, and raisiny.

MACKESON STOUT

The world's most widely known sweet stout was developed with the help of a dietician in 1907. It was originally made by the Mackeson brewery, in the small English port of Hythe, Kent. After several changes of ownership, the product came into the hands of the national brewer Whitbread. Mackeson Stout contains lactose, and a milk churn is shown on the label. The beer is light, smooth, and creamy, with hints of evaporated milk and coffee essence, and a liqueurish finish.

Region of origin
Southeast England, UK

Style Sweet Stout

Alcohol content
3.0abv (2.4w)
Export version
5.0abv (4.0w)

Ideal serving temperature
13°C (55°F)

GUERNSEY MILK STOUT

"Milk Stout" was a popular colloquialism after World War II. The UK Ministry of Food eventually deemed it misleading, but such legislation does not apply on the Channel Islands. With their reputation for dairy cattle, it seems appropriate that they still have a Milk Stout. Disappointingly, this does not contain lactose. It nonetheless has a deliciously creamy flavour, drying in a chewy, licorice-toffee finish.

Region of origin
Guernsey, Channel Islands

Style Sweet Stout

Alcohol content
3.3abv (2.6w)

Ideal serving temperature
13°C (55°F)

Polo pint
The trademark of the brewery is a polo pony, reflecting a past owner's enthusiasm.

CSARDA SWEET STOUT

Csarda is Hungarian for inn. Travels in Europe inspired a Japanese clothing manufacturer to open a brewery making a range of beers stretching from a Pilsner and wheat beer to a bitter and this sweet stout, which contains lactose. It has a yoghurty aroma and milky, peaches-and-cream flavours, but is beautifully balanced. The Csarda brewery and country-style restaurant is in the heart of downtown Yokohama.

Region of origin
Honshu, Japan

Style Sweet Stout

Alcohol content
5.0abv (4.0w)

Ideal serving temperature
13°C (55°F)

Dancing beer
The label image reflects the traditional costume of a dancer at a Hungarian inn, or Csarda.

YOUNGER OF ALLOA SWEETHEART STOUT

aA famous old name in Scottish brewing, George Younger, is kept alive in this product. Among several different Younger breweries, the Alloa brewery was acquired and then closed by Tennent, of Glasgow, in the 1960s. Tennent, in turn, is owned by Bass. Aptly, Sweetheart Stout is the most sugary example of the style: with vanilla, caramel, and medicinal notes. In a style that is typically low in alcohol, this example is especially modest.

Region of origin
Scotland, UK

Style Sweet Stout

Alcohol content
2.0abv (1.6w)

Ideal serving temperature
13°C (55°F)

WINTER WARMERS: BOCK BEERS

THE STRONG LAGERS (AND COMPARABLY STRONG WHEAT BREWS) identified as Bock are sometimes intended specifically for spring, but more often they are understood as winter warmers. Some are launched each year in October or November; others appear at Christmas, New Year, or February; and several are available all year round. These beers are rich and malty, sometimes sweet, and sustaining. The Bock tradition is German, but it has also spread to nearby countries, notably The Netherlands and Norway. It is also widely followed in German areas of the US and Canada, and there is even the odd Bock in Australia. In the southern hemisphere, it probably tastes best in the relatively cool months of June and July.

BURRAGORANG BOCK BEER

As the aboriginal-sounding name suggests, this is an Australian beer. It is produced near Burragorang Lake, in Picton, 80 km (50 miles) southwest of Sydney, and is possibly the biggest-tasting beer in Australia. In 1978, the first application to licence a micro-brewery in Australia was made by Geoff Scharer, a fourth-generation Australian from a family who originated from Zurich, Switzerland. In 1987, Scharer finally made beer, advised by the late Otto Binding, Germany's micro-brewery pioneer. Made with three malts and German Spalt hops, Burragorang Bock Beer pours with a huge head; has a silky body; a perfumy, appetizing, malt character; suggestions of treacle toffee; and a resiny, hop balance. The brewery also has a very hoppy, Pilsner-style brew.

Region of origin	New South Wales, Australia
Style	Bock
Alcohol content	6.4abv (5.1w)
Ideal serving temperature	9°C (48°F)

IT'S THE WATER

THE DEPICTION OF THE Burragorang Valley on the Burragorang Bock Beer label shows a tract of land owned by the brewery's proprietor. The Valley is the main source of Sydney's water. The painting was commissioned by the Water Board from artist Robin Collier.

Painting by Robin Collier

KNEITINGER BOCK

A charitable foundation benefiting orphans and sick children has operated this family brewery, in the town of Regensburg, Bavaria, since the death, in 1991, of the last Kneitinger. The brewery dates from 1530, and had been in the Kneitinger family since 1876. The brewery and its adjoining original inn are a listed landmark.

The inn taps the first cask of a new Bock on the first Thursday in October. Kneitinger Bock is very rich and layered in its complex malt character, with a faint smokiness.

Region of origin
Regensburg, Bavaria, Germany

Style Bock

Alcohol content
6.0abv (4.8w)

Ideal serving temperature
9°C (48°F)

AUGUST SCHELL DOPPEL BOCK

The German-accented August Schell brewery, in New Ulm, Minnesota, has in recent years done much to rediscover its heritage. In addition to a tawny, rummy Bock (5.8abv; 4.6w), there is now this well-balanced *Doppel*. It has an appetizing balance of faintly citric hop and cookie-like malt in the aroma; a smooth, medium body; clean, syrupy notes in the palate; and an underpinning of dryness and hoppiness in the finish. The *Doppel* is available from January to March.

Region of origin Midwest US

Style Double Bock

Alcohol content 6.8abv (5.4w)

Ideal serving temperature
9°C (48°F)

BRICK BOCK

Jim Brickman founded this sizeable new-generation brewery in the old beer and whisky town of Waterloo, Ontario, in 1984. Although its Bock recipe has been varied from one year to the next, its typical characteristics include a very malty aroma; a light but firm palate; and a depth of dark-malt flavours, developing licorice, rooty, peaty, burnt, whiskyish notes. The beer is said to be matured for three months.

Region of origin
Province of Ontario, Canada

Style Bock

Alcohol content
7.0abv (5.6w)

Ideal serving temperature
9°C (48°F)

Seal of strength
Some Brick Bock bottlings have an attractive wax seal.

AASS BOCK

Aass (pronounced "orse") means "summit" in Norwegian, but is in this instance a family name. This old brewery is in Drammen, near Oslo, and produces a good example of a Norwegian Bock. Aass Bock has a sweet, licorice-toffee, malt aroma and palate, and a smooth creaminess. It is made with a double-decoction mash, a long boil, and six months' maturation. It is sometimes served with marzipan cake, a Norwegian favourite.

Region of origin
Norway

Style Bock

Alcohol content
6.5abv (5.2w)

Ideal serving temperature
9°C (48°F)

JOPEN BOK BIER

The word *Jopen* was used in Haarlem, once a great brewing city in The Netherlands, to describe a size of beer barrel. This unusual "four-grain" beer is made from barley, wheat, rye (all malted), and raw oats, and is top-fermented and bottle-conditioned. Although developed in Haarlem, it is produced at the Schaapskooi Trappist brewery. To experience its fragrant, orangey aroma is like biting into the fruit itself. The beer is lightly syrupy and malty in the palate, with spicy, dry flavours (but no spices are used).

Region of origin
Province of North Holland, The Netherlands

Style
Top-fermenting Bock

Alcohol content
5.5abv (4.4w)

Ideal serving temperature
9°C (48°F)

AMSTEL HERFSTBOCK

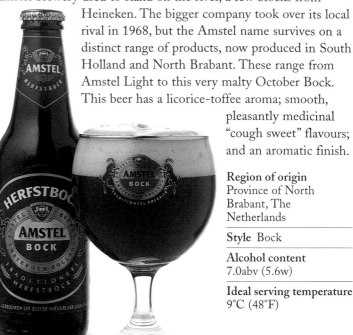

The Amstel is the river that gives Amsterdam its name. The Amstel brewery used to stand on the river, a few blocks from Heineken. The bigger company took over its local rival in 1968, but the Amstel name survives on a distinct range of products, now produced in South Holland and North Brabant. These range from Amstel Light to this very malty October Bock. This beer has a licorice-toffee aroma; smooth, pleasantly medicinal "cough sweet" flavours; and an aromatic finish.

Region of origin
Province of North Brabant, The Netherlands

Style Bock

Alcohol content
7.0abv (5.6w)

Ideal serving temperature
9°C (48°F)

HEINEKEN TARWEBOK

One of the most distinctive, flavoursome, and complex beers made by Heineken is this wheat Bock. No fewer than four types of barley malt are used, along with 17 per cent wheat malt. The result is a silky-smooth beer, with suggestions of cream, coffee, chocolate, prunes, and rum. This Dutch interpretation of the style does not have the phenol smokiness or bubble-gum flavours that might be found in a typical German *Weizenbock*.

Region of origin
Province of North Brabant, The Netherlands

Style Wheat Bock

Alcohol content
6.5abv (5.2w)

Ideal serving temperature
9–10°C (48–50°F)

SCHNEIDER AVENTINUS

When the famous Schneider family was brewing in Munich, their bottling hall was on Aventinstrasse, which provided an ideal name for this "double" *Weizenbock*. With its alcoholic warmth and layers of malty complexity, balanced by clovey spiciness, figgy, raisiny fruitiness, sparkle, and champagne-like acidity, Aventinus is a truly remarkable beer.

Region of origin Munich, Upper Bavaria, Germany

Style Wheat Double Bock/*Weizenbock*

Alcohol content
7.7abv (6.2w)

Ideal serving temperature
9–10°C (48–50°F)

BOCK BEERS

COUGAN'S BOCK

Far from Germany can be found an astonishingly drinkable, Irish-sounding Bock, made in a brewery and pub (more a neighbourhood bar) called Cougan's, in Phoenix, Arizona. Cougan's is owned by the fashionable brewpub chain, Hops! Talented brewer and beer historian Daniel Rothman created this lively brew, with its rocky head; deep amber colour; malty fruitiness of aroma; cookie-like flavours; and leafy, hoppy, balancing dryness.

Region of origin Southwest US

Style Bock

Alcohol content 5.9abv (4.7w)

Ideal serving temperature 9°C (48°F)

DENISON'S BOCK

The Denison's brewery at the Growler's Pub, in Toronto, Ontario, produces a full range of German styles, in consultation with Prince Luitpold of the Kaltenberg brewery, in Bavaria. These include a ruby-coloured Bock that pours with a big head; has a nutty, syrupy, creamy aroma and flavour; developing a deep, peppery dryness towards a lively finish. There is also a tawny *Dunkler Weizenbock* with a toffeeish, fruity palate, finishing with a touch of clove.

Region of origin Province of Ontario, Canada

Style Bock

Alcohol content 6.5abv (5.2w)

Ideal serving temperature 9°C (48°F)

DOCK STREET ILLUMINATOR

Wry twists on the Salvator tradition are offered by many North American breweries, with names such as Hibernator, Terminator, and Liberator. This enlightening example, Illuminator, from the Dock Street brewery and pub in Philadelphia, is a dark amber Double Bock: creamy, with vanilla notes, and pruney flavours.

Region of origin Northeast US

Style Double Bock

Alcohol content 7.2abv (5.8w)

Ideal serving temperature 9°C (48°F)

FORDHAM CALVINATOR

Benjamin Fordham was an immigrant from London who made English-style ales in the earliest days of Annapolis, Maryland. The brewery named after him is at a 1740s' tavern called the Ram's Head. Despite its English heritage, the brewery makes German styles, produced according to the Purity Law. Its Calvinator has a deep, ruby colour; a huge, rocky head; a perfumy, malt aroma; a very smooth body; and lively, assertive malt flavours, finishing with a powerful hop bitterness. The name? "Calvinists would like beer if they tasted ours."

Region of origin Northeast US

Style Double Bock

Alcohol content 7.5abv (6.0w)

Ideal serving temperature 9°C (48°F)

GORDON BIERSCH BLONDE BOCK

This California-based chain of brewery restaurants produces beers in classic German styles. Its Blonde Bock is bright gold in colour, with a malty aroma; has barley-sugar notes and whiskyish flavours; a light, flowery finish; and a late hit of warming alcohol. Try it as a dessert beer or the last beer on a winter's night.

Region of origin California, US

Style Bock

Alcohol content 7.0–7.2abv (5.6–5.8w)

Ideal serving temperature 9°C (48°F)

GROLSCH HERFSTBOK

The well-known Dutch brewer has in its wide range several variations on the Bock theme. This "Harvest" Bock for late autumn and early winter has a very attractive, tawny, reddish colour; a big, well-retained, rocky head; a fresh, malty aroma; a very sweet but nutty and appetizing palate; and a pleasantly medicinal, warming finish.

Region of origin Eastern Netherlands

Style Bock (*Bok*)

Alcohol content 6.5abv (5.2w)

Ideal serving temperature 9°C (48°F)

HOSTER'S CAPTIVATOR

In the lively brewing town of Columbus, Ohio, Hoster's was once a famous name. It bids to be so again, having been revived in 1989. A wide range of mainly German styles is produced. The Captivator has an attractive garnet colour; a smooth, syrupy, textured palate; and a complex of satisfying flavours, drying into light smokiness, leafy hoppiness, and warming alcohol.

Region of origin Midwest US

Style Double Bock

Alcohol content 8.5abv (6.8w)

Ideal serving temperature 9°C (48°F)

SPECULATOR

This Double Bock is spiced with ginger, cloves, cinnamon, nutmeg, and pepper: the spices typically used in the Dutch national cookie, called *speculaas*. The beer is cerise to black in colour, with a big, warm, dusty, spicy, cherryish aroma. It has a smooth palate, with bitter-cherry, rooty, licorice-like flavours; and a menthol, herbal finish. It is made by the North Holland Foundation of Alternative Brewers.

Region of origin North Holland, The Netherlands

Style Double Bock (*Dubbel Bok*)

Alcohol content 8.5abv (6.8w)

Ideal serving temperature 9°C (48°F)

WÜRZBURGER HOFBRÄU SYMPATOR

The wine-growing town of Würzburg banned brewing "for ever" in 1434, but to no avail. In the 1600s, when the vineyards could not quench the thirsts of the military in the 30 Years' War, the local bishop decreed that the town should have a brewery, which was sited in the royal armoury. The brewery later became a private business, and its present buildings date from 1882. The Sympator has a deep, chestnut colour; a creamy, well-retained head; a brandyish aroma; and very clean, complex, malty flavours, and fudgy notes.

Region of origin Franconia, Bavaria, Germany

Style Double Bock (*Doppelbock*)

Alcohol content 7.9abv (6.3w)

Ideal serving temperature 9°C (48°F)

WINTER WARMERS: SPICED BEERS

BEFORE HOPS BECAME THE BREWER'S FAVOURITE HERB, many of the spices used in beer were those that bring the hot flavours of sunny lands to a more wintry world. Ginger, nutmeg, cinnamon, and cloves are mentioned in laws concerning brewing in the seventh century, and were no doubt used long before that. None of these has ever totally vanished from the brewery, and all have enjoyed a revival in recent years. Some of today's spiced beers are even intended to be tasted warm, as mulled ales.

Cherry Christmas
The typical Liefmans tissue comes in Christmassy colours for this brew, but Glühkriek might better be enjoyed with winter sports. The Ardennes are less suitable than the Alps, Aviemore, or Aspen.

LIEFMANS GLÜHKRIEK

Anyone who has ever been skiing has been offered *Glühwein* – a "glow wine", served warm and spiced, typically with cloves and cinnamon. The German prefix *Glüh* is used by the otherwise Flemish-speaking, Belgian brewery Liefmans to promote the same notion. This beer, based on the cherry brew Liefmans Kriek, contains the same two spices, but also anise. The cinnamon seems most obvious in the aroma, with iron-like, medicinal flavours giving way to sweet, sugared-almond notes, balanced by fruity acidity and a clovey finish. The aromas increase and the sweetness diminishes if the beer is mulled. It is intended to be heated as though it were hot chocolate. This is best done in a double boiler (bain-marie), though a simple pan, or even microwave, can be used.

Region of origin
Province of East Flanders, Belgium

Style Spiced Cherry Beer

Alcohol content 6.5abv (5.2w)

Ideal serving temperature 70°C (158°F)

SAINTLY PLEASURES

THE BEERS OF THE St Peter's brewery are available in London at a tavern named after the Priory of St John of Jerusalem. Behind the 1800s' shopfront of the Jerusalem Tavern is a building from the early 1700s. The name is much older. There was a Jerusalem Coffee House in the 1600s and an earlier tavern in the 1300s.

UNIBROUE QUELQUE CHOSE

The Belgian company that owns Liefmans was originally a consultant to this very adventurous Quebecois brewery. Unibroue has some truly remarkable beers, and this is one of them. Liefmans Glühkriek and Quelque Chose have much the same base beer, but the latter is blended with a paler, stronger brew, with a complex malt specification including some whisky malt. The resultant beer is therefore stronger, but it also seems lighter-bodied, fruitier, and tarter.

Region of origin
Province of Quebec, Canada

Style Spiced Cherry Beer

Alcohol content 8.0abv (6.4w)

Ideal serving temperature
70°C (158°F)

Something else...
"Is it a wine or a beer, or something else?" people asked. "It's something else! Really something!!" replied the brewer.

MÅRTEN TROTZIG'S ÖL

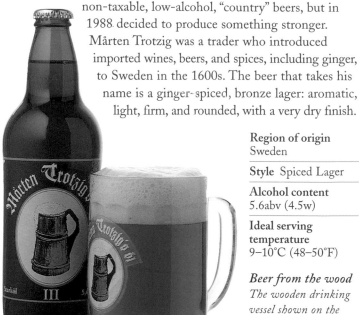

The brewery Sofiero is in the small Swedish town of Laholm, and is named after the castle at nearby Hälsingborg. It originally made non-taxable, low-alcohol, "country" beers, but in 1988 decided to produce something stronger. Mårten Trotzig was a trader who introduced imported wines, beers, and spices, including ginger, to Sweden in the 1600s. The beer that takes his name is a ginger-spiced, bronze lager: aromatic, light, firm, and rounded, with a very dry finish.

Region of origin
Sweden

Style Spiced Lager

Alcohol content
5.6abv (4.5w)

Ideal serving temperature
9–10°C (48–50°F)

Beer from the wood
The wooden drinking vessel shown on the label is a powerful symbol of the deeply forested Baltic countries.

ST PETER'S SPICED ALE

The 13th-century St Peter's Hall is a manor house, near Bungay, Suffolk, England. It was acquired in 1995 by an expert on marketing, with an enthusiasm for the drinks industry, and turned into a brewery, bar, and restaurant. A wide range of beers has been produced, one of the most assertive being this dark ale spiced with cinnamon and apple. It has a deep ruby colour; a very aromatic, dark-chocolate bouquet; an oily, smooth body; a palate suggesting mocha, nuts, and port; and a very dry, tannic finish.

Region of origin
Eastern England, UK

Style
Spiced Dark Ale

Alcohol content
6.5abv (5.2w)

Ideal serving temperature
10–13°C (50–55°F)

GROLSCH WINTERVORST

"Winter Frost" is a distinctive and flavoursome strong ale in a "Four Seasons" range from this Dutch brewer. Wintervorst is spiced with clover, honey, and orange peel. It pours with a big, rocky, well-retained head; an aromatic, malty bouquet; rich, sweet, appetizing, licorice-like flavours; a lightly oily, soothing, smooth body; and a gently herbal, flowery finish.

Region of origin
Eastern Netherlands

Style Spiced Ale

Alcohol content
7.5abv (6.0w)

Ideal serving temperature
10°C (48°F)

Vorst of both worlds
"Frost" and "first" sound as similar in Dutch as in English. The wintry king (the "first" person) on the label and glass depicts this word-play.

WINTER WARMERS: OLD ALES

FLAVOURSOME, OFTEN DARK BROWN ALES, usually malt-accented, sweet, and relatively full-bodied but only medium-to-strong in alcohol, are typically regarded as winter warmers. Brews in this style are most often described as old ales. This can imply an old style of beer, or it can suggest a longer-than-usual ageing. One or two brews labelled "old ale" are much stronger, and can be matured in the bottle. A great many beers in this style have the term "Old" or "Winter" in their brand-names, and some are also identified as barley wines: the styles blur into each other. The purist might argue that old ales are typically the darker, less potent of the two, and frequently available on draught; while barley wines are stronger brews more often found in the bottle.

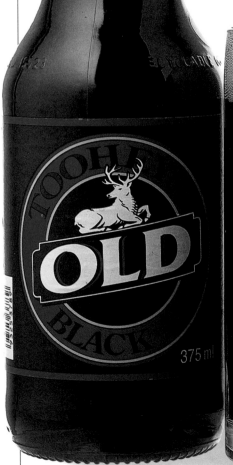

Ale halo
Amid Australia's sea of bland, sweet lagers, Tooheys Old emphasizes its status as an ale by declaring, on the neck-label, that it is made with top-fermenting yeast.

TOOHEYS OLD BLACK ALE

Irish-Australian brothers founded the Tooheys brewery, in Sydney, in the mid-1800s. It became known as the city's "Catholic" brewery and still thrives as part of the national group Lion Nathan. Tooheys has maintained the tradition of an old ale, which was at one stage brewed north of Sydney in the city of Newcastle, where it was popular with miners. Toohey's Old has a modest alcohol content and light but smooth body. The flavours are very gentle, but there are touches of bitter-chocolate, cream, and oloroso sherry spiciness, nuttiness, and fruitiness. It finishes toasty and dry and has more complexity than its local rival, from the Tooth's brewery. The latter, established in 1835 by an Englishman, became Sydney's "Protestant" brewery. Tooth's is now owned by the national group Fosters.

Region of origin
New South Wales, Australia

Style Old Ale

Alcohol content 4.4abv (3.5w)

Ideal serving temperature 10°C (50°F)

OLD WOOD

THE FAMOUS OLD ALE brewery, Theakston, in North Yorkshire, England, uses wooden casks for some local deliveries. It employs two coopers to maintain, and occasionally build, casks. Some of the wood used is up to 80 years old.

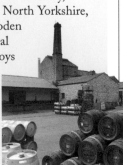

MARSTON'S OWD RODGER

Who was "Owd" (Old) Rodger? The renowned Marston's brewery, in Burton, England, does not know, except that his name has been used since at least the 1950s, and perhaps even before that. Several such beers are named after long-gone brewers, drinkers, cellarmen, publicans, or local characters. Owd Rodger is the stronger style of old ale and has a warming alcohol note. It pours with a dense head, leaving good lacework; has an almost purple colour; a licorice aroma; a rooty palate; a lightly creamy body; and a juicy, fruity, port-like finish.

Region of origin Trent Valley, England, UK

Style
Old Ale/Barley Wine

Alcohol content
7.6abv (6.1w)

Ideal serving temperature
10–13°C (50–55°F)

YOUNG'S WINTER WARMER

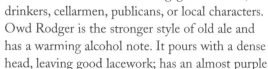

This seasonal brew from the famous London brewery has had several names, including Old Ale, but adopted the identity Winter Warmer in the early 1970s. It is a registered name in the UK, but has been copied in the US. Young's Winter Warmer is drinkable, light and smooth in body, and deceptively powerful. It has pronounced cookie-like, malt flavours, developing to raisiny fruitiness; with a faintly smoky, dry finish.

Region of origin
London, England, UK

Style Old Ale

Alcohol content
5.0abv (4.0w)

Ideal serving temperature
10–13°C (50–55°F)

THEAKSTON OLD PECULIER

The best-known example of an old ale as a dark brown, full-bodied, sweet, malty brew, medium-to-strong, and widely available on draught, is Old Peculier from Theakston. The tiny 1870s' brewery, in Masham, North Yorkshire, England, is now owned by Scottish Courage. Old Peculier (reviving a medieval spelling) has a soft and oily body; flavours reminiscent of milk chocolate; and a raisiny, blackcurrant dryness in the finish. It is a soothing and sustaining brew.

Region of origin
Northern England, UK

Style Old Ale

Alcohol content
5.6abv (4.5w)

Ideal serving temperature
13°C (55°F)

GRANITE BREWERY PECULIAR

Inspired by Theakston's Old Peculier, but opting for a more conventional spelling, this Canadian beer is similar in style but slightly paler in colour and lighter in body. It pours with a lively, bubbly head; has a fresh, minty, hop aroma; very nutty, creamy, toffeeish, satisfying flavours; and an appetizing, leafy dryness in the finish. The beer was first made in the Granite brewpub in rocky Nova Scotia. There are two breweries there, in Halifax, and a third in Toronto, Ontario.

Region of origin
Nova Scotia, Canada

Style
Old Ale/Strong Ale

Alcohol content
5.6abv (4.5w)

Ideal serving temperature
10–13°C (50–55°F)

WINTER WARMERS: WHISKY-MALT BEERS & STRONG SCOTTISH ALES

ALTHOUGH SCOTLAND MAKES BEERS of all colours and strengths, its most famous brews are dark, rich ales potent enough to fight the country's gusty, snowy weather. An example similar to an English barley wine is usually known in Scotland as a *wee* ("small") *heavy*. The romance of Scotland, and the renown of its distilled spirit, has in recent years inspired brewers in other countries to use peat-dried malts like those typically employed in whisky. These represent a style in their own right (*page 116*). Some North American brewers use similar peated malts in Scottish-style ales (*page 117*).

Winged warmer
This enamel long pre-dates Nussdorf's whiskyish brew.

MITCHELL'S OLD 90/- ALE

The spread of the Scottish people has done much to introduce their beer styles to a wider world. Alexander Angus Mitchell was from Blairgowrie, in Perthshire. He fought in the famous Highland regiment, the Black Watch, in the wars between the British and Dutch farmer (*Boer*) settlers in Southern Africa at the turn of the century. He married locally, and his grandson Lex founded the Mitchell's brewery, in Knysna, Western Cape, in 1984. The term 90/-, on his Scottish ale, refers to the old British unit of currency, the shilling. Traditionally, a "Ninety Shilling" was a strong ale. This unfiltered, unpasteurized example is spiced with cinnamon. It has an aroma reminiscent of Scotch whisky; a malty palate; and a dry, slightly tart finish.

Region of origin	South Africa
Style	Strong Scottish Ale
Alcohol content	7.0abv (5.6w)
Ideal serving temperature	Store at 5°C (41°F) Serve at 10°C (50°F)

THE LADY OF TRAQUAIR

THE ENERGY OF **Catherine Maxwell Stuart** has done much to promote interest in the beers made at her family's castle, Traquair House. A *quair* is a winding stream. The house is alongside a stream running into the River Tweed. Lady Catherine is seen here with brewer Ian Cameron.

BROUGHTON OLD JOCK

To Americans, the name sounds unsavoury, but Scots are called "Jock" (or, in Glasgow, "Jimmie") the way people in B-movies are called "Mack". This alcoholic manifestation might variously be regarded as an old ale, barley wine, or, in the more typically Scottish parlance, a wee heavy. It has more hop aroma than many Scottish ales; an appetizing, smooth, tasty maltiness; and a soothing, whiskyish, warm finish.

Region of origin
Scottish Borders, UK

Style
Strong Scottish Ale

Alcohol content
6.7abv (5.4w)

Ideal serving temperature
10–13°C (50–55°F)

BORVE ALE

A hugely distinctive, characterful, complex beer from a tiny brewery in a former school at the hamlet of Ruthven, near Huntley, in the Grampian mountains. Borve Ale is matured in casks that have previously been used to age first Bourbon then Scotch whisky. It emerges with an oaky, "hop-sack" aroma; a relatively light but clingy body; orangey flavours; and a big finish that is charcoal-like, peppery, and even salty.

Region of origin
Highlands, Northern Scotland, UK

Style
Strong Scottish Ale

Alcohol content
10.0abv (8.0w)

Ideal serving temperature
10–13°C (50–55°F)

Gaelic Ale
The Scottish Gaelic text on the label says "Brought to life on the Isle of Lewis".

TRAQUAIR HOUSE ALE

Beer from the castle at Traquair was first mentioned in 1566. The brewery was revived in 1965, by the 20th Laird ("Lord") of Traquair, Peter Maxwell Stuart. It is now managed by his daughter, Lady Catherine. The brewery's principal product has a lightly oaky aroma; touches of fresh earthiness, pepperiness, and nutty maltiness in the palate; and some woody, rooty tartness in the finish.

Region of origin
Scottish Borders, UK

Style
Strong Scottish Ale

Alcohol content
7.2abv (5.8w)

Ideal serving temperature
10–13°C (50–55°F)

Label lore
The back-label reveals that Traquair's main gates will remain closed until a Stuart returns to the British throne.

GORDON HIGHLAND SCOTCH ALE

The Christmas beer under the Gordon name has this year-round counterpart with a marginally less hefty alcohol content but a big, fresh, rich maltiness and toasty balance. Both are made for the Belgian market by Scottish Courage. A similar beer, slightly less strong (7.3abv; 5.8w) but with all the richness of a fruit-filled chocolate praline, was launched in the British market in 1998 under the name McEwan's No 1 Champion Ale.

Region of origin
Southern Scotland, UK

Style
Strong Scottish Ale

Alcohol content
8.6abv (6.9w)

Ideal serving temperature
10–13°C (50–55°F)

HOEPFNER BLUE STAR

This beer was first brewed, in 1996, on New Year's Eve, a very important day for the Scots. It does not identify itself as being Scottish in style, but is in character very similar to the various whisky-malt brews. The beer contains a proportion of beech-smoked malt, and has a subtly sappy dryness in the finish. It is oily, malty, and lightly nutty, with a touch of flowery elegance. Blue Star is produced by Hoepfner, of Karlsruhe, Germany.

Region of origin
Baden-Württemberg, Germany

Style Smoked *Altbier*

Alcohol content 5.5abv (4.4w)

Ideal serving temperature
9°C (48°F)

NUSSDORFER OLD WHISKY BIER

Having Anglicized his name for "Sir Henry's", a vaguely Irish stout, Baron Henrik Bachofen von Echt next turned his Vienna brewery to a Scottish theme with this satisfyingly malty brew. Among whisky-malt beers, this example has notably lively, fruity, complex flavours. Though the smokiness is very restrained, it is just enough to provide a good, balancing dryness.

Region of origin
Austria

Style
Whisky-malt *Altbier*

Alcohol content
6.1abv (4.9w)

Ideal serving temperature
9°C (48°F)

PELFORTH AMBERLEY

This *bière aromatisée au malt à whisky* is made by Pelforth, in Lille, France. Amberley is smooth, firm, and dry. Among European

examples of the style, it has perhaps the most obvious late smokiness. Whisky-malt beer was pioneered in Alsace, France, by the lightly grainy-peaty Adelscott. There is a companion brew of a much darker style called Adelscott Noir. These beers are produced at the Adelshoffen brewery.

Region of origin
Northern France

Style Whisky-malt Lager

Alcohol content
7.0abv (5.6w)

Ideal serving temperature
9°C (48°F)

MAC QUEEN'S NESSIE

The mythical monster Nessie is said to live in a Scottish loch, not a lake in the Alps, but its fame captures the imagination far and wide. The beer called Nessie is made by the castle brewery of Eggenberg, in lake country at Vorchdorf, between Salzburg and Linz, Austria. This incarnation of Nessie is a deep gold or bronze rather than the full "red" extravagantly promised on the label, but there is a real heftiness of malt in both the aroma and palate, with a late dryness and faint smokiness.

Region of origin Austria

Style Whisky-malt Lager

Alcohol content
7.3abv (5.8w)

Ideal serving temperature
9°C (48°F)

Monstrously royal
Just in case Nessie is not sufficiently Scottish-sounding, the brewery has invented the company name, Mac Queen's.

WHISKY-MALT BEERS & STRONG SCOTTISH ALES

BELHAVEN WEE HEAVY

Oily, creamy, grainy, toasty, nutty (almondy?), and fruity (pineapple?)...this has all the richness and flavour of a classic wee heavy, though it is less strong than some. Despite this, it is headily alcoholic and a good winter brew. Belhaven occasionally produces a stronger (8.0abv; 6.4w) draught-only version under the name 90/-. There is also a less potent (6.0abv; 4.8w) bottled wee heavy under the Fowler's name, brewed for the Bass subsidiary, Tennent's. This is pleasant enough, but a shadow of the beer produced by the long-gone Fowler's of Prestonpans.

Region of origin
Southern Scotland, UK

Style Wee Heavy

Alcohol content 6.5abv (5.2w)

Ideal serving temperature
13°C (55°F)

FISH POSEIDON OLD SCOTCH ALE

The Fish brewery, in Olympia, Washington, produces this hugely assertive, peated Scottish ale. An unusually large proportion of the malt used, about eight per cent, is peated. While many such beers employ only a lightly peated malt, this contains the heavily kilned style. The result is a remarkable blend of sweetish, treacle-toffee maltiness; earthy chewiness; and woody smokiness.

Region of origin Northwest US

Style Strong Scottish Ale

Alcohol content 8.0abv (6.4w)

Ideal serving temperature
13°C (55°F)

MASH AND AIR SCOTCH ALE

Britain's first American-style brewpub opened in Manchester in 1997, with a London branch the following year. "Mash" refers to the infusion of grains in the making of beer, not to the food. "Air" was inspired by the building, a former textile mill, towering over Manchester's nightlife quarter. One of the most characterful among the early beers was the Scotch Ale, very smooth and silky, developing some medicinal warming notes, and with a slightly smoky finish. Chocolate malt is used, along with Maris Otter, and hops from both England and Washington State.

Region of origin
Northwest England, UK

Style Strong Scottish Ale

Alcohol content 6.0abv (4.8w)

Ideal serving temperature
10–13°C (50–55°C)

MOUNT HOOD PITTOCK WEE HEAVY

Surrounded by ski resorts, in national forest in the Cascade Mountains of Oregon, the oddly-named town of Government Camp has since 1992 had its own brewery. Its Pittock Wee Heavy is named after the first man to reach the summit of Mount Hood (378 m/1,239 ft), in 1857. Henry L. Pittock was a businessman, writer, and mountaineer. This beer contains oats, peated malt, and

East Kent Goldings, and has a relatively cool fermentation and maturation. It is a delicious brew, garnet-to-brown in colour, with the aroma of cherry nougat; a fudgy palate, with lots of flavour development; and a caramel dryness in the finish.

Region of origin Northwest US

Style Wee Heavy

Alcohol content 8.0abv (6.4w)

Ideal serving temperature
13°C (55°F)

ORKNEY SKULLSPLITTER

Many skulls were said to have been split by a Viking ruler of Orkney in the ninth century. During renovations of the island's cathedral in 1919, a split skull was found sealed into a pillar. This beer, if taken in excess, seems to promise an eternal sleep. The Orkney brewery's Skullsplitter is a wee heavy. It has a raisiny, sweet aroma; a very creamy taste, developing flavours like a Dundee fruit cake dunked in port; and a toasty finish.

Region of origin
Orkney Islands, Scotland, UK

Style Strong Scottish Ale/Wee Heavy

Alcohol content 8.5abv (6.8w)

Ideal serving temperature
13°C (55°F)

PYRAMID SCOTCH ALE

A thistle in front of Egyptian pyramids makes an odd conjunction on this Scotch Ale from Seattle. The neck-label light-heartedly proposes it as a drink after caber-tossing (the Highland sport in which pine trunks are thrown). The beer is made with a proportion of peated malt and some roasted barley. It has a cerise-to-burgundy colour; a creamy, chocolate aroma; coffee-essence flavours; and a perfumy, smoky, port-like, oaky, dryish, warming finish.

Region of origin Northwest US

Style Strong Scottish Ale

Alcohol content 6.0abv (4.8w)

Ideal serving temperature
13°C (55°F)

UNIBROUE RAFTMAN

The lumberjacks who cut timber and rafted it down the St Lawrence river were always willing to settle their differences over a beer, according to the neck-label of this woody tasting brew. It is, in fact, a peat-smoked *bière au malt de whisky*, and perhaps the most assertive example of this style. It has an orangey, resiny aroma; a light, firm, malty middle; and an oaky, sappy, smoky finish. Raftman is one of the many individualistic beers from Unibroue, of Chambly, near Montreal.

Region of origin
Province of Quebec, Canada

Style Peat-smoked Ale

Alcohol content 5.5abv (4.4w)

Ideal serving temperature
13°C (55°F)

VERMONT PUB AND BREWERY WEE HEAVY

Lager expert and beer writer Greg Noonan established this brewery with his wife Nancy, who now runs it. The brewery, in Burlington, Vermont, has a wide range of very individualistic beers. Its Wee Heavy is tawny to red; has a rich, fruity, syrupy maltiness; and a medicinal, peppery, warming finish. The beer varies slightly each winter, its original gravity matching the year (such as 1098 for 1998). Classic "vintages" have popped up in some states at very high strengths.

Region of origin Northeast US

Style Wee Heavy

Alcohol content 8.0abv (6.4w)

Ideal serving temperature
13°C (55°F)

WINTER WARMERS: BALTIC PORTERS AND STOUTS

THE MOST WINTRY BEERS OF ALL are the extra-strong, almost tar-like porters and stouts originally made in Britain for export to the cold countries of the Baltic and Scandinavia. Because these beers were favoured by the royal court in St Petersburg, names such as Russian Stout and Imperial Stout are often used. In these hugely rich beers, the typical roastiness of stout develops into a burnt currant fruitiness, with a warming embrace of alcohol.

A "Great" beer
Catherine II is mentioned on the label, which is partly rendered in Russian. The beer is a last vestige of a 200-year-old export trade.

COURAGE IMPERIAL RUSSIAN STOUT

Britain's biggest brewing company, Scottish Courage, is the current owner of this label. Behind it lies a powerful beer that is produced only occasionally and vintage-dated. Courage inherited the product from the now-defunct Barclay's brewery, in London. That brewery exported the beer to the Baltic during the time of Empress Catherine II. With her encouragement, British-style porter, the most sophisticated beer of the day, was introduced to the Russian Empire. Today's Courage Imperial Russian Stout is winey, sherryish, raisiny, woody, and sappy. The most recent vintages have been made at Courage's subsidiary brewery, John Smith's, in Tadcaster, Yorkshire. That brewery's neighbour and independent rival, Samuel Smith's, produces an imperial stout that is slightly less strong but richer, more creamy, and peppery.

Region of origin	London, England, UK
Style	Imperial Stout
Alcohol content	10.0abv (8.0w)
Ideal serving temperature	13–18°C (55–64°F)

IMPERIAL THIRSTS

EMPRESS CATHERINE II was also known as Catherine the Great. Her appetites matched her name: she was said to breakfast on vodka-laced tea and a caviar omelette. A letter still exists from a later empress, Alexandra Feodorovna, thanking a British supplier for 5,000 bottles of stout donated to local hospitals.

SINEBRYCHOFF PORTER

When Nikolai Sinebrychoff founded this brewery (also known as "Koff") in Helsinki, in 1819, the city was under Russian rule. Koff has brewed porter from the start, apart from a period of prohibition in Finland in the early part of the 20th century. The porter was reintroduced for the 1952 Olympics. It is lively and flavoursome: dry, smooth, oily, coffeeish, and flowery, with fresh wood notes. It is rich and warming in the finish.

Region of origin
Finland

Style Baltic Porter/
Imperial Stout

Alcohol content
7.2abv (5.8w)

**Ideal serving
temperature**
13–18°C (55–64°F)

BALTIKA PORTER

The capital of imperial stout is home to this beer from the Baltika brewery, established in St Petersburg as recently as 1990. Baltika Porter is soft, starting with a cereal-grain sweetness, but in the end proving to be lightly dry, with some whiskyish notes. A fruitier, winier imperial porter is made by the nearby Vienna brewery. A firmer, spicier, more warming example comes from Stepan Razin, the city's oldest brewery, founded in 1795.

Region of origin
St Petersburg, Russia

Style
Baltic Porter/Imperial Stout

Alcohol content 7.0abv (5.6w)

Ideal serving temperature
13–18°C (55–64°F)

OKOCIM PORTER

The district of Okocim is in the town of Brzesko, to the east of Cracow, Poland. The brewery there was founded in 1845 and makes a porter in the northerly, Baltic tradition. It has a soothing, almost medicinal character, with hints of cinnamon, drying in a cedary, appetizing finish. Other Polish strong porters include a notably smooth example from the town of Zywiec and a more raisiny interpretation from the Elblag brewery.

Region of origin
Province of Galicia,
Poland

Style Strong Porter/
Imperial Stout

Alcohol content
8.1abv (6.5w)

**Ideal serving
temperature**
13–18°C (55–64°F)

Imperial helmet?
*This grandiose mug
was designed to mark
one of the brewery's
anniversaries.*

NORTH COAST OLD RASPUTIN RUSSIAN IMPERIAL STOUT

Grigori Rasputin was a mystic who influenced the royal family prior to his assassination. He is celebrated with some irony in this rich, buttery, toffeeish, rummy imperial stout. Along with an excellent dry stout called Old No 38, it is produced by the North Coast brewery, in the one-time whaling port of Fort Bragg, California. Founded in 1987, the brewery began life in an old Presbyterian church and mortuary.

Region of origin
California, US

Style Imperial Stout

Alcohol content
8.9abv (7.1w)

**Ideal serving
temperature**
13–18°C (55–64°F)

NIGHTCAP BEERS: BARLEY WINES

BARLEY WINE IS A TERM USED in the English-speaking world for the strongest of ales. They are beers, but some of them are as strong as wines and do have winey flavours. These derive from the behaviour of ale yeasts at high strengths, often over long periods of fermentation and maturation. Some American brews in this style use wine yeasts, which are capable of creating more alcohol. Barley wines are best enjoyed in a small goblet, with a book at bedtime or a late-night movie.

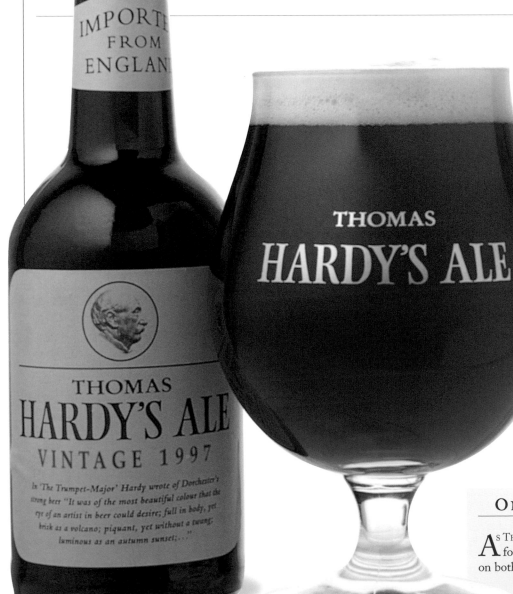

ELDRIDGE POPE THOMAS HARDY'S ALE

The ultimate book-at-bedtime beer. This brew is named after the novelist and poet Thomas Hardy, who wrote admiringly of the Eldridge Pope beer. In 1968, a festival to celebrate Hardy was held in his home town of Dorchester, and this beer was launched as a commemorative brew. Thomas Hardy's Ale is a beer that will mature in the bottle. When young, it can be as rich, creamy, and meaty as beef broth. There may also be apple-wood smokiness. After about five years, it develops Madeira flavours, and samples left to mature for 25 years have proven lean, warming, and elegant.

Region of origin West of England, UK

Style Barley Wine/Old Ale

Alcohol content 12.0abv (9.6w)

Ideal serving temperature
Store at 13°C (55°F)
Serve at 13–18°C (55–64°F)

ONE FOR THE LIBRARY

As THOMAS HARDY'S is typically stored for bottle-ageing, the presentations on both left and right may be seen. In the 1980s, the beer was served at the National Theatre, London, to celebrate a play about the brewery by David Edgar.

BASS NO 1

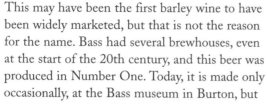

This may have been the first barley wine to have been widely marketed, but that is not the reason for the name. Bass had several brewhouses, even at the start of the 20th century, and this beer was produced in Number One. Today, it is made only occasionally, at the Bass museum in Burton, but it is commercially available. It is firm, smooth, oily, oaky, and at first tasting shockingly bitter, but strangely addictive.

Region of origin
Trent Valley, England, UK

Style Barley Wine

Alcohol content
10.5abv (8.4w)

Ideal serving temperature
Store at 13°C (55°F)
Serve at 10–13°C (50–55°F)

WHITBREAD GOLD LABEL

Traditionally, barley wines were full in colour, with the rich, treacly flavours that come from dark malts. Gold Label was the first pale one, launched in 1951, by a brewer that later became part of the Whitbread national group. It has an amber or bronze colour, but its flavours speak of pale malts. Gold Label has a firm creaminess, with shortbread flavours, developing to a fruity, spicy dryness with hints of apricot and aniseed. Originally made in Sheffield, Yorkshire, this beer now comes from a brewery near Blackburn, Lancashire.

Region of origin
Northern England, UK

Style Barley Wine

Alcohol content
10.9abv (8.7w)

Ideal serving temperature
10–13°C (50–55°F)

COTTAGE NORMAN'S CONQUEST

Chris Norman, an airline pilot, took early retirement and started a brewery with his wife Helen in 1993. It was not quite in a cottage, but was initially in a garage at their house at Little Orchard, West Lydford, Somerset. Two years later, their barley wine was judged Champion Beer at the Great British Beer Festival. For a big beer, it is remarkably appetizing, with fresh cinnamon, sultana, and apple aromas. It has a clean, creamy palate and a spicy, peppery, balancing dryness.

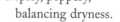

Region of origin
West of England, UK

Style Barley Wine

Alcohol content
7.0abv (5.6w)

Ideal serving temperature
Store at 13°C (55°F)
Serve at 10–13°C (50–55°F)

YOUNG'S OLD NICK

Once, every regional brewery in England had its own barley wine. Many have since dropped this traditional style, on the grounds that it is a minor speciality, but the London brewery Young's – a famously stubborn enterprise – has remained loyal to the style. This example is a rich, toffeeish brew, with a banana-liqueur finish. As the label suggests, this is one to enjoy in front of the fire before retiring for the night.

Region of origin
London, England, UK

Style Barley Wine

Alcohol content
6.8abv (5.4w)

Ideal serving temperature
13°C (55°F)

The old devil
An "old" ale in name, Old Nick is strong enough to wear the neck-label barley wine.

HERTOG JAN GRAND PRESTIGE

Hertog means duke, and the name recollects the Jan who ruled Flanders and Brabant. This strong Dutch ale is broadly in the style of a barley wine. It was an early speciality after the 1980s' revival of the Arcen brewery, in the Limburg town of the same name. The beer has a dense head; a garnet colour; a spicy malt aroma; a surprisingly light, soft body; and a sweetish, very slightly meaty, port-like finish.

Region of origin
Province of Limburg, The Netherlands

Style Barley Wine

Alcohol content
10.0abv (8.0w)

Ideal serving temperature
13°C (55°F)

CHELSEA OLD TITANIC

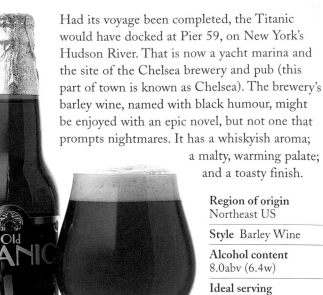

Had its voyage been completed, the Titanic would have docked at Pier 59, on New York's Hudson River. That is now a yacht marina and the site of the Chelsea brewery and pub (this part of town is known as Chelsea). The brewery's barley wine, named with black humour, might be enjoyed with an epic novel, but not one that prompts nightmares. It has a whiskyish aroma; a malty, warming palate; and a toasty finish.

Region of origin
Northeast US

Style Barley Wine

Alcohol content
8.0abv (6.4w)

Ideal serving temperature
13°C (55°F)

Not to be iced
Icebergs loom on the label, but this ale is to be served at a natural cellar temperature.

ANCHOR OLD FOGHORN

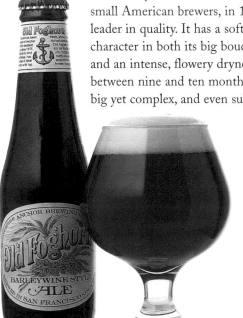

Any vessel sailing into misty San Francisco Bay might welcome a warning foghorn. So would any drinker of discernment. This brew led the way in the introduction of barley wines by small American brewers, in 1975, and remains a leader in quality. It has a soft, oily, apricot-citrus character in both its big bouquet and juicy palate, and an intense, flowery dryness. The beer has between nine and ten months on dry hops. It is big yet complex, and even subtle. Drink it with a Jack London novel.

Region of origin
California, US

Style Barley Wine

Alcohol content
8.7abv (7.0w)

Ideal serving temperature
13°C (55°F)

Late warning
The maritime name of this big beer came later than that of the famous brewery.

BIG TIME OLD WOOLY

Mammoths might have been more common in icy Alaska than in rainy Washington State, but the hairy pachyderm makes an appropriate symbol for this big, strong winter warmer. The Big Time pub and brewery in Seattle is noted for beers with extravagant names and flavours to match. This one has beautifully combined aromas and flavours of fragrant hop, grapefruit rind, and layered maltiness. It is smooth, and hoppy enough to be dazingly soporific.

Region of origin
Pacific Northwest US

Style Barley Wine

Alcohol content
10.0abv (8.0w)

Ideal serving temperature
13°C (55°F)

Prehistoric nip
Old Wooly is vintage-dated, and unusual in that it develops with age.

BARLEY WINES

BOULDER CREEK DIZZY LIZZY

A dryish but well-balanced, astonishingly drinkable barley wine is among the British-accented beers from this Californian brewery and pub in the logging town of Boulder Creek, in the Redwood Hills, north of Santa Cruz. Dizzy Lizzy starts soft and slightly syrupy, with a very clean maltiness; seems to slim down to quite a lean, firm, nutty character; then dries into a rounded finish with some flowery hoppiness. It is made mainly from pale ale malt, with a touch of crystal malt, and some brown sugar in the brew kettle.

Region of origin California, US

Style Barley Wine

Alcohol content 10.6abv (8.5w)

Ideal serving temperature 13°C (55°F)

BRIDGEPORT OLD KNUCKLEHEAD

A celebrated barley wine from the pioneering brewery and pub in Portland, Oregon. An assertive, delicious, juicy maltiness is cut by grassy, peppery hop flavours, and rounded in a warming finish. A bottling is released in November, and each year's label features a different local celebrity. One year, the mayor of Portland was asked if he would like to be the next Knucklehead; "It's a lot better than being Bud," he replied.

Region of origin
Pacific Northwest US

Style Barley Wine

Alcohol content 9.1abv (7.3w)

Ideal serving temperature 13°C (55°F)

MARIN "OLD DIPSEA"

In laid-back Marin County, across the water from San Francisco, this brewery and pub, at Larkspur Lang, makes many flavoursome specialities. The jokingly named "Old Dipsea" has an attractive, bright amber colour, and a herbal hop accent in its aroma, flavour, and long dryness. This emphatic hop character is balanced by a firm, lean, juicy maltiness. It is very drinkable.

Region of origin California, US

Style Barley Wine

Alcohol content 9.5abv (7.6w)

Ideal serving temperature 10–13°C (50–55°F)

PIKE OLD BAWDY

A house of ill repute once occupied the Seattle building that became the first site of the Pike brewery, hence Old Bawdy as a name for its robust barley wine. This is an unusual example of the style in that it contains a proportion of peated malt and is aged in oak. The beer has a peaty brown colour and a sweetly malty aroma, becoming earthy and oaky, and finishing with a suggestion of a salty Scotch whisky. A bedtime beer for someone who might otherwise favour a Laphroaig or Lagavulin.

Region of origin
Pacific Northwest US

Style Barley Wine

Alcohol content 10.0abv (8.0w)

Ideal serving temperature 13°C (55°F)

RICHBRAU POE'S TELL TALE ALE

The Gothic horror stories of Edgar Allan Poe may not be best for bedtime reading, but they do go well with this unusual beer. Poe worked briefly in Richmond, Virginia, as assistant editor of the Southern Literary Messenger. This beer comes from Richbrau, a brewery and pub in that town. The brew is aged in casks that previously held red wine, and that is reflected in its character. It has a pinkish russet colour; a cellar aroma; a surprisingly light body with a firm, malty background; and an oaky, extraordinarily winey finish.

Region of origin Mid Atlantic US

Style Barley Wine

Alcohol content 10.0abv (8.0w)

Ideal serving temperature 10–13°C (50–55°F)

SIERRA NEVADA BIGFOOT ALE

Probably the world's hoppiest barley wine, especially in its bouquet. A remarkably aromatic interpretation of the style, with flavours that seem to explode on the tongue. Typically lemon-grassy, citric, grapefruity, tangerine-like American hop notes, and plenty of bitterness, combine with a huge maltiness and a crisp, clean yeast character in a big, bottle-conditioned brew that develops great complexity.

This is a world classic from the respected Sierra Nevada brewery in Chico, California.

Region of origin California, US

Style Barley Wine

Alcohol content 10.0abv (8.0w)

Ideal serving temperature 10–13°C (50–55°F)

SMITHWICK'S BARLEY WINE

A little-known speciality from the ale brewery in Kilkenny, Ireland. This barley wine, already of modest strength for the style, is often served in a mix with the regular Smithwick's Ale. The barley wine has a distinctly Burgundyish colour; a full body; and notes of chocolate, toffee, Turkish delight, and fruit.

Region of origin Republic of Ireland

Style Barley Wine

Alcohol content 5.5abv (4.4w)

Ideal serving temperature 10–13°C (50–55°F)

WOODFORDE HEADCRACKER

Whimsically aggressive name for a "very strong pale ale" (or barley wine) from Woodforde, a very successful new-generation brewery in Norfolk, England. This beer is relatively light but smooth; starting malty, developing to a dry, medicinal, peppery hoppiness; and finishing with a marmalady fruitiness.

Region of origin Eastern England, UK

Style Barley Wine/Strong Pale Ale

Alcohol content 7.0abv (5.6w)

Ideal serving temperature 10–13°C (50–55°F)

APERITIFS: EXTRA-DRY PILSNER LAGERS

MANY GOLDEN LAGERS call themselves Pilsners (sometimes spelled Pilsener or abbreviated to Pils), but this term should be reserved only for a truly hoppy example: this means a flowery bouquet and an appetizingly dry finish. The bitterness of the best examples arouses the gastric juices and awakens the appetite. All borrow their designation from the world's first golden lager, which was made in 1842 in the Bohemian city of Pilsen, in the Czech Republic.

PILSNER URQUELL

The term *Urquell* means "original source" in German, the official language of Bohemia when it was a part of the Austrian empire. Bohemia now forms, with Moravia, the Czech Republic. In Czech, the beer is called Plzeňský Prazdroj. This is the original Pilsner, copied throughout the world, often by lesser, blander beers. Its golden colour was a novelty at the time when glass vessels were replacing stoneware steins and pewter tankards, but the beer's fame was also due to its quality. The famous Bohemian Saaz hop imparted the flowery, spicy aroma and bitter finish; the equally renowned Moravian barley malt provided a soft, delicious balance. Both characteristics have diminished slightly in recent years, but Pilsner Urquell is still one of the world's great beers.

The Pilsner glass
Tall, conical glasses
are often used to
present Pilsner-style
beers. This shape helps
to sustain the sparkle.

Region of origin
Pilsen, Bohemia, Czech Republic

Style Pilsner

Alcohol content 4.4abv (3.5w)

Ideal serving temperature 9°C (48°F)

TRIUMPHAL BREW

WITH ITS MAGNIFICENT, Napoleonic-looking arches, the Pilsner Urquell brewery reflects the pride inspired by its famous beer. In the former Austrian Empire, Germany and Scandinavia, several great breweries have similar architectural features...like Victorian industrial buildings in Britain.

MORAVIA PILS

Although the name honours the Czech barley-growing region, it is the export of Bohemian hops down the river Elbe that seems to have inspired the especially assertive Pilsners of north Germany. Moravia Pils is one of the best-known examples. It has a flowery, minty aroma; a light, firm, clean, dry maltiness; a big hit of hop bitterness; and a gently dry finish. The Moravia brewery, in Lüneburg, is owned by Holsten.

Region of origin
Lower Saxony, Germany

Style Pilsner

Alcohol content
4.8abv (3.8w)

Ideal serving temperature
9°C (48°F)

JEVER PILSENER

The town of Jever (pronounced "yayver") is in the German part of Friesland, a region that also straddles Denmark and The Netherlands. The people of Friesland are reputed to have a taste for food and drink with strong flavours. Jever Pilsener is famous among beer lovers worldwide for its bitterness. It pours with the blossoming head favoured on German Pilsners, and has a tingling, almost rough dryness on the tongue.

Region of origin
Northern Germany

Style Pilsner

Alcohol content 4.9abv (3.9w)

Ideal serving temperature
9°C (48°F)

RADEBERGER PILSNER

The King of Saxony was supplied with beer from this brewery in Radeberg, northeast of Dresden. The area, with its own history of hop-growing, is close to the Czech region of Bohemia. The brewery dates from 1872, and its Pilsner survived as a speciality during East Germany's 40-odd years of communism. Radeberger Pilsner is aromatic, with earthy hop flavours, a firm body, and a crisp, dry finish.

Region of origin Saxony, Germany

Style Pilsner

Alcohol content 4.8abv (3.8w)

Ideal serving temperature 9°C (48°F)

Head fit for a king
Radeberger pours with a huge head, half-filling its elegant flute glass.

WERNESGRÜNER PILS LEGENDE

This beer is a legend because it remained an intensely bitter speciality during the Communist period. It is made at Wernesgrün, south of Zwickau and nearer to Auerbach. It has a bubbly head; an almost quinine-like, tonic-water dryness in the bouquet; a cleansing palate; and a peppery punch of arousal in the finish. As the label says, it is "fresh and spritzy", and as appetizing as a gin and tonic.

Region of origin
Saxony, Germany

Style Pilsner

Alcohol content 4.9abv (3.9w)

Ideal serving temperature
9°C (48°F)

DAS FEINE HOFMARK WÜRZIG HERB

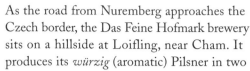

As the road from Nuremberg approaches the Czech border, the Das Feine Hofmark brewery sits on a hillside at Loifling, near Cham. It produces its *würzig* (aromatic) Pilsner in two versions. The *mild* is beautifully flowery, with a gently perfumy dryness; but this *herb* ("bitter") version of the beer is a touch firmer in its dry finish.

Region of origin
Bavaria, Germany

Style Pilsner

Alcohol content
5.6abv (4.5w)

Ideal serving temperature
9°C (48°F)

HOEPFNER PILSNER

The family name derives from "hop farmer", though the member who founded this brewery, in Karlsruhe, Germany, was a priest. The brewery was established in 1798, has seen six generations of Hoepfners, and is now in an 1898 building that looks like a castle. Hoepfner Pilsner is very well hopped, but the bitterness is balanced by a mint-creme aroma and light, marshmallow maltiness. Its complexity may owe something to the use of traditional open fermenters.

Region of origin
Baden-Württemburg, Germany

Style Pilsner

Alcohol content 4.8abv (3.8w)

Ideal serving temperature
9°C (48°F)

ST GEORGEN KELLER BIER

In Germany, Pilsner beers are normally filtered; this beer is not, and therefore it is, strictly speaking, a *Kellerbier* (taken from the cellar while still hazy). Nonetheless, it is of a typical Pilsner strength, with a superbly appetizing, fresh, flowery, hop character. The hop is balanced by a lightly nutty maltiness and a yeasty acidity in the finish. The beer is made by St Georgen, at Buttenheim in Bavaria, near the great brewing town of Bamberg.

Region of origin
Franconia, Bavaria, Germany

Style *Kellerbier/* Unfiltered Pilsner

Alcohol content
4.9abv (3.9w)

Ideal serving temperature
9°C (48°F)

A seasonal saint
St George's Day sometimes marked the season's last brew.

CHRISTOFFEL BLOND

One of the world's hoppiest Pilsner-style beers, made at Roermond, in Dutch Limburg, near the German border. The town's saint is St Christopher. This new-generation brewery was founded in 1986 by Dutch brewer Leo Brand. Its Blond beer has spicy, piney, hop aromas; very lively flavours; and an appetizingly robust bitterness in the finish. In The Netherlands, the term Pils often indicates a bland beer; the brewery avoids this description.

Region of origin
Province of Limburg, The Netherlands

Style Pilsner

Alcohol content
5.0abv (4.0w)

Ideal serving temperature
9°C (48°F)

CON DOMUS

A beer with Domus? The student clientele of the Domus brewery and pub in Leuven, Belgium, is no doubt amused by the sexy pun, but the beer is perfectly serious. It has a flowery, oily, hop aroma; a rich malt background; and a spicy, minty finish. It is very dry indeed and an excellent aperitif. A cheekily assertive Pilsner-style beer made in the shadow of the town's Stella Artois brewery.

Region of origin Province of Flemish Brabant, Belgium

Style Pilsner

Alcohol content 5.0abv (4.0w)

Ideal serving temperature 9°C (48°F)

Hoppy students
The Catholic University of Leuven, dating from 1425, and boasting Erasmus and Mercator among its alumni, awards doctorates in brewing science.

STOUDT'S PILS

Not a stout brewery – the family name is spelled with a "d", and is originally German. Mrs Carol Stoudt runs this brewery, in Adamstown, Pennsylvania, and has won awards for many styles of beer. Her Pils ("assertively hopped with Saaz", according to the label) is one of America's best examples. It has an excellent hop character in its aroma, flavour, bitterness, and finishes with a very late, lingering, lemony dryness. The brewery adjoins a steak restaurant and a Sunday antiques market.

Region of origin Northeast US

Style Pilsner

Alcohol content 4.5abv (3.6w)

Ideal serving temperature 9°C (48°F)

DOCK STREET BOHEMIAN PILSNER

The Dock Street brewery and pub, in Philadelphia, produces two Pilsner-style brews: a regular Bohemian and an occasional German version. Bohemian Pilsner is softly aromatic, with a sweet, malt background and a crisply hoppy finish. The signature hop is the Bohemian variety Saaz. The German version is firmer and drier, and features Tettnang hops.

Region of origin Northeast US

Style Pilsner

Alcohol content 5.1abv (4.1w)

Ideal serving temperature 9°C (48°F)

VICTORY PRIMA PILS

The stylized hop on the label is appropriate for this very bitter Pilsner, made in Downingtown, Pennsylvania, by the Victory brewery and pub. It has a "fresh sea air" aroma of Saaz hops; almost gritty, hop flavours; a lean malt background; and a firm, bitter finish. This Pilsner was inspired by the very hoppy example of the style made by the Vogelbräu brewery and pub, in Karlsruhe, Germany.

Region of origin Northeast US

Style Pilsner

Alcohol content 5.4abv (4.3w)

Ideal serving temperature 9°C (48°F)

Pennsylvania prime
The state of William Penn was once the heart of German brewing in the US. It bids to be so again.

APERITIFS: DRY ABBEY BEERS

AMONG THE TRAPPIST ABBEYS of Belgium and The Netherlands, only Orval restricts itself to just one beer: an intensely dry, amber, strong ale that is a superb aperitif. The abbey of Chimay has three principal beers, with a distinctly dry speciality in the middle of its range. The abbey of Westmalle has a golden "single" for the monks to drink with their meals; a stronger, sweeter, dark "double"; and a yet more potent, pale, fruitily-dry aperitif "triple". Terms such as single, double, and triple date from times before widespread literacy, and correspond to the strength of the beer.

A touch of glass
The Orval glass was designed by Henri Vaes, the abbey's architect.

ORVAL

The abbey's name derives from *Vallée d'Or* (Valley of Gold). Legend has it that a countess lost a gold ring in a lake there, and vowed that she would establish a monastery if it were ever returned. A trout appeared from the waters with her gold ring in its mouth, and she was as good as her word. Monks have occupied the site in the Ardennes, since 1070. Today's 1930s' abbey is an architectural gem, and the beer a classic. It gains its colour from its own specification of malt, and is dry-hopped. The hop-sack aroma derives from the use of a semi-wild yeast, Brettanomyces, which adds a light, firm body and fresh acidity of finish.

Region of origin
Province of Luxembourg, Belgium

Style Abbey (Authentic Trappist)

Alcohol content 6.2abv (5.0w)

Ideal serving temperature
Store at around 14°C (57°F)
Serve no colder than 10°C (50°F)

ON GOLDEN POND

THE COUNTESS WAS MATILDA of Tuscany (*c.* 1046–1115), who married the Duke of Lorraine. Her husband was assassinated by the Duke of Flanders, and she was mourning him when she found the "Valley of Gold". She is depicted here by the great Belgian artist Camille Barthélémy (1890–1961).

CHIMAY CINQ CENTS

The best-known of the Trappist abbey breweries dates from the mid-1800s. It became known for dark, sweet brews, but in the 1960s decided to add a drier beer to its range. This version was originally known by the white cap on the bottle, but an additional champagne-style presentation was added to celebrate the 500th anniversary of the nearby town of Chimay. Cinq Cents has a remarkably fluffy body; a light but firm hit of malt; and an intense, late, junipery dryness.

Region of origin
Province of Hainaut, Belgium

Style Abbey (Authentic Trappist)

Alcohol content 8.0abv (6.4w)

Ideal serving temperature
Store at around 14°C (57°F)
Serve no colder than 10°C (50°F)

It's a corker
Chimay beers in the original bottles do not seem to gain quite the softness in maturation imparted by this larger, corked version.

WESTMALLE TRAPPIST

The Westmalle abbey dates from 1794. This pale beer was added to its range of beers in the period following the Second World War. Westmalle Trappist has become a classic, much imitated for its orangey-gold colour; its combination of high strength and drinkability; and its complex of appetizing aromas and flavours. A sea-air freshness in the nose, from Saaz hops; herbal, sage-like notes; and an orange-skin fruitiness are just some of the elements.

Region of origin Province of Antwerp, Belgium

Style Abbey (Authentic Trappist) Triple

Alcohol content 9.0abv (7.2w)

Ideal serving temperature Store at around 14°C (57°F). Serve no colder than 10°C (50°F)

BOSTEELS TRIPEL KARMELIET

A Belgian Carmelite abbey reputedly made a three-grain beer, at Dendermonde, in the 1600s. This inspired the Bosteels brewery, in nearby Buggenhout, to create, in 1997, a *tripel* made from barley, wheat, and oats. Each is used both raw and malted, and the beer is also heavily spiced. Tripel Karmeliet is a brew of some finesse and complexity: with a wheaty lightness, sweet lemons, an oaty creaminess, and a spicy, medicinal dryness.

Region of origin Province of East Flanders, Belgium

Style Abbey Triple

Alcohol content 8.0abv (6.4w)

Ideal serving temperature Store at around 14°C (57°F) Serve no colder than 10°C (50°F)

VILLERS TRIPPEL

Villers-la-Ville is a ruined Cistercian Abbey, southeast of Brussels, that brewed in 1215. Today the abbey is remembered in a range of beers made in Liezele, near Puurs, north of the city. The brewery dates from 1727, and three of its past owners were mayors of the town. Villers Trippel is very fruity, with suggestions of apples, apricots, and honey. It is one of the drier examples of this style produced outside monasteries, but not especially complex.

Region of origin Province of Antwerp, Belgium

Style Abbey Triple

Alcohol content 8.5abv (6.8w)

Ideal serving temperature Store at around 14°C (57°F). Serve no colder than 10°C (50°F)

APERITIFS: STRONG GOLDEN ALES

T HE FLOWERIEST OF APERITIF BEERS are the Belgian-style strong golden brews originally inspired by the classic, Duvel. The flowery character of these ales arises from hop varieties normally used in lagers – and from aromas created during the fermentation of such strong brews. Their distinctive character shines through because, despite their strength, these beers are lean in body: pale malts and highly fermentable sugars are used, and there is a maturation in the bottle. The Belgians regard beers in this style as an elegant aperitif, even where wine is to be served with the lunch or dinner. They can also be served after the meal, chilled, like the "white alcohol" brandies of Alsace.

DE HOPDUVEL KAFFEE

Belgium's devil
In local lore, the devil shown above is said to haunt hop-growers. The image is from the Hopduvel, a famous beer café in Ghent.

MOORTGAT DUVEL

The strange case of a dark brown beer that turned to gold. When British beers were fashionable in Belgium, the family-owned Moortgat brewery, at Breendonk, north of Brussels, produced a Scottish ale, using McEwan's yeast. The brewery later decided to re-style this, keeping the Scottish yeast and ale fermentation, and the high strength, but using pale malts to meet a tide of golden lagers. The beer is hopped with the Styrian Goldings variety (often used in English ales) and Saaz (typically preferred in lagers). An elaborate sequence of warm and cold fermentation and maturation lasts for well over three months and sometimes more than four. "The Devil of a Beer!" someone in the brewery observed of the first experimental batch, hence the Flemish corruption *Duvel* (pronounced Doov'l). The brew is extremely fragrant, and has flavours reminiscent of orange zest, pear brandy, green apples, and the lightest touch of smooth, stony dryness.

Region of origin
Province of Antwerp, Belgium

Style Belgian-style Strong Golden Ale

Alcohol content 8.5abv (6.8w)

Ideal serving temperature 10°C (50°F)

LOUWAEGE HAPKIN

Named after an axe-wielding Count of Flanders, Boudewijn Hapkin. (All beers in this style have names that are in some way diabolical.) In complexity, Hapkin perhaps comes closest to Duvel. This beer has a very perfumy aroma; a soft maltiness; a clean, smooth fruitiness; a persistent bead; and a spritzy, very dry finish. Hapkin is made by the family-owned Louwaege brewery, at Kortemark, southwest of Bruges.

Region of origin
Province of West Flanders, Belgium

Style Belgian-style Strong Golden Ale

Alcohol content
8.5abv (6.8w)

Ideal serving temperature
10°C (50°F)

ALKEN-MAES JUDAS

Deceitful? Well, deceptively potent, true to the style. Judas is made by the Belgian national brewer Alken-Maes, and has a fruity, hop dryness; a distinct, sweet-orange palate; and a dry finish. Julius – winier, spicier, and drier – is its national rival from Interbrew (Artois). The makers of Judas suggest a serving temperature of 6–8°C (43–46°F) and Julius 5–6°C (41–43°F). At these temperatures, all that can be tasted is the sensation of cold.

Region of origin
Province of Antwerp, Belgium

Style Belgian-style Strong Golden Ale

Alcohol content
8.5abv (6.8w)

Ideal serving temperature
10°C (50°F)

ARCEN HET ELFDE GEBOD

The name means "The Eleventh Commandment". This ordination is: "Enjoy!", and refers to food and drink. Het Elfde Gebod is a bright Dutch beer, more restrained in alcohol than its competitors, with a perfumy apple aroma; some banana and honey notes in the palate; and a teasing interplay of sweetness and dryness. The beer was originally produced by Breda/Oranjeboom, and is now made by the Arcen brewery, which long ago made Skol.

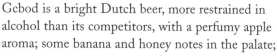

Region of origin
Province of Limburg, The Netherlands

Style Belgian-style Strong Golden Ale

Alcohol content
7.0abv (5.6w)

Ideal serving temperature
10°C (50°F)

JEANNE D'ARC BELZEBUTH

"Beelzebub" is from the ancient Greek and Hebrew for the Devil, or his alternate the "Lord of the Flies". He is graphically shown on the label of this beer, from a French brewery with the combustible name Jeanne d'Arc. This immensely strong, bright beer is said to be all-malt (that is, not to contain other sugars). It is smooth, almost fluffy, starting candyish, with peppery alcohol flavours perhaps contributing to a spicy, surprising dryness. Belzebuth is less thick than might be expected at its strength, but is very heady.

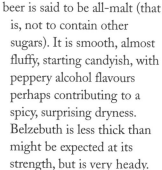

Region of origin
Northern France

Style Belgian-style Strong Golden Ale

Alcohol content
15.0abv (12.0w)

Ideal serving temperature
10°C (50°F)

APERITIFS: INDIA PALE ALES

MANY DRINKERS HAVE ENCOUNTERED THE TERM "IPA" without realizing that the initials stand for "India Pale Ale". When pale ales became fashionable, the British Empire in India was at its height, and a special version of the style was made for the British colonial rulers. India Pale Ales were stronger than usual, so that they could continue fermenting during the long sea journey round Cape Horn. Additionally, because hops are a preservative, they were used especially heavily, and that made the beer particularly bitter. In most British examples, the bitterness is no longer extreme, but the US revivalists make some of the world's driest, and most appetizing, beers.

Bombay Bomber...
...is made by Teri Fahrendorf at Steelhead.

Bravura bitterness
The name 1812 is whimsically intended to suggest an "overture" of hop aroma.

EMERSON'S 1812 INDIA PALE ALE

Not from India, but certainly round the Horn. This new-generation brewery is in the New Zealand city of Dunedin (the old name for Edinburgh). It makes some of New Zealand's best beers. Emerson's 1812 India Pale Ale is very appetizingly aromatic, with a spicy hop bouquet. There is also a great deal of hop flavour, rather than pure bitterness. The hop notes are set against a light, smooth, juicy, malt background. The flavours are beautifully combined, and the finish is fresh, dry, and faintly lemony. The inspiration for the brewery was a visit by George Emerson, a bio-chemist, to Edinburgh in 1983. He travelled with his son Richard, 18 at the time, who later established the business. Richard, who is almost entirely deaf, has nonetheless been a voluble publicist for his products.

Region of origin
South Island, New Zealand

Style India Pale Ale

Alcohol content 4.9abv (3.9w)

Ideal serving temperature 12°C (54°F)

THIRST CLIPPER

PALE ALE WAS PERFECTED by brewers like Allsopp and Bass in Burton, from the 1820s. Burton is in the middle of England, but was linked by canal and river to the sea. India Pale Ales were shipped to Calcutta to quench the thirsts of British plantation owners there. The clippers came back with tea.

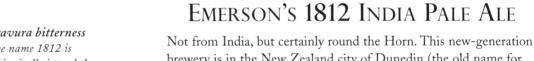

BURTON BRIDGE EMPIRE PALE ALE

Although pale ale is said to have been first produced in London, the style was made famous by the great breweries of Burton, helping this small town in the Midlands to become Britain's beer capital. The new-generation brewery Burton Bridge has sought to revive the tradition of strong, hoppy IPA in Britain. There is a distinct "hop sack" aroma and taste to this lively, leafy, peppery, orangey, bitter brew.

Region of origin
Trent Valley, England, UK

Style India Pale Ale

Alcohol content
7.5abv (6.0w)

Ideal serving temperature
10–13°C (50–55°F)

COBBOLD IPA

Coastal, barley country brewery, in Ipswich, England. The enterprise was founded by country gentry, and traces its history to 1723, but was reborn as a micro-brewery in a management buy-out in 1990. The IPA pours with a very well-retained head; has a good English, slightly peppery, hop aroma; a smooth, light body; a light palate, with a touch of clean apple; and a firm hit of dryness in the finish. There is some appetizingly lingering bitterness.

Region of origin
Eastern England, UK

Style India Pale Ale

Alcohol content
4.2abv (3.4w)

Ideal serving temperature
10–13°C (50–55°F)

MCNEILL'S DEAD HORSE INDIA PALE ALE

Cellists Ray and Holiday McNeill run a brewery and pub in a former police station in Brattleboro, Vermont. Their beers are wonderfully appetizing, despite off-putting names. Dead Horse IPA is aromatic, with long, oily, hop flavours; a firm, malt background; and a cedary, dry finish. It is dry-hopped with East Kent Goldings. This is one of the best IPAs on the East Coast (Brooklyn's East India Pale Ale being another fine manifestation), but the US is dense with outstanding examples.

Region of origin
Northeast US

Style India Pale Ale

Alcohol content
5.8abv (4.6w)

Ideal serving temperature
10–13°C (50–55°F)

BIG TIME BHAGWAN'S BEST INDIA PALE ALE

Several American breweries use jocular Indian names for their IPAs. Big Time, in Seattle, pays wry tribute to Bhagwan Shree Rajneesh, who established a commune in nearby Oregon in the 1980s. The beer has the grapefruit-zest American hop aroma typical in many northwestern beers; perfumy, sweet-orange flavours; a light, soft body; and a lemony, stony, appetizingly dry finish.

Region of origin
Pacific Northwest US

Style India Pale Ale

Alcohol content
5.8abv (4.6w)

Ideal serving temperature
10°C (50°F)

APERITIFS: EXTRA-HOPPY ALES

Framed by hop poles
"The Brewer" statue in Watou, near Poperinge, in West Flanders.

NOT EVERY HOPPY ALE is labelled as an IPA. Some of the hoppiest are not identified as belonging to any formal style. They are simply ales designed to highlight the hop. An intensely hoppy beer can be so aromatic, dry, and bitter as to frighten many consumers. Why would a brewer make such a product? The answer is that most brewers themselves love hops. Many would like to make their beers far hoppier than the marketing men advise. The beers on these two pages are expressions of brewers' hoppiest ambitions.

ANCHOR LIBERTY ALE

This world classic has its origins in a pilgrimage made in the early 1970s by Anchor's owner Fritz Maytag to several great English ale breweries, among them Young's, of London. Inspired by the hoppy ales of England, he began to work on a brew that would highlight American varieties of hop. His Liberty Ale was first produced in 1975, to commemorate Paul Revere's ride of 1775. (Revere rode from Boston to Lexington, to warn the American revolutionaries that the British were coming to arrest them; thus started the War of Independence.) Anchor Liberty is hugely aromatic, though its perfumy bouquet is complex and rounded. The body is surprisingly light, but smooth and oily. The palate gradually develops cleansing, lemon-rind, angelica, appetizing flavours, building to an intense finish as dry as a Martini cocktail.

Region of origin West US

Style American Ale

Alcohol content 6.1abv (4.9w)

Ideal serving temperature 10°C (50°F)

Taking a Liberty
The American eagle seems to have made a nest from barley and hops on the label of Anchor Liberty. The hops are of the variety Cascade, from Washington State.

TUPPERS' HOP POCKET ALE

Bob Tupper is a history teacher who gives lectures on beer at a famous bar, The Brickskeller, in Washington DC. He and his wife Ellie, an editor, designed this beer, which is produced by the local Old Dominion brewery. It has a flowery aroma; a crisp, cedary, malt background; and wood-bark bitterness in its big, lingering finish. A hop "pocket" is the long sack in which pressed hops are packed. It looks like a boxer's punchbag: this beer hops and hits with the best.

Region of origin
Mid Atlantic US

Style American Ale

Alcohol content 6.0abv (4.8w)

Ideal serving temperature
10°C (50°F)

YOUNG'S SPECIAL LONDON ALE

London beer-maker John Young is married to a Belgian, and once made a superbly hoppy English ale for her local brewery near Liège. The product survives in Britain as Young's Special London Ale, though it can today be easier to find in the US. The drily aniseedy, spicy English hop is extremely powerful, but cushioned by a malty creaminess and a lively, fruity, yeast character, with suggestions of banana and orange zest. The fruitiness softens the final, peppery punch of hop bitterness.

Region of origin
London, England, UK

Style English Ale/ Strong Pale Ale

Alcohol content
6.4abv (5.1w)

Ideal serving temperature
10°C (50°F)

POPERINGS HOMMEL BIER

Near to the World War I graves around Ypres, the town of Poperinge is the centre of a small hop-growing region. Although the word hop is used in Flemish, there is also a local variation, *hommel*, from the Latin *humulus*. This beer, highlighting the local hops, is made by the Van Eecke brewery, in nearby Watou. It is a bottle-conditioned ale, with a rose-like floweriness, honeyish notes, orange-zest hop flavours, and a late spicy, cumin-seed dryness.

Region of origin
Province of West Flanders, Belgium

Style
Strong Golden Ale

Alcohol content
7.5abv (6.0w)

Ideal serving temperature
10°C (50°F)

BUSH 7%

The name facilitates a word-play in French. "Bush Sept" sounds like "Bouchette", implying a mini-mouthful. Only in Belgium could a beer of such a potency (actually, 7.5 per cent) be deemed small, but this is a lower strength version of the regular 12 per cent Bush. The drop, in gravity as well as alcohol, diminishes the maltiness, and allows the yeasty floweriness (violets?) to come through, and the minty, peppery hop. There is also added coriander.

Region of origin Province of Hainaut, Belgium

Style Strong Golden Ale, with spice

Alcohol content 7.5abv (6.0w)

Ideal serving temperature
10°C (50°F)

Fit for a king
Bush 7% is sold as Clovis in the US, after the King of the Franks.

BEER AND FOOD

CHOOSE THE RIGHT BEER AND YOU HAVE ONE of the world's great aperitifs – more effective in this respect than even dry sherry or champagne. Although wine is a fine accompaniment to good food, many dishes are better illuminated by beer: starters such as asparagus, scrambled eggs, smoked salmon, or sausages; spicy dishes and many ethnic foods; and chocolate desserts are just a few examples. Some of these are among the items that might be found in a *brasserie* – French for brewery, but the term has come to mean a certain style of restaurant. The first brasseries were taverns attached to breweries. Their eclectic approach to dining is mirrored in contemporary lunch spots from London to New York and Tokyo to Sydney. Small wonder that interesting selections of beer are increasingly nudging the wine list.

BEERS WITH APPETIZERS & SOUPS

IN THEIR HOME COUNTRIES, several styles of beer are typically served with specific snacks or appetizers, often featuring cheese and sausages. This is notably true of two similar-sounding traditional styles: Germany's *Gose*, associated with Leipzig and nearby towns; and Belgium's *gueuze*, from the Brussels area. *Gueuze* suits such appetizers in the way that fino sherry goes with tapas, and is often served with steamed mussels or with the classic Belgian dish, *waterzooi*, a soup or stew made with fish or chicken.

Savoury start
The more acidic styles of beer are in perfect harmony with the sharper, more lactic, cheeses.

CANTILLON GRAND CRU BRUOCSELLA 1900

The Cantillon family arrived in Brussels, "Bruocsella" in Latin, in 1900. This beer has a toasty aroma and start, with suggestions of Madeira, drying into fino sherry, fresh apple, and lemon notes. It is the perfect accompaniment to sharp cheeses and the lighter soups.

Region of origin
Province of Flemish Brabant, Belgium

Style *Lambic*

Alcohol content 5.0abv (4.0w)

Ideal serving temperature 13°C (55°F)

GEUZE BOON

The shorter spelling of *g(u)euze* is preferred by Frank Boon. Being a *gueuze*, this beer is a blend of young and old *lambics* that ferments in the bottle, causing carbonation and sparkle. It has great finesse: a soft floweriness of aroma (rhubarb?); a momentary gingery sweetness; and a long, dry, oaky, faintly salty finish.

Region of origin
Province of Flemish Brabant, Belgium

Style *Gueuze-lambic*

Alcohol content 6.0abv (4.8w)

Ideal serving temperature 13°C (55°F)

GUEUZE GIRARDIN

From an aristocrat's estate brewery, now run by the Girardin family. The brewery, at St Ulriks-Kapelle in the traditional region of *gueuze* production, grows its own wheat, and still has a mill that grinds the grain between stones. Gueuze Girardin is elegant, lean, and complex; perfumy and dry; with unfolding flavours of cedar, hay, and acacia honey.

Region of origin
Province of Flemish Brabant, Belgium

Style *Gueuze-lambic*

Alcohol content 5.0abv (4.0w)

Ideal serving temperature 13°C (55°F)

EVERY MAN'S DREAM WOMAN

THE LADY DEPICTED in the postcard (*right*) is a good prospect for marriage. She has a curvaceous figure, comprising bottles of *Gose* beer, her legs are glasses of the brew, and she is rich, judging from the bag of money in her hand. *Gose* beer features, too, in her punning name: Fräulein Gosella. With her, "anything goes", according to her motto, *Gosi van Duti*, a play on the title of Mozart's famous opera. Male fantasies have changed little over the ages. The card is from a whimsical collection of eight published between 1896 and 1905. The artist is unknown.

GOSE OHNE BEDENKEN

The German town of Goslar, Lower Saxony, is said to have given its name to this style of wheat beer, which was once popular in Leipzig. The style has recently been revived by Goslar's Ohne Bedenken taproom and beer garden. *Gose* is a wheat beer, lightly spiced with salt. It is flavoured with coriander and emerges with a citric palate. Traditionally, it is matured in flasks with a narrow neck, so that the yeasty head acts as a bung to foster carbonation.

Gose is often served with Camembert cheese, sometimes with a digestif of *Allasch*, an almond-flavoured version of the caraway liqueur *Kümmel*.

Region of origin Lower Saxony, Germany

Style *Gose*

Alcohol content 4.8abv (3.8w)

Ideal serving temperature 9–10°C (48–50°F)

Belgian broth
This chicken waterzooi *includes cream, shallots, leeks, carrots, and bay leaves among its ingredients.*

LINDEMANS CUVÉE RENÉ

Because *lambic* beers can be quite dry, many of the more popular labels are sweetened. While this is true of the regular Lindemans products, Cuvée René is in a drier style. Owner René Lindemans gives his name to a delicious, full-flavoured beer: foamy and lively, with the nuttiness of a Palo Cortado sherry. It has a soft, rounded sweetness; then a long, drying finish.

Region of origin
Province of Flemish Brabant, Belgium

Style *Gueuze-lambic*

Alcohol content 5.0abv (4.0w)

Ideal serving temperature 13°C (55°F)

BEERS WITH SHELLFISH

THEY MAY BE FAMOUSLY sociable beers, but in Britain and Ireland, porters and stouts have been partners to oysters since Georgian and Victorian times. The very combination speaks of Charles Dickens dining in a chop-house. In those days, porter was the everyday beer, and oysters were so plentiful as to be a cheap snack, often served free in pubs. Oysters can be very expensive today, but dry porters and stouts are also delicious accompaniments to mussels, clams, scallops, and crustaceans.

GUINNESS EXTRA STOUT

The world's most famous dry stout. Irish country brewer Arthur Guinness set up in Dublin in 1759. Among the many versions of Guinness, the 7.5abv (6.0w) Foreign Extra Stout has a particular tangy acidity. The bottled Extra Stout sold in Ireland best highlights the oaky-seeming dryness that is distinctive to Guinness.

Region of origin Republic of Ireland

Style Dry Stout

Alcohol content 4.2abv (3.4w)

Ideal serving temperature 10–13°C (50–55°F)

Pepper and salt
The peppery intensity of the drier porters and stouts counterpoints the sea-salt flavours in a mixed shellfish platter.

BEAMISH IRISH STOUT

A stout from what was once Cork city's "Protestant" brewery, founded in 1792, on a site even older than that. As its competitors have become sweeter, in deference to "modern" tastes, Beamish Irish Stout has seemed by comparison drier. The beer is toasty, with buttery, creamy, and peppery notes in a late, lingering, dry finish.

Region of origin Republic of Ireland

Style Dry Stout

Alcohol content 4.3abv (3.4w)

Ideal serving temperature 10–13°C (50–55°F)

MURPHY'S IRISH STOUT

From what was Cork city's "Roman Catholic" brewery, named after a well consecrated to Our Lady. Murphy's brewery was established in the 1850s, and has on occasion produced an oyster stout, made by adding a broth of the shellfish to the brew-kettle. Its regular stout is mildly dry, with soda-bread graininess and a hint of peat.

Region of origin Republic of Ireland

Style Dry Stout

Alcohol content 4.0abv (3.2w)

Ideal serving temperature 10–13°C (50–55°F)

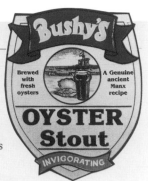

AN APHRODISIAC IN THE GLASS

Diners and drinkers who feel that only champagne is a fit accompaniment to oysters might enjoy a Black Velvet. This classic cocktail blends champagne half and half with stout. Guinness Foreign Extra Stout (*left*) is used for its power and strength. Its richness requires a very dry champagne as a balance. Some brewpubs offer stout with a whole oyster in the glass, as a "mixed drink". A handful of stouts are actually produced with oysters as an ingredient, imparting a salty, gamey note. Murphy's has on occasion made an example. So has Bushy's, on the Isle of Man.

MARSTON'S OYSTER STOUT

This bottle-conditioned beer, from the famous Marston's brewery of Burton, England, does not contain oysters, but is offered by the brewery as a perfect accompaniment to the shellfish. Among the stouts shown here, it has the fruitiest of flavours, with hints of onion or shallot, and a firm, woody, cedary background.

Region of origin Trent Valley, England, UK

Style Dry Stout

Alcohol content 4.5abv (3.6w)

Ideal serving temperature 10–13°C (50–55°F)

ELGOOD'S FLAG PORTER

Taste the sea in this porter? It is fermented in part with a yeast recovered from bottles of porter found in an 1825 shipwreck on the bed of the English Channel. Flag Porter is produced by the Elgood's brewery of Wisbech, Cambridgeshire. The beer is lively and fruity, with woody, sooty, leathery, oily notes. It is perfect with the gamier varieties of oyster.

Region of origin Eastern England, UK

Style Porter/Dry Stout

Alcohol content 5.0abv (4.0w)

Ideal serving temperature 10–13°C (50–55°F)

COOPERS BEST EXTRA STOUT

Most Australian breweries have a stout in their range, and the famously traditionalist Coopers, of Adelaide, makes a most characterful example. Coopers Stout is woody, oily, and strong, but very drinkable with the oysters and mussels of the South Seas.

Region of origin South Australia

Style Dry Stout

Alcohol content 6.8abv (5.4w)

Ideal serving temperature 10–13°C (50–55°F)

BEERS WITH SALADS & STARTERS

BROWN ALES MAY SOUND MACHO but, being the nuttiest of all beers, they provide an appetizing accompaniment to a crunchy salad: crudités, palm hearts, or artichokes, for example. Not the sweeter type of brown ale, but the style typically made in the US and around Newcastle, England. In Europe, seasonal asparagus is often served with beer as a starter or light meal. Hoppy, fruity, strong amber or golden ales in the Belgian style provide a tastier complement than the blander lagers often offered.

Classic combo
In season, asparagus is celebrated in continental Europe, often with scrambled eggs or ham (or both).

UNIBROUE MAUDITE

Inspired by the Belgian strong golden ale, Duvel, this bottle-conditioned brew has a name meaning "damned" in French. The beer is made by Unibroue of Chambly, near Montreal. Maudite is a darkish interpretation of the style; fruity, spiced (orange peels, coriander, pepper?), and dry. It is a flavoursome beer to accompany crudités or roasted peppers.

Region of origin
Province of Quebec, Canada

Style Strong, spiced Belgian-style Ale

Alcohol content 8.0abv (6.4w)

Ideal serving temperature
10–13°C (50–55°F)

ROMAN SLOEBER

Sloeber, "joker" in Flemish, is made at Mater, near Oudenaarde, Belgium. This complex beer pours with a massive head; is aromatic, smooth, firm, and malty; with a dry, orange-zest finish, in part deriving from Styrian hops. Big enough in flavour to accompany a robust antipasto.

Region of origin
Province of East Flanders, Belgium

Style Strong Belgian Ale

Alcohol content 7.5abv (6.0w)

Ideal serving temperature 10°C (50°F)

CELIS GRAND CRU

When revivalist Pierre Celis set up the Hoegaarden brewery in Belgium, he made a strong golden ale, with orange peel and coriander, hints of peach and honeydew melon, flowery and dryish, called Grand Cru. When he moved to Austin, Texas, he created the similar Celis Grand Cru. The beer is spicy (sorrel?), but less delicate, more robust, grassier, and more lemony. Either is delicious with asparagus.

Region of origin Southwest US

Style Strong, spiced Belgian-style Ale

Alcohol content 8.8abv (7.0w)

Ideal serving temperature
7–10°C (45–50°F)

BROWN BEERS AND BIG BRIDGES

SALADS ARE LESS TRADITIONAL than leek puddings (with beef suet) in Newcastle, a northern English city associated in the public mind with coal and heavy engineering even in the post-industrial era. Its Newcastle Brown Ale has over the years used variations on a label design featuring the city's symbol, the "New" Tyne Bridge. Big bridges are a muscular symbol for beers thought by consumers to be full-bodied and strong. While Newcastle Brown Ale actually has a modest alcohol content (*see below*), its transatlantic counterpart, Brooklyn Brown Ale, is bigger in both its nutty, hoppy flavours and its alcohol content (5.5abv, 4.4w).

NEWCASTLE BROWN ALE

The most popular bottled ale in Britain, with a macho image and a great student following. This paler, drier style of brown ale was launched in 1927 by a head-brewer whose not-quite appropriate name was Colonel Porter. If it is not excessively chilled or gulped, this beer has a surprisingly nutty, flowery, winey delicacy.

Region of origin
Northeast England, UK

Style Brown Ale

Alcohol content 4.7abv (3.8w)

Ideal serving temperature 10°C (50°F)

BOSTON BEER WORKS BEANTOWN NUT BROWN ALE

The baked bean, prepared with pork and molasses (sometimes beer), is a traditional Boston dish; hence the name Beantown. This beer might go well with such a simple dish. It starts sweetish, with a cherryish fruitiness, but dries out, with hints of cedar and cinnamon. It has a smooth texture, lightish body, and satisfying flavours.

Region of origin Northeast US

Style Brown Ale

Alcohol content 5.5abv (4.4w)

Ideal serving temperature 10°C (50°F)

Walnut brown
The nuttiest of beers deserves a salad to match. This one features walnuts, crispy bacon, and mixed leaves.

VAUX DOUBLE MAXIM

Newcastle's immediate neighbour is Sunderland, a city that makes marine engines and beer, and has a fiercely rival soccer team. Sunderland's Vaux brewery has a brown ale called Double Maxim, named after a type of machine-gun used by Captain Ernest Vaux in the Boer War. The beer is quite pale, but assertive in its nutty, fruity, dry flavours.

Region of origin
Northeast England, UK

Style Brown Ale

Alcohol content 4.7abv (3.8w)

Ideal serving temperature 10°C (50°F)

BEERS WITH PICKLES & PÂTÉS

EVEN WINE LOVERS TEND TO recommend beer with dishes such as pickled herrings, but which brew? Beers with a long maturation in unlined wood gain varying degrees of sourness, and sometimes iron-like flavours, that can stand up to vinegary dishes. Some of the best are made near North Sea ports with a tradition of serving herring. Another starter course might be a terrine or pâté, or foie gras. Grape lovers might suggest a rich wine, classically a Sauterne. Beer lovers could try an extra-strong Bock.

Sweet treat
The custom of serving sweetish dessert wines with goose liver shocks the uninitiated. With this game pâté, try a similarly luscious strong beer.

SAM ADAMS TRIPLE BOCK

Sauterne wines are said to be scented, intensely sweet and oily, and to become Madeira-like with time. This beer has a minty aroma, chocolatey maple and vanilla flavours, and all the fatness and power of such a wine. Californian "champagne" yeast ferments the brew, which might better be described as barley wine; it is not a Bock. Try it with a rich, nutty terrine.

Region of origin Northeast US

Style Barley Wine

Alcohol content 17.5abv (14.0w)

Ideal serving temperature 9°C (48°F)

EKU 28

"The strongest beer in the world", boasts the slogan on the glass. The initials EKU indicate in German the First United Brewery of Kulmbach, a great brewing town. The figure 28 represents the beer's original gravity (in German degrees), not alcohol. Such a high gravity makes it syrupy, but its complex, tangerine flavours are surprisingly fresh and clean.

Region of origin
Franconia, Bavaria, Germany

Style Double Bock/Strong Lager

Alcohol content 11.0abv (8.8w)

Ideal serving temperature 9°C (48°F)

SCHLOSS EGGENBERG URBOCK 23°

The castle brewery of Eggenberg, at Vorchdorf, between Salzburg and Linz, Austria, dates from the 1100s. Its Urbock has an original gravity of 23; a bubbly, well-retained head for such a strong beer; a shimmering gold colour; a light creaminess, with hints of lemon, pink grapefruit, melon rind, and perhaps cinnamon.

Region of origin Austria

Style Double Bock

Alcohol content 9.6abv (7.7w)

Ideal serving temperature 9°C (48°F)

BEER FROM THE WOOD

IN A WINERY, OR BRANDY distillery, the ceiling-high wooden tuns at Rodenbach might not seem exceptional. In a brewery, they are far more unusual. No brewery has remotely as many as Rodenbach, where they fill 11 halls. The vessels vary in size from 100 to 600 hectolitres (2,200 to 13,200 gallons), and the veterans among them are more than 150 years old. They are made from oak, variously from the Vosges region of France and from Poland. They are maintained by a team of three permanent coopers, who work with numbered staves, hoops, reeds, and beeswax. Other breweries in the region have wooden tuns, but far fewer of them, to make the local reddish-brown, sourish ale.

RODENBACH GRAND CRU

While Rodenbach's regular ale is a blend of old and young beers, Grand Cru is a straight bottling of the long-matured, stronger component. It is aged in vast oak tuns for over two years. The result is a lively bouquet, with vanilla oakiness that extends into the palate; passion-fruit flavours; and a clean, sharp acidity.

Region of origin Province of West Flanders, Belgium

Style Flemish Red Ale

Alcohol content 6.0abv (4.8w)

Ideal serving temperature 10°C (50°F)

GREENE KING STRONG SUFFOLK

Many English breweries once aged beer in wooden tuns, blending old with new for equilibrium: Greene King is the last to do so. The beer's key ingredient is a strong ale matured in wooden tuns for one to five years. The beer is less sour than those made across the North Sea, but iron-tasting, sappy, peppery, and winey.

Region of origin Eastern England, UK

Style Old Ale

Alcohol content 6.0abv (4.8w)

Ideal serving temperature
10–13°C (50–55°F)

Acid attack
It takes a very iron-tasting, acidic beer to cope with vinegary dishes. The three on the left are perky enough to deal even with pickled herrings.

DOCK STREET GRAND CRU

The Dock Street brewery and pub, in Philadelphia, intends this occasional brew as a tribute to Rodenbach. It succeeds magnificently, though it is less aggressively acidic. Dock Street Grand Cru is aged in wine casks; has firm, plant-stem flavours, with a hint of sloe gin; and a cherryish, sweet-and-sour finish.

Region of origin Northeast US

Style Flemish Red Ale

Alcohol content 7.5abv (6.0w)

Ideal serving temperature 10°C (50°F)

BEERS WITH SAUSAGES

THE GERMANS DO MORE with beer than serve it with sausages (and often sauerkraut), but no combination of brew and food crosses borders so readily: from the brasseries of Paris to the Germanic restaurants of Chicago to the brewpubs of Tokyo. The lightest of German-style brews does the trick with a veal *Weisswurst*, but anything meatier, coarser, smokier, or more spicy deserves a bigger brew: a Munich-style dark lager, with its subtle combination of malty richness and burnt flavours.

Baroque dazzler
The interior of the monastery at Weltenburg has won the admiration of such distant critics as present-day artist Jeff Koons.

WELTENBURGER KLOSTER BAROCK-DUNKEL

The oldest "cloister" (monastery) brewery in the world, tracing its history to the 600s and its brewing to at least 1050. Weltenburg is on the Danube, near Kelheim. The Barock Dunkel ("Dark") beer is light-bodied and smooth, with a very good malt character suggesting cookies or crackers. It has a toasty, smoky, roast-malt finish.

Region of origin
Upper Bavaria, Germany

Style Munich Dark Lager

Alcohol content 4.5 abv (3.6w)

Ideal serving temperature 9°C (48°F)

STAROPRAMEN DARK

This Czech brewery, a classic of the mid-1800s, is close to the centre of Prague. Staropramen ("Old Spring"), is widely known for its golden lager, but it also produces a dark version. This is light-bodied, but soft and smooth; with malty licorice or aniseed notes; and an underlying flowery hop.

Region of origin
Bohemia, Czech Republic

Style Dark Lager

Alcohol content 4.6 abv (3.7w)

Ideal serving temperature 9°C (48°F)

The best Wurst
The plate includes Bierschinken (ham sausage with pistachios). Green beans are typically served with beer in Japan.

HACKER-PSCHORR ALT MUNICH DARK

Composer Richard Strauss was the son of Josephine Pschorr, and he dedicated his most famous work, *Der Rosenkavalier,* to the brewing family that financed him. Hacker-Pschorr's "Old" Munich Dark has a creamy aroma and flavour, with notes of cinnamon, and a lightly syrupy body. Try it with veal sausages.

Region of origin
Munich, Upper Bavaria, Germany

Style Munich Dark Lager

Alcohol content 5.2 abv (4.2w)

Ideal serving temperature 9°C (48°F)

PASTRAMI ON RYE

DARK LAGERS ARE NOT the only beers to go well with sausages and *charcuterie*. The spicier type of sausage, with pepper or fennel, or pastrami, may find a better balance with the minty, bittersweet character of rye beers. Historically, the Russians and Finns used rye in country brews. In 1988, a brewery owned by the German aristocratic family Thurn und Taxis launched a beer made with rye and wheat. This is called Roggen ("rye") Bier. It is grainy, slightly smoky, fruity, and spicy, with a bittersweet rye character (5.0abv; 4.0w). An ale called Rye Beer is made by King & Barnes, of Horsham, England. This is packed with oily, grainy, spicy flavours (5.5abv; 4.4w).

SILLAMÄE MÜNCHEN

Made in Estonia, in a micro-brewery established in 1993, in the Russian-speaking town of Sillamäe, once a defence industry centre. München is German for Munich. The beer is a remarkable dark lager, so assertive and strong that it could equally be regarded as a Bock. It has a rich, malty aroma; a surprisingly light and smooth drinkability; and a clean, toasted-nut dryness; developing to a juicy, warming finish.

Region of origin Estonia

Style Munich Dark Lager/Bock

Alcohol content 6.5abv (5.2w)

Ideal serving temperature 9°C (48°F)

TABERNASH MUNICH

There is a town of Tabernash, west of Denver, Colorado, named after a Native American Ute chief. It gives its name to a Denver micro-brewery specializing in German beers. One of its founders studied brewing at Weihenstephan, near Munich. Tabernash Munich is very smooth, with some fruity maltiness and toastiness. It has a well-rounded finish, with a hint of hoppy dryness.

Region of origin Southwest US

Style Munich Dark Lager

Alcohol content 4.9abv (3.9w)

Ideal serving temperature 9°C (48°F)

SAGRES DARK

Outside of the main beer countries, many breweries have in their ranges both golden and dark lagers. This is true in Spain and Portugal, for example. Portugal's two biggest breweries both have dark lagers. The brew shown here, Sagres, has a toffeeish, caramel character, while its rival Cristal Preta has more of a fresh-bread, malt-loaf note.

Region of origin Portugal

Style Munich Dark Lager

Alcohol content 4.3abv (3.4w)

Ideal serving temperature 9°C (48°F)

BEERS WITH SMOKED FOODS

ONCE, OPEN FIRES WERE widely used to dry the grains in the malting process. Another technique that imparts a smoky flavour is the use of hot rocks to heat the brew, dating from the days of wooden vessels, which could not be set over a flame.

Beers made by these two methods, including some newcomers, are an unusually appropriate accompaniment to smoked foods or even barbecues.

CHRISTIAN MERZ SPEZIAL RAUCHBIER

The heartland of smoked beer is the German region of Franconia, and especially the town of Bamberg. Beechwood from nearby forests is used to smoke the malt. This bottled *Märzen*-style *Rauchbier* ("Smoked Beer") has a treacle-toffee aroma; a clean, dry, creamy palate; and a fragrant smokiness in the big finish. It is perfect with Bavarian smoked ham.

Region of origin
Franconia, Bavaria, Germany

Style *Bamberger Rauchbier*

Alcohol content 5.3abv (4.2w)

Ideal serving temperature 9°C (48°F)

AECHT SCHLENKERLA RAUCHBIER

The Schlenkerla tavern, dating from 1678, is an institution in Bamberg, and is noted for regional food. Schlenkerla is the most widely known *Rauchbier*. It has a firm beechwood smokiness, from its aroma through its palate to a clean, dry, long finish.

Region of origin
Franconia, Bavaria, Germany

Style *Bamberger Rauchbier*

Alcohol content 4.8abv (3.8w)

Ideal serving temperature 9°C (48°F)

Holy protection
This plaque, outside Christian Merz, warns that Heinrich the Holy protects the brewery.

Taking the pulse
Smoked foods such as this ham are typical of Bavaria. It is shown here with pease pudding, similar to the German Erbseneintopf.

BOSCOS FLAMING STONE

An American pioneer of stone beer. The Boscos brewery and restaurant was opened in 1992, in the suburbs of Memphis, Tennessee. Colorado granite is heated in a wood-burning pizza oven in the making of Boscos Flaming Stone, which is based on a wheat ale. It has a pale colour; a toffeeish, nutty palate; and a very late development of a refreshing, slightly sour, smoky dryness.

Region of origin South US

Style Stone Beer

Alcohol content 4.8abv (3.8w)

Ideal serving temperature 10°C (50°F)

WHERE THERE'S SMOKE THERE'S BEER

IN THE MORE WIDELY produced type of smoked beer, the grains are smoked during the malting process. Among this type, the long-established style is the *Rauchbier* of Bamberg. This is a smoked lager. Newer variations, such as the Smoked Porter (*left* and *below*) of Alaska, and the Smoked Ale of Japan, are made in the same way but with top-fermenting yeasts. Stone beers, such as Rauchenfelser Steinbier, apply the smoky, more caramelly, character by heating rocks (*right*) and placing them in the brew-kettle. This method was revived by the enterprising Bavarian brewer Gerd Borges in 1982.

RAUCHENFELSER STEINBIER

This wheat beer was first made near Coburg and is now produced near Augsburg. Hot rocks are craned into the brew-kettle to bring it to the boil. The brew caramelizes around the rock. The caramel later induces a secondary fermentation in the lagering vessel. The resultant beer is light, with a clean, softly burnt, toffeeish finish.

Region of origin
Upper Bavaria, Germany

Style Stone Beer

Alcohol content 4.9abv (3.9w)

Ideal serving temperature 9°C (48°F)

ALASKAN BREWING CO. SMOKED PORTER

A pioneer of smoked beers in the New World. The brewery, in Juneau, state capital of Alaska, is opposite a fish smokery. The malt is smoked there, over alder. This big, complex, unfiltered brew was launched in 1988. It starts oily, with hints of bitter chocolate and burnt fruits, then explodes with smokiness.

Region of origin Pacific Northwest US

Style Smoked Porter

Alcohol content 5.9abv (4.7w)

Ideal serving temperature
10–13°C (50–55°F)

MOKU MOKU SMOKED ALE

This Japanese brewery's name is a reference to the use of smoke screens by Ninja warriors. The ale is earthy and oily, with a late surge of fresh smoke. Scottish peated malt is used. The brewery is part of a co-operative that smokes ham and makes sausages; these can be tasted, with the beer, in its restaurant in Ayama, near Ueno.

Region of origin Honshu, Japan

Style Smoked Ale

Alcohol content 5.0abv (4.0w)

Ideal serving temperature
10–13°C (50–55°F)

BEERS WITH FISH

LIKE THE CHARDONNAYS of the wine world, the more delicate examples of Pilsners and other dry, clean-tasting, golden lagers are perfect with fish. The comparison is apt in more than just the colour: their fresh, flowery palates highlight the flavours of fish without dominating them. In Bavaria, a local Pilsner might accompany pike-perch caught near Munich; in the Rhineland, Bitburger Pils is often served with local trout; and in the Czech Republic, Budweiser Budvar is offered with carp from the Bohemian lakes.

BITBURGER PREMIUM PILS

This brewery, in Bitburg, claims to be the first in Germany to have used the term Pilsner, in 1883. Its Pils is very light, soft, and clean. It appears at first to be accented towards a clean, sweet maltiness, but finishes with a firm, elegantly rounded, hoppy dryness. Some of the malting barley is grown locally; so is a proportion of the hops. In early days, the lagering cellars were cooled with ice from the Eifel lakes.

Region of origin
Rhineland-Palatinate, Germany

Style Pilsner

Alcohol content 4.6abv (3.7w)

Ideal serving temperature 9°C (48°F)

CRISTAL ALKEN

Names such as "crystal" have been used by several brewers of golden lager. This particularly fine example is brewed in the town of Alken, and was the first Belgian Pilsner, launched in 1928. True to its name, Cristal tastes at first almost like spring water; then comes a clean hit of hoppy dryness; and a refreshing, crisp finish.

Region of origin
Province of Limburg, Belgium

Style Pilsner

Alcohol content 4.8abv (3.8w)

Ideal serving temperature 9°C (48°F)

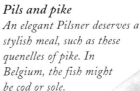

Pils and pike
An elegant Pilsner deserves a stylish meal, such as these quenelles of pike. In Belgium, the fish might be cod or sole.

HALLERTAU AUER PILS

Germany's best-known hop-growing region is Hallertau, just to the north of Munich. In the heart of the region, in the village of Au, there has been a castle brewery since 1590. Today, it produces a lively, bubbly Pilsner with a fresh aroma; textured malt character; and well-combined flavours of leafy, dry hop. A hop-country classic.

Region of origin
Upper Bavaria, Germany

Style Pilsner

Alcohol content 4.9abv (3.9w)

Ideal serving temperature 9°C (48°F)

BIRTH OF THE BUDWEISER BEERS

THE CITY OF BUDWEIS, in Bohemia, was known for beer as early as the 1200s. One of its two present breweries, Budweiser Bürgerbräu, founded in 1795, was among the pioneers of golden lager, in 1853. The second of today's breweries, Budweiser Budvar (*right*), dates from 1895. By then, Adolphus Busch, a German-American, was in Missouri already marketing a beer inspired by the city of Budweis.

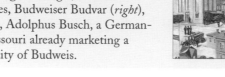

BUDWEISER BUDVAR

In the Czech Republic, only beers from Pilsen may use the name of that city. While they emphasize the hop, their rivals from Budweis (in Czech, České Budějovice) lean towards a light maltiness. The beers from both the Czech Budweiser breweries are bigger in malt and hop (but not alcohol) than their US namesake.

Region of origin
Bohemia, Czech Republic

Style Golden Lager

Alcohol content 5.0abv (4.0w)

Ideal serving temperature 9°C (48°F)

FREEDOM PILSENER

British brewers generally regard lager as a style to be made cheaply for drinkers who respond less to flavour than advertising. One of the few British lagers made with any seriousness is Freedom Pilsener, from a London micro-brewery established in 1995. This beer has been variable, but at its best has a smooth maltiness and late dry, flowery hoppiness.

Region of origin London, England, UK

Style Pilsner

Alcohol content 5.0abv (4.0w)

Ideal serving temperature 9°C (48°F)

CREEMORE SPRINGS PREMIUM LAGER

Creemore Springs is a ski resort north of Toronto. In 1987, its 1890s' hardware store was turned into a micro-brewery. Its Premium Lager has a deliciously fresh malt aroma; a smooth, clean, textured, lightly nutty body; and an elegant balance of hoppy dryness.

Region of origin
Province of Ontario, Canada

Style Golden Lager/Pilsner

Alcohol content 5.0abv (4.0w)

Ideal serving temperature 9°C (48°F)

BEERS WITH CHICKEN

THE BRONZE, SWEETISH, MALTY, medium-strong lagers traditionally brewed in March (in German, *März*) and matured through the summer, are typically served at the *Oktoberfest* with spit-roast chicken. The combination works because the reddish, Vienna-style malts employed have a spicy sweetness that goes well with meats such as chicken. In recent years, many beers in this style have become lighter in character. Today, some of the richest *Märzen* and *Oktoberfest* lagers are made in the US.

CATAMOUNT OCTOBERFEST

This Vermont micro-brewery makes a beautifully balanced *Oktoberfest*, lighter in colour and body than many American examples, but fuller than most German ones. The beer is made with Munich malt, Northern Brewer and Tettnang hops, and a lager yeast.

It has a fresh, appetizing aroma; starts very smooth and dryish; has a long development of flavours, with a spicy maltiness; and finishes crisply.

Region of origin Northeast US

Style *Märzen-Oktoberfest* Lager

Alcohol content 5.3abv (4.2w)

Ideal serving temperature 9°C (48°F)

OLD DOMINION BREWING CO. OCTOBERFEST

The *Oktoberfest* produced by this lager-oriented micro near Washington DC has a malty smoothness, firmness, and nuttiness. Among the malts used is a Vienna type, and its contribution is evident in the beer's "barley sugar" sweetness and spiciness. The overall malt character is very good. There is a late, herbal, fragrant hop balance.

Region of origin Mid Atlantic US

Style *Märzen-Oktoberfest* Lager

Alcohol content 5.8abv (4.6w)

Ideal serving temperature 9°C (48°F)

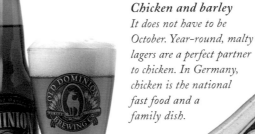

Chicken and barley
It does not have to be October. Year-round, malty lagers are a perfect partner to chicken. In Germany, chicken is the national fast food and a family dish.

PENN OKTOBERFEST

Some of America's finest German-style lagers are made by the Penn brewery and pub, established in the old German quarter of Pittsburgh, Pennsylvania, in 1986. Its wide range of classic styles includes this *Oktoberfest*. The beer has a deliciously fresh malt aroma; a smooth, lightly sweet, appetizingly nutty palate; and a spicily dry hop finish.

Region of origin Northeast US

Style *Märzen-Oktoberfest* Lager

Alcohol content 5.8abv (4.6w)

Ideal serving temperature 9°C (48°F)

Pulling for Variety

Once, the bars of the US boasted tap handles announcing only familiar names such as Budweiser, Miller, and Coors. Today, more demanding beer lovers flock to the inelegantly-named "multi-tap" bars and restaurants. As each new micro-brewery seeks to attract attention, tap handles can become elaborate, inventive, and witty in their design, but a forest of them can also be confusing. The tap handle on the right is a model of simplicity and clarity, perhaps because the Gordon Biersch beers are most readily found in their own brewery-restaurants, where they do not have to fight the clamour of competition.

Gordon Biersch Märzen

Some of the best beer-friendly food in the US is found in the small chain of brewery-restaurants founded in Palo Alto, California, in 1988 by Dan Gordon and the restaurateur, Dean Biersch. Gordon is a brewing graduate of Weihenstephan, Bavaria.

Their *Märzen* has a bronze-red colour; a light but smooth body; a spicy, fruity, malt character; and a dry, whiskyish finish.

Region of origin California, US

Style *Märzen-Oktoberfest* Lager

Alcohol content 5.8abv (4.6w)

Ideal serving temperature 9°C (48°F)

Independence Franklinfest

In Philadelphia in 1776, Benjamin Franklin helped draft America's Declaration of Independence. The Independence brewery was founded there 219 years later. Franklinfest lager has a depth of malt aroma and spicy flavour; is light and smooth; with a clean, sweet finish.

Region of origin Northeast US

Style *Märzen-Oktoberfest* Lager

Alcohol content 5.5abv (4.4w)

Ideal serving temperature 9°C (48°F)

Thomas Kemper Oktoberfest

Among new-generation American breweries, Thomas Kemper was an early lager producer, in 1984. The Kemper beers now share a pub and brewery in Seattle with Pyramid. This beer forms a rocky head; has a peachy aroma; a nutty malt character, becoming grainy then creamy; and a late balance of flowery hop dryness.

Region of origin Pacific Northwest US

Style *Märzen-Oktoberfest* Lager

Alcohol content 5.6abv (4.5w)

Ideal serving temperature 9°C (48°F)

BEERS WITH PIZZA

To Americans, pizza and beer (usually a very ordinary, "regular" lager) is by far the best known combination of food and brew. It is a transatlantic marriage: the tomatoes, originally from the Americas, may have been introduced by Neapolitan mariners to the oregano, basil, and flat bread of Italy. Beer being "liquid bread", the marriage works. It is happiest if the doughiness of the pizza base and the flavours of the topping are matched by a lager or ale with the spiciness and chewiness of a succulent amber malt.

MORETTI LA ROSSA

While pizza originates in south Italy, the country's most characterful beers come from the north. Moretti has its origins in Udine, Friuli, northeast of Venice. Its La Rossa almost has the aroma of straight-from-the-oven pizza dough; a fresh, sweetish, lively, smooth malt character; finishing with a spicy dryness. The definitive pizza beer, were it not so deceptively strong.

Region of origin Northern Italy

Style Vienna Lager/*Maibock*

Alcohol content 7.2abv (5.8w)

Ideal serving temperature 9°C (48°F)

MOHRENBRÄU SCHLUCK

One of the Three Wise Men was said to have been a Moor, and the Moor's Head is a common name for an inn. Mohrenbräu, in Dornbirn, Austria, makes a soft, smooth, light, balanced, rounded, Vienna-style beer, under the name Schluck (implying a quick drink).

Region of origin Rhine Valley, Austria

Style Vienna Lager

Alcohol content 5.2abv (4.2w)

Ideal serving temperature 9°C (48°F)

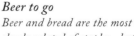

Beer to go
Beer and bread are the most closely related of staples...but a brew with malty sweetness and spiciness is needed to stand up to pizza toppings.

RICKARD'S RED

Signed by E.H. Rickard, of the Capilano Brewing Company, of Barrie, Ontario, and Vancouver, British Columbia. The locations of the brewery sites betray the fact that this is a confection of the Canadian national brewer, Molson. Rickard's Red is light in body and flavour, with a pleasantly sweet, caramelly maltiness in the middle. An easily drinkable beer to enjoy with pizza.

Region of origin
Province of Ontario, Canada

Style Red Beer/Vienna Lager

Alcohol content 5.2abv (4.2w)

Ideal serving temperature 9°C (48°F)

FOR THE GOOD OF THE CITIZENS

THE GANG-BUSTER in the 1950s' TV series and 1980s' movie, *The Untouchables*, Eliot Ness (*right*) was the grandly-titled "Director of Public Safety" in Cleveland, Ohio. The city's Great Lakes brewery, known for making local allusions in the names of several of its beers, honours him with The Eliot Ness (*below*). Great Lakes' Burning River Pale Ale recalls the day the polluted local waterway caught fire. Cleveland has become a much smarter, livelier city since then. A great contribution to this revival was made by Great Lakes; its beers are a source of civic pride.

GREAT LAKES BREWING CO. THE ELIOT NESS

Cleveland's Great Lakes brewery and pub, proud of its bullet-holes from the gang-busting days of Eliot Ness, gives his name to their serious Vienna-style lager. It is rich, creamy, and malty in aroma and palate, with a late balance of whiskyish oakiness and acidity. A big beer to go with a Chicago-style deep-pan pizza or focaccia bread.

Region of origin Midwest US

Style Vienna Lager

Alcohol content 5.6abv (4.5w)

Ideal serving temperature 9°C (48°F)

CHELSEA SUNSET RED

This pub and brewery is in the Chelsea district of Manhattan, New York. Specialities include brick-oven pizzas and this reddish, malty, spicy ale. Sunset Red marries a clean, very smooth, chewy, nutty, crystal-malt character with toasty and fruity-ale notes. It is quite dry for the style. Perhaps one for the grilled vegetable and tomato pizza.

Region of origin Northeast US

Style Red Ale

Alcohol content 5.0abv (4.0w)

Ideal serving temperature 10°C (50°F)

LAKEFRONT RIVERWEST STEIN BEER

Milwaukee, with its several rivers that flow into Lake Michigan, was once infamous for watery beers. Today, it has big-tasting beers from little breweries, such as Lakefront. Riverwest Stein Beer is a superb lager, with a lovely balance of bigness and drinkability; anise-like malt flavours; and a crisp finish.

Region of origin Midwest US

Style Vienna Lager

Alcohol content 5.9abv (4.7w)

Ideal serving temperature 9°C (48°F)

BEERS WITH CHEESE

SOME TRAPPIST MONASTERIES in Belgium make both beer and cheese. Abbeys of other orders have these products made for them. The beers are strong ales, some of which develop a port-like character during maturation. Several of the cheeses are typically semi-soft and mild (*see facing page*), though flavoured variations, some with beer added, and cheddar types can also be found. The biggest, fruitiest abbey beers are even better with tasty blue cheeses such as Stilton and Roquefort. Some of the abbeys also make bread.

LEFFE RADIEUSE

Notre-Dame de Leffe is a Norbertine abbey in Belgium. It has not brewed beer since the French Revolution, but in the 1950s the abbot licensed a local brewer to make Leffe beer. It is now made by Interbrew, at Leuven. Radieuse, meaning halo, is the biggest in flavour. The beer has a cherry-like fruitiness, a portish texture, and a faintly roasty, cinnamon-tinged finish.

Region of origin
Province of Namur, Belgium

Style Abbey

Alcohol content 8.2abv (6.6w)

Ideal serving temperature
15–18°C (59–64°F)

Hop snack
Not only the cheese but also the finest crackers have an affinity with beer: these Bath Oliver biscuits contain hops.

WESTVLETEREN 8° (BLUE CAP)

Belgium's smallest Trappist monastery is St Sixtus, at Westvleteren, near the war graves around Ypres. Its beers have no labels, but are identified on the crown. The blue-capped 8° is the fruitiest, with hints of plum wine or brandy, and an almondy dryness in the finish. Try it with a sweet, soft cheese.

Region of origin
Province of West Flanders, Belgium

Style Abbey (Authentic Trappist)

Alcohol content 8.0abv (6.4w)

Ideal serving temperature
15–18°C (59–64°F)

LA TRAPPE QUADRUPEL

This beer is made at the Schaapskooi brewery of the Koningshoeven Trappist monastery, near Tilburg, in The Netherlands. The strongest of its beers, Quadrupel, is very long, smooth, oily, syrupy, and fruity; with a dry, warming, coriander-like finish.

Region of origin Province of North Brabant, The Netherlands

Style Abbey (Authentic Trappist)

Alcohol content 10.0abv (8.0w)

Ideal serving temperature
10–14°C (50–57°F)

SMOOTH AND SAVOURY

CHIMAY IS ONE of several Belgian abbeys that make cheese. Its principal cheese (*right*) is in the classic style known as Trappist. Made from cow's milk, it has a slightly lactic aroma; a velvet-smooth texture, which melts in the mouth; and an appetizingly savoury, very mild flavour. The style was first made by Trappists at the monastery of Port-du-Salut, at Entrammes, in Normandy, France, after the Napoleonic period. The monks later sold the brand-name Port Salut to a commercial dairy.

CHIMAY GRANDE RÉSERVE

The port-like Grande Réserve is made by the Trappist monastery of Notre-Dame, near Chimay, south Belgium. The port flavours develop if the beer is laid down for five years or more. This lively, rich ale has a medium-sweet middle, with suggestions of thyme, pepper, sandalwood, and nutmeg in the finish. It is a complex classic, and a delight with Roquefort cheese.

Region of origin
Province of Hainaut, Belgium

Style Abbey (Authentic Trappist)

Alcohol content 9.0abv (7.1w)

Ideal serving temperature
15–18°C (59–64°F)

BUDELS CAPUCIJN

The Dutch town of Budel once had a Capuchin monastery, but this beer honouring the order was launched by the local brewery in the 1980s. The beer is very lively, and has a fresh, hoppy aroma; a lightly syrupy palate; dessert-apple sweetness; and rooty, woody dryness in the finish.

Region of origin Province of North Brabant, The Netherlands

Style Abbey

Alcohol content 6.5abv (5.2w)

Ideal serving temperature 10°C (50°F)

ECHIGO LAND BRAUEREI ABBEY-STYLE TRIPEL

Many "abbey-style" beers have been made in the New World in recent years, most of them in the US. This example is from the Japanese Echigo brewery, at Makimachi in the Niigata prefecture. Tripel has an aroma of raspberries; a suggestion of morello cherries in its oily palate; and an intense almondy dryness in the finish.

Region of origin Honshu, Japan

Style Abbey

Alcohol content 9.0abv (7.2w)

Ideal serving temperature
10–14°C (50–57°F)

BEERS WITH FRUITY DESSERTS

THE IDEA OF BEER WITH DESSERTS may surprise, but it can work beautifully. Try a raspberry or cherry beer with a fruit tart, pie, or pudding. While the sharpest, driest fruit beers are best as a party-greeting or aperitif, more rounded ones can highlight the flavours of desserts containing similar ingredients. Apart from the beers suggested here, "white" Belgian wheat beers accompany orangey dishes well; their German counterparts are good with apple desserts; and a *Dunkelweizen* is a delight with banana dishes.

Two bites...
The cherry is the most traditional fruit flavouring used in beer. It is also widely used in desserts. These tartlets are half of a marriage made in heaven.

RODENBACH ALEXANDER

For years, Belgium's Rodenbach brewery fretted that some consumers, finding its regular beer just too tart, "spoiled" it by adding grenadine syrup. Finally, the brewery realized the value of making a sweetened version. The background of its oak-aged Grand Cru brings a "live yoghurt" tartness and an iron-like, passion fruit balance to the clean, sweet, syrupy, cherry character. It is both sharp and sweet.

Region of origin
Province of West Flanders, Belgium

Style Flemish Red, with fruit essence

Alcohol content 6.0abv (4.8w)

Ideal serving temperature 12°C (53°F)

LINDEMANS FRAMBOISE

A raspberry beer based on the *lambic* of this Belgian farmhouse brewery. It has the typically seed-like, stemmy, woody, tobaccoish fragrance of real raspberries. The flavour begins flowery, then becomes very sweet, suggesting a heavy hand with the fruit juice. In the finish, the sherryish acidity and tartness of the *lambic* emerges as a late, surprising balance.

Region of origin
Province of Flemish Brabant, Belgium

Style *Framboise/Frambozen-lambic*

Alcohol content 2.5abv (2.0w)

Ideal serving temperature 9–10°C (48–50°F)

DE TROCH
CHAPEAU PÊCHE

The farmhouse brewery De Troch makes crisp *gueuze-lambic* beers in the Belgian village of Wambeek. It also has a sweeter range, Chapeau. This peach beer is very sweet indeed, but has the "fresh apple" flavours of *lambic* beers, and a dry, "fino sherry" finish.

Region of origin
Province of Flemish Brabant, Belgium

Style Peach *Lambic*

Alcohol content 3.0abv (2.4w)

Ideal serving temperature
9–10°C (48–50°F)

NEW WORLD WINNER

DEBORAH AND DAN CAREY (*left*) and their Belgian-style Cherry Beer have twice in succession won the prize for the world's best speciality brew. The awards were made at a contest judged by brewers from all over the world, in Britain's brewing capital, the town of Burton. The Careys typify the enthusiasm and creativity being brought to the world of beer by young American brewers. Other products from their New Glarus brewery, near Madison, Wisconsin, include a *Weissbier*, a Bock, and an *Oktoberfest* lager.

NEW GLARUS WISCONSIN CHERRY BEER

Cherries grown around Brussels, Wisconsin, are used in this award-winning brew, which also uses wheat, barley-malt, and yeasts from Belgium. The beer has almondy, cherry-stone aromas; sweet, fresh-fruit flavours; a textured maltiness; and notes of iron and tart acidity in the finish.

Region of origin Midwest US

Style Belgian-style Cherry Beer

Alcohol content 5.0abv (4.0w)

Ideal serving temperature 9–10°C (48–50°F)

HUYGHE NINKEBERRY

Ninke is not a fruit, but a child's name. The beer, made near Ghent, Belgium, is in the Florisgaarden range of fruit-flavoured, "white" wheat brews. It is most obviously flavoured with peach, but also apricot and mango. It is syrupy but refreshing, with a spicy, minty balance.

Region of origin
Province of East Flanders, Belgium

Style
Belgian Wheat Beer, with fruit essences

Alcohol content 3.0abv (2.4w)

Ideal serving temperature
9–10°C (48–50°F)

Sweet treat
An eclectic beer such as Ninkeberry (left) *would suit the treat below: banana fritters with lime-and-caramel syrup.*

McAUSLAN RASPBERRY ALE/BIÈRE À LA FRAMBOISE

This fruit beer has a genuine raspberry colour and aroma, but a less obviously raspberryish flavour, even though real fruit (purée) is used. There is even a hint of blackberries (which are not used). Because it is based on an ale, it lacks the tartness of *lambic* fruit beers.

Region of origin
Province of Quebec, Canada

Style Raspberry Ale

Alcohol content 5.0abv (4.0w)

Ideal serving temperature
9–10°C (48–50°F)

BEERS WITH CREAMY DESSERTS

THE USE OF ONLY a tiny proportion of oatmeal in the brewing gives beer a delicious creaminess of both texture and flavour. The type of brew in which oatmeal is most often used is stout. Here, the creaminess is married with the typically coffeeish, chocolatey, toasty flavours of the style. A stout clearly labelled as containing oatmeal can be the perfect accompaniment to a creamy dessert. The style has its origins in the fashion for "nutritious" beers in Britain after World War II.

Move over, Marsala
Oatmeal stouts are not only accompaniments but also ingredients of dishes like zabaglione, in place of the more usual Moscato or Marsala wines.

SAMUEL SMITH OATMEAL STOUT

The fashion of using oatmeal in stout waned in the 1960s and vanished in the 1970s, but was revived in the 1980s by Samuel Smith's, in the brewing village of Tadcaster. This brew has a fresh, flowery, oloroso sherry aroma; a clean, sweet creaminess; and a silky dryness in the finish.

Region of origin	Northern England, UK
Style	Oatmeal Stout
Alcohol content	5.0abv (4.0w)
Ideal serving temperature	13°C (55°F)

MACLAY OAT MALT STOUT

Oatmeal stouts are usually made with rolled oats, but Maclay uses the malted version to give a fuller, sweeter character. Its stout has a malted-milk aroma, a well-rounded palate, and a light body. It finishes with a buttery, toasty dryness. It is delicious with the Scottish dessert Atholl Brose, which contains cream, honey, and whisky.

Region of origin	Central Scotland, UK
Style	Oat Malt Stout
Alcohol content	4.5abv (3.6w)
Ideal serving temperature	13°C (55°F)

MIDDLESEX BREWING CO. OATMEAL STOUT

The Middlesex Brewing Company, established in 1992, is in the former hop-growing town of Wilmington, Massachusetts. Its Oatmeal Stout has a particularly solid ebony colour and a dark head. It has the aroma of cinnamon-dusted cappuccino and a firm, smooth, long, coffee-chocolate palate with a good, balancing dryness.

Region of origin	Northeast US
Style	Oatmeal Stout
Alcohol content	4.2abv (3.4w)
Ideal serving temperature	13°C (55°F)

...AND WITH HONEY CAKE

Honey has long been used as an addition to beer. Because honey is very fermentable, much of its obvious flavour quickly vanishes, but some traces always remain. In addition, the interaction of yeast and honey creates new, flowery, creamy flavours. Honey beers are made in several countries, especially Belgium and the US, but the two brews shown on the left are both from England. The notably flowery Enville Ale (4.5abv, 3.6w) is made on the estate of the Earls of Stamford, near Stourbridge. Vaux, of Sunderland, produces the sweeter, more overtly honeyish-tasting Waggle Dance (5.0abv, 4.0w).

BOSTON BEER WORKS BUCKEYE OATMEAL STOUT

Among the Boston Beer Works' very assertive beers is this full-bodied, rich, oily, oatmeal-tasting, marshmallow-like, sweetish stout. In its rotating range of 30 or 40 products, the Beer Works has brewed a wide selection of porter and stout variations. These have included a creamy, peppery Imperial Stout; and a Cherry Stout with semi-sweet and milk chocolate, for Valentine's Day.

Region of origin Northeast US

Style Oatmeal Stout

Alcohol content 5.5abv (4.4w)

Ideal serving temperature 13°C (55°F)

ADLER BRAU OATMEAL STOUT

Adler, of Appleton, Wisconsin, grew out of a German-American lager tradition, but today also makes British styles such as this oatmeal stout. It is medium-sweet, with a rooty, gingery, fruity aroma; a firm, smooth, creamy palate; and a "toasted cookie" finish.

Region of origin Midwest US

Style Oatmeal Stout

Alcohol content 4.9abv (3.9w)

Ideal serving temperature 13°C (55°F)

Kiss Kahlúa goodbye?
Tiramisu means "pick me up", so it should contain alcohol. It can be infused with stout instead of the more usual Kahlúa.

OASIS ZOSER STOUT

With its ancient Egyptian theme, this respected brewery and pub in Boulder, Colorado, names its oatmeal stout after the mythical gatekeeper to heaven. The beer, which has an almost tar-like appearance and a very dense head, has a fragrant, perfumy, bitter-chocolate aroma and palate; a firm body; and a smoky finish reminiscent of a smooth Scotch malt whisky.

Region of origin Southwest US

Style Oatmeal Stout

Alcohol content 5.0abv (4.0w)

Ideal serving temperature 13°C (55°F)

BEERS WITH CHOCOLATE & COFFEE

IT IS HARD TO FIND a dessert wine robust enough to accompany the powerful flavours of chocolate mousses, puddings, or cakes, but many stouts are perfect for the job. The stout chosen must be big, rich, and not too dry. In many stouts, the dark malts used mirror the flavours of chocolate. This alone can create a powerful illusion of chocolate flavours. In recent years, some brewers have begun to add actual chocolate or coffee to speciality stouts – creating the perfect beer for this purpose.

BROOKLYN BLACK CHOCOLATE STOUT

This outstanding strong stout, from the Brooklyn Brewery, New York, was launched in 1994. It achieves an astonishingly chocolatey taste from malt alone. It is rich, spicy, textured, and fruity. To drink it is like eating the Viennese classic, Sacher Torte.

Region of origin Northeast US

Style Chocolate/Imperial Stout

Alcohol content 8.3abv (6.6w)

Ideal serving temperature 13°C (55°F)

Classic cake
Sacher Torte, the famous Viennese chocolate cake with apricot preserve, finds an echo in the flavours of some fruity "chocolate" stouts, especially the one from Brooklyn.

YOUNG'S DOUBLE CHOCOLATE STOUT

The first stout to be made with added chocolate – both bars and essence – introduced by Young's, of London, in 1997. It is silky smooth and textured, with a lively complexity. The aromas and flavours begin with faint hints of ginger, becoming fudgy and creamy, then balancing this sweetness with a round, bitter-chocolate finish.

Region of origin London, England, UK

Style Chocolate Stout

Alcohol content 5.0abv (4.0w)

Ideal serving temperature 13°C (55°F)

MCMULLEN'S CHOCOLATE STOUT

A lighter-bodied example that nonetheless has a very good dark chocolate character, especially when served at room temperature. This beer also has raisiny, sherryish notes: the flavours of a chocolatey trifle or Italian panettone cake. It was introduced by the English country brewery McMullen's, of Hertford, in 1997, initially for the US market.

Region of origin Southern England, UK

Style Chocolate Stout

Alcohol content 5.0abv (4.0w)

Ideal serving temperature 13°C (55°F)

PERFECTION IN PRALINES

Gouden Carolus ("Golden Charles") is a strong (7.5–8.2abv, 6.0–6.6w), dark ale from the city of Mechelen, Belgium. It is named after Holy Roman Emperor Charles V. The beer's toffeeish, orangey flavours go well with petit fours or chocolates. The sweetmeats shown here are made by Pâtisserie Christian Meyer, of Strasbourg, France. The marzipan "hop flowers" have a curiously authentic perfume (they are aromatized with hop oil). The "mugs" are flavoured with beer; the pralines with powdered malt. Beer seems to be an inspiration to Pâtisseur Christian...perhaps because his premises are opposite a famous beer café, The Twelve Apostles.

CEYLON LION STOUT

Several tropical countries have rich, strong stouts. Perhaps the tastiest is this one, from Ceylon Breweries, of Sri Lanka. Lion Stout is bottle-conditioned, and has big, pruny, mocha aromas and flavours; developing an intense bitter-chocolate finish. In Sri Lanka, it is sometimes laced with the local *arrack*, a spirit made from coconuts.

Region of origin Sri Lanka

Style Strong Tropical Stout

Alcohol content 7.5abv (6.0w)

Ideal serving temperature 13°C (55°F)

PYRAMID ESPRESSO STOUT

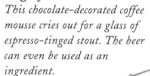

In espresso-loving Washington State, the Pyramid brewery produces a stout with the local flavour. The espresso character is achieved by the use of dark malts and highly roasted barley. These seem to mimic one of the fruitier varieties of coffee-bean. The beer has coffee-like flavours, right through to a long, dry finish.

Region of origin Pacific Northwest US

Style Coffee Stout

Alcohol content 5.6abv (4.5w)

Ideal serving temperature 13°C (55°F)

Mighty mousse
This chocolate-decorated coffee mousse cries out for a glass of espresso-tinged stout. The beer can even be used as an ingredient.

RED HOOK DOUBLE BLACK STOUT

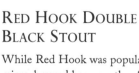

While Red Hook was popularizing micro-brewed beer, another Seattle company, Starbucks, was leading the espresso movement. Both companies were the idea of Seattle entrepreneur Gordon Bowker. His two notions are married in this Red Hook beer flavoured with Starbucks coffee. It has a smooth, nutty middle, and a rounded espresso bitterness in the finish.

Region of origin Pacific Northwest US

Style Coffee Stout

Alcohol content 6.9–7.0abv (5.5–5.6w)

Ideal serving temperature 13°C (55°F)

COOKING WITH BEER

BEER WAS FIRST MADE FOR its nutritional value, and it is central to the world of food and drink. Like wine, it also adds a sensuous element to the kitchen. Beers that accompany foods well are often also a useful addition to the dish itself, whether as a braising liquid or marinade; an ingredient in a vinaigrette, soup, or sauce; a yeasty raising agent in a batter, bread, or cake; or a flavour in a dessert. The possibilities extend far beyond the commonly suggested beer batters and Belgian beef stews. As with wine, there are no hard-and-fast rules. The recipes that follow are simply ways of having more fun with beer and exploring its diversity.

BEERS FOR VINAIGRETTES

VINEGAR ORIGINATED FROM SOUR WINE, but is now more often brewed from malt, like a sour beer. Before refrigerators, beer that had gone sour at the brewery was sometimes sold as malt vinegar. Some breweries today deliberately make such a product, or offer beer-flavoured condiments. There is, therefore, every logic in using sour styles of beer as an alternative or complement to vinegar.

BEERS TO TRY

The classic oil-and-vinegar dressing is given a new twist by the addition of beer. The most obvious beers to use are the *Berliner Weisse* type (*pages 82–83*). Bürgerbräu's example is insufficiently acidic, but examples in this style from Kindl or Schultheiss will do the trick.

In Belgium, the *lambic* family of beers offers many possibilities. Straight, unblended *lambic* is normally available only on draught, though Cantillon has a bottled version, Bruocsella 1900 (*page 140*). The tarter examples of *gueuze* or fruit *lambics* can substitute for raspberry vinegar, as in the recipe below.

The sweet-and-sour "red" ales of Flanders, such as Rodenbach (*page 94*), especially in its Grand Cru version, can also substitute for vinegars. In this instance, distinct acetic characteristics and malty notes emerge.

CANTILLON KRIEK LAMBIC

Although it is well balanced, this is the tartest-tasting cherry beer, and therefore the most suitable for a fruity vinaigrette. It is based on a very traditional *lambic* (*page 75*), with a distinctly lemony note. There is no lemon added, but this character develops during fermentation. There are also cherry-skin notes; a fresh fruitiness that also hints at raspberry; plenty of intensity; a powerful, oily, zesty aroma; and an attractive cerise colour. Cantillon's Rosé de Gambrinus would make a good raspberry vinaigrette.

Region of origin
Province of Flemish
Brabant, Belgium

Style Fruit *Lambic*

Alcohol content
5.0abv (4.0w)

Ideal serving temperature
13°C (55°F)

ENDIVE SALAD WITH A KRIEK VINAIGRETTE

Both the *kriek* cherry and Belgian endive are especially associated with Schaarbeek, a neighbourhood of Brussels. The endive is the whitish-green bud of the chicory root. Its bitter, earthy, yet delicate flavour adds sophistication to a simple salad.

Ingredients

The vinaigrette:
2 tsp Dijon mustard
1 tsp sugar
½ tsp salt
170 ml (6 fl. oz) olive oil
1 clove garlic, crushed
Juice from ¼ lemon
150 ml (5 fl. oz) kriek lambic

The salad:
Freshly ground pepper, to taste
6 heads endive
6 black olives, stoned
3 radishes, sliced
Chopped chives
1 poached egg
Fried croutons

1 Pour the *kriek lambic* beer into the oil. Olive oil must be used: a lighter oil, such as sunflower, will not mix with the beer.

LIQUID COLOUR
Only a hint of the very attractive cerise colour of the kriek *lambic, but all of the flavours, will be evident in the finished vinaigrette.*

2 Add the Dijon mustard, sugar, salt, lemon juice, and garlic. A German mustard, or any other creamy mustard, can be substituted, but a grainy mustard should be avoided. Blend well with a fork, then strain out the garlic flesh (it is very strong, and will overpower the other flavours). Season with freshly ground pepper (black or white) to taste.

3 Cut the ends off the endive, wash, dry, and then arrange the leaves on a flat plate. Poach an egg. (To make a perfect poached egg, add a teaspoon of vinegar to the water. Swirl the boiling water round with a spoon, then drop in the egg. The water will wrap the white round the yoke.)

4 Scatter the olives, fried croutons, and sliced radishes on top of the endive, place the poached egg in the centre, sprinkle with chives, then dress the salad with the kriek vinaigrette.

SEASONAL SIMILARITY
With its poached egg centrepiece, this endive salad is similar to the Flemish dish of hop shoots typically offered in March.

BEERS FOR MARINADES

THE ACIDITY IN BEERS CAN TENDERIZE MEATS and other raw materials in cooking. Acids are created by fermentation, but they are also derived from hops, which also contribute piney elements similar to the flavours in some balsamic vinegars. If a relatively vinegary marinade is required, try the types of beer suggested on page 176. To tenderize red meats, an English ale might be more suitable, but look for one with some acidity.

BEERS TO TRY

Ales such as Adnams' Extra, Bateman's XXXB, Marston's Pedigree, Timothy Taylor's Landlord, and McMullen's Castle Pale Ale, from England, all have enough acidity to work as a marinade. So do St-Ambroise Pale Ale, from Canada, and US ales such as Oliver's or BridgePort ESB. Very hoppy ales, especially some IPAs, might be just too bitter for long contact with meat. A malty *Helles*, *Oktoberfest*, or *Maibock* will impart both sweetness and lightly herbal hop flavours to pork, a meat that can easily seem dry. While the beer will tenderize the meat, this action can also be drying – so also use some beer in a sauce. In the recipe below, a beer marinade is used partially to "cook" a salmon, and to impart a smoky flavour. Any smoked beer would make an interesting contribution, but Alaskan Smoked Porter is especially apposite. The malts in this beer are dried over alder, in a smokery whose normal function is to prepare Alaskan salmon.

VINTAGE BREWS

ALASKAN SMOKED PORTER (*page 151*) is one of the few beers to be vintage dated. It is unfiltered, and will develop with age. Although it is not hugely strong, it has enough residual sugar, and sufficiently complex flavours, to round out. It has at least some living yeast still working in the bottle. When young, it is explosively sooty, with tinges of bitter chocolate and burnt fruits. This is not a beer to lay down for long periods, but a bottle of one or two years old might work better in a marinade than a fresh example. With most beers, exactly the opposite would be the case.

SALMON IN SMOKED PORTER

Caribous, king crab, and – especially – salmon are the indigenous foods of Alaska. According to American food historian Waverley Root, the most traditional method of cooking salmon in Alaska was to sandwich the fish between planks of alder and set them over glowing embers.

BOTTLE-SMOKED SALMON
Marinading salmon in alder-smoked porter imparts flavours associated with the traditional method of cooking salmon in Alaska.

Ingredients

1.8–2.3 kg (4–5 lb) whole salmon, gutted and cleaned	2 lemons, sliced
	6 large red onions, sliced
1.4 litres (2½ pints) smoked porter	To dress:
	2 cucumbers, as thinly sliced as possible
Few sprigs fresh dill	
Few sprigs fresh tarragon	3 lemons, as thinly sliced as possible

1 Line a large baking tray with foil. Allow sufficient overlap on each side of the baking tray to form a rolled-back "pocket", which will prevent the marinade from spilling. Lay the sliced red onions, sliced lemons, and sprigs of fresh tarragon in the baking tray. Place the salmon on top, and cover with the sprigs of fresh dill. Pour the smoked porter over the salmon, and leave to marinade for at least one hour.

2 Preheat the oven to gas mark 6 (200°C/ 400°F). Place another large piece of foil under the baking tray. Wrap it fairly loosely around, and seal it at the top. Place the baking tray on the top shelf of the oven, and bake for 30 minutes.

3 Remove the baking tray from the oven. Carefully place the salmon on a suitable plate. Peel off the skin, which should come away easily in your fingers. To dress the salmon, cover it in overlapping slices of thinly sliced cucumber, with occasional rows of thinly sliced lemon.

A BIG FISH

"Beer-smoked" salmon makes a wonderful dish for a summer party...or perhaps served with bagels and cream-cheese for a Sunday brunch. A more European treatment might use crème fraiche and perhaps rye bread.

BEERS FOR SOUPS

THE COMBINATION OF MALTY SWEETNESS and texture with grassy, herbal hop flavours, and sometimes yeasty tastes, makes beer an excellent base for soups. Malty, sweetish lagers are employed in soups based on barley or other grains, such as sweetcorn, or on shellfish such as crab, clams, or oysters. Lactic-tasting beers such as a *Berliner Weisse* or a *lambic* can even be employed in chilled fruit soups.

BEERS TO TRY

For chilled fruit soups, use a Kindl or Schultheiss Weisse, or a Cantillon or Boon Kriek, or a US brew such as the New Belgium or New Glarus cherry beers. An earthy, yeasty ale such as Orval Trappist makes a wonderful onion soup. Orval's own cookbook proposes a "Brewer's Soup", marrying the beer with beef stock, egg yolks, bread, chicory essence, nutmeg, and parsley. The Shepherd Neame brewery has a soup recipe using its Bishop's Finger strong ale, beef stock, potatoes, and cinnamon-spiced apples. Try a rye brew such as Thurn und Taxis Roggen Bier in a thick bean soup with bacon, pepper, and dill; serve it with rye bread. A French *bière de garde* or an Irish ale would add flavour if plenty of potatoes and salt pork were used in a clam chowder. For a lighter version, try a touch of Samuel Adams' Boston Lager.

RIDLEYS ESX BEST

The Ridley family brewery has its origins in a grain mill in the 1700s at the hamlet of Hartford End, near the town of Great Dunmow, in the more rural part of Essex, England. The present buildings date from 1842. Ridleys' beers are typically fruity, with suggestions of blackberry and apple emerging from the house yeast. As a change from beers called ESB, Triple X, or Four X, Ridleys plays on the county's name with ESX. This beer has very lively flavours: beginning malty, developing lots of fruit, and finishing long and hoppy.

Region of origin
Eastern England, UK

Style Bitter/Pale Ale

Alcohol content
4.3abv (3.4w)

Ideal serving temperature
13°C (55°F)

ONION AND CHEESE SOUP

Variations on this theme are found in several brewing nations. British styles such as bitter or ESB are often suggested in the US, where beer cheese soup is a classic. In this recipe, the cheese is on croutons in an onion soup. The traditional version involves whisking grated cheddar or Wisconsin Jack into a chicken broth, seasoned with thyme. This calls for great care in the cooking: over-heating will damage the flavour, and will also make the cheese become "stringy".

Ingredients

4 large white onions, thinly sliced	Pinch of sugar
2 red onions, thinly sliced	4–8 slices French bread, depending on size, thickly cut
60–90 g (2–3 oz) butter	
1 chicken or beef stock cube	120 g (4 oz) Gruyère cheese, grated
900 ml (1½ pints) pale ale	1 tbsp chopped parsley

SIMMERING, NOT BOILING
Overheating or boiling this soup will excessively concentrate the bitterness of the beer, and will spoil the tasty, savoury flavours.

1 Preheat the oven to gas mark 5 (190°C, 375°F. Melt 40 g (1½ oz) butter in a large, heavy frying pan (ideally, one with a lid). Gently sauté the red and white onions with the sugar until they have collapsed, and are soft and golden brown. Keep stirring to stop them sticking to the frying pan. Dissolve the chicken or beef stock cube in the beer.

2 Stir the dissolved beer stock into the onions, cover the frying pan with a lid, and simmer for about 30 minutes.

3 Generously spread the thick slices of French bread with the remaining butter and bake them in the top of the oven until they are golden brown. Sprinkle the grated Gruyère cheese over the slices of bread, and grill them until the cheese is bubbling. Place the slices of bread in bowls and pour over the soup. Serve with a fine sprinkling of chopped parsley.

LIQUID LUNCH
This thick onion and cheese soup is from the tradition of inexpensive, hearty, filling dishes to go with beer. It makes an excellent snack lunch with ham or tomatoes and French or sourdough bread.

BEERS FOR STEWS

BEER CAN ADD PIQUANCY TO STEWS. This even works in relatively light dishes such as stewed mussels. A dry, hoppy beer like an IPA, if used with a light touch, also performs well with stews based on oily fish such as eel or salmon. Meat stews need something richer, like an Irish ale, French *bière de garde*, *Märzenbier*, or *Bockbier* for pork or chicken, or a French, English, Scottish, or Belgian ale for lamb or beef.

BEERS TO TRY

For fish dishes, the American IPAs are often lighter bodied and drier than the British versions. Anchor Liberty is an American beer in broadly this style that can be found in Europe. As fish is cooked only gently, there should not be excessive reduction. To go with meat, the most full-flavoured Irish ales are McNally's, from Canada, and McGuire's, from Florida. The latter brewery also makes its own malt vinegar as a culinary ingredient. The ales actually made in Ireland are less big, but still tasty. Among the widely available *bières de garde*, Jenlain has the fullness of flavour to be very food-friendly. With lamb, consider using a beer in this style with juniper berries or even a splash of gin. The Celebrator Doppelbock from the Ayinger brewery, near Munich, or that city's Paulaner Salvator, also have plenty of flavour to add to a stew. The same is true of Black Sheep Ale, from England, Caledonian's Flying Scotsman, or Belgium's Cuvée De Koninck.

GRANTED A GIFT

BERT GRANT WAS BORN in Scotland but his family left when he was two. He has spent a lifetime in the hop and brewing businesses, in Canada and the US. When he established his own brewery in 1982, his first product was a Scottish ale, but he soon moved on to an extremely hoppy IPA (*page 135*). Grant was the first small brewer in the US to revive the term IPA. The hoppiness is appropriate not only because of Grant's background in the hop industry, but also because his brewery is in Yakima, the hop capital of Washington State.

MUSSELS IN INDIA PALE ALE

Like most shellfish, mussels lend themselves very well to beer. The slightly salty, seaweedy flavours of mussels are a match for a dry, savoury, and acidic brew. In northern France or Belgium, a *lambic* or *gueuze* is typically used. In Britain, an acidic bitter might be considered; in Ireland a dry stout. American IPAs also have the appropriate qualities, especially in their homelands of Oregon and Washington, northwestern states renowned for shellfish.

Ingredients

1.8 kg (4 lb) mussels, cleaned	3 tbsp chopped flat-leafed parsley
70 g (2½ oz) salted butter	Pinch of salt
1 clove garlic, crushed	Pinch of sugar
2 medium-sized red onions, finely chopped	Freshly ground black pepper
400 ml (14 fl. oz) IPA	French bread, to serve
1 tsp fresh thyme	

GENTLY DOES IT
When pouring the IPA into the pan, gently lift up the mussels with a spoon, allowing the appetizing flavours of the IPA to permeate every shell.

1 Buy the mussels cleaned, if possible, but if cleaning them yourself, scrub and rinse them thoroughly, and pull off any barnacles and "beardy" attachments. The mussels must be closed – never cook open mussels.

2 Melt the butter in a pan and fry the onions and garlic until soft. Add the thyme, 200ml (7 fl. oz) IPA, one third of the parsley, and pepper. Simmer for 10 minutes. Strain, then return to the pan. Add the mussels and the rest of the IPA, and cook until the mussels are open. Discard any mussels that are closed or less than quarter-open. Remove the mussels and keep them warm.

3 Add the rest of the parsley to the liquid in the pan. Reduce just a little, then pour the liquid over the warm mussels. Serve in individual soup bowls, with plenty of French bread to soak up the liquid.

SCOOP AND SERVE
In Belgium, mussels are often eaten straight from the pan in which they are prepared. The shell is used as a spoon, and the cooking liquid is scooped up as a sauce.

USEFUL ADDRESSES

INFORMATION

The Beer Hunter®
News and articles from Michael Jackson, with beer reviews.
www.beerhunter.com

Beer Paradise
In English, French, and Flemish. Consumer-friendly information from the Belgian Confederation of Brewers.
www.beerparadise.be

Bier.de
Consumer-oriented site in English and German. Contains information on retailers.
www.bier.de

Breworld
Principal site covering UK brewing industry and consumer issues. Contains information on retailers.
www.breworld.com

Campaign for Real Ale (CAMRA)
A consumer organization dealing with traditional UK beers. Publisher of the monthly *What's Brewing*, the annual *Good Beer Guide*, and organizers of the Great British Beer Festival.
230 Hatfield Road
St Albans
Hertfordshire
AL1 4LW
tel: 01727 867201
fax: 01727 867670
e-mail: camra@camra.org.uk
internet: www.camra.org.uk

Deutsche Brauerbund on-line
German language site produced by the German brewing industry's professional organization.
www.brauer-bund.de

The Real Beer Page
The principal worldwide web publication for beer lovers. Links to many other sites.
www.realbeer.com

RETAILERS

High-street wine merchant Oddbins has in recent years paid particular attention to speciality beers, but there are growing ranges in supermarkets such as Asda, Morrisons, Safeway, Sainsbury, Tesco, and Waitrose. In London, the department store Selfridges has a good range.
* Indicates a UK mail-order service available.

Cumbria (Kendal)
Beers in Particular
151 Highgate
Kendal
Cumbria
LA9 4EN
tel: 01539 735714

Cumbria (Windermere)
The Masons Arms (also a brewpub)
Strawberry Bank
Cartmel Fell
Grange-over-Sands
Cumbria
LA11 6NW
tel: 015395 68486

Lancashire (Preston)
The Real Ale Shop
47 Lovat Road
PR1 6DQ
tel: 01772 201591

Leicestershire (Leicester)
The Bottle Store *
77 Queens Road
LE2 1TT
tel: 0116 270 7744

Lincolnshire (Grimsby)
Small Beer
199 Grimsby Road
Grimsby
DN35 7HB
tel: 01472 699234

Lincolnshire (Lincoln)
Small Beer
91 Newland Street West
LM 1 1QF
tel: 01522 528628

London
The Beer Shop and Pitfield Brewery *
14 Pitfield Street
N1 6EY
(near Old Street)
tel: 0171 7393701

Norfolk (Norwich)
The Beer Cellar *
31 Norwich Road
Strumpshaw
NR13 4AG
tel: 01603 714884

Yorkshire (Knaresborough)
Beer Ritz *
17 Market Place
HG5 8AL
tel: 0142 386 2850
e-mail: sales@beerparadise.ltd.uk
internet: www.beerparadise.ltd.uk

Yorkshire (Leeds)
Beer Paradise *
Granary Wharf
The Canal Basin
LS1 4BR
tel: 0113 2429572
e-mail/internet: as above

Yorkshire (Sheffield)
The Archer Road Beer Stop *
57 Archer Rd
S8 0JT
tel: 0114 2551356

Barrels & Bottles *
The Wicker Arches
S3 8GZ
tel: 0114 2769666
e-mail: manorh.@aol.com
(International mail order service available)

The Dram Shop
21 Commonside
S10 1GA
tel: 0114 2683117

Yorkshire (Wakefield)
M & D Homebrew
Fernades Brewery
Beerhunters Paradise
The Old Malt House
5 Avison Yard
WF1 1UA
tel: 01924 369547

Yorkshire (York)
York Beer Shop
28 Sandringham Street
(off Fishergate)
YO10 4BA
tel: 01904 647136

SCOTLAND

Aberdeen
Wine Raks (Scotland) Ltd
231 Springfield Road
Aberdeen
AB15 7RJ
tel: 01224 311460
fax: 01224 312186

Edinburgh
Villeneuve Wines
49a Broughton Street
EH1 3RJ
tel: 0131 558 8441
e-mail: wines@villeneuvewines.com

Peckham & Rye
155–159 Bruntsfield Place
EH10 3DG
tel: 0131 229 7054

Glasgow
Peckham & Rye
21 Clarence Drive
G12 9QN
tel: 0141 334 4312

Southwest of Glasgow, on the coast at Fairlie, Ayrshire:-
Octopus at Fence Bay
Fence Foot Farm
Fairlie, Ayrshire.
tel: 01475 568918
fax: 01475 568921
E-mail: fencebay@aol.com

BELGIUM

Stephen D'Arcy of The Campaign for Real Ale (Brussels) produces a highly informative and regularly updated newsletter *A Selective Guide to Belgian Bars*. Contact PO Box 5, Rue des Atrébates, B-1040, Brussels, Belgium.
tel: +32 2 736 72 18 fax: +32 2 296 36 49
e-mail: Stephen.D'Arcy@dg1.cec.be

Drink Market Delépine
13 Rue Eugène Cattoir
Brussels 1050
tel: +32 2 640 45 64
fax: +32 2 640 36 23

NETHERLANDS

De Bierkoning
Paleisstraat 125
1012ZL Amsterdam
tel: +31 20 625 23 36
fax: +31 20 627 06 54

D' Oude Gekroonde Bier en Wijnwinkel
Rosmarijn Steeg 10
1012RP Amsterdam
tel: +31 20 623 77 11
(International mail order service available; tasting room upstairs)

The Beer Shop
Gier Straat 83
2011GC Haarlem
tel: +31 23 531 41 80
fax: +31 23 524 78 68

GERMANY

Haus der 131 Biere
Karlshöhe 27
D-22175 Hamburg
tel: +49 40 640 72 99
fax: +49 40 640 20 71
e-mail: 131biere@bier.de
internet: www.biershop.de
(Offers a beer of the month club and an international mail order service)

Bruno Maruhn
Pfungstädter Straße 174-176
D-64297 Darmstadt-Eberstadt
tel: +49 61 51 5 72 79
fax: +49 61 51 59 54 95
(Mail order service available)

INDEX

ACKNOWLEDGMENTS

Author's Acknowledgments
All the beers in this book were chosen by the author on the basis of past tastings. The brewers were then requested to supply current bottles for re-tasting and photography. The author and publishers would like heartily to thank all of the brewers who supplied beer, especially those whose products for one reason or another did not make the final selection. In the longer term, we hope to produce further editions, in which some of these beers will feature. Many of the glasses were supplied by the brewers but a large number were provided directly by the Rastal company, of Höhr-Grenzhausen, Germany; special thanks to them. For this book and over the years, the following have all offered great help:

Larry Baush, Stephen Beaumont, Eugene Bohensky, Kathleen Boyen, Ian Burgess, Vince Cottone, Tom Dalldorf, Stephen D'Arcy, Erich Dederichs, René Descheirder, Alan Dikty, Sarah and Phil Doersam, Jim Dorsch, Pierre-André Dubois, Drew Ferguson, David Furer, Gary and Libby Gillman, Geoff Griggs, Thomas Halpin, Ainsley Harriot, Erik Hartman, Dr Alfred Haunold of Oregon State University, Bob Henham, Hans J. Henschien, Graham Howard, Miles Jenner, Eric Källgren, Nirbhao Khalsa, Alan Knight, Konishi Brewing, Jim Krecjie, Michiko Kurita, Graham Lees, Lars Lundsten, Rob Maerz, Franz Mather, Peter McAuslan, Ed McNally, Bill Metzger, Steve Middlemiss, Mikko Montonen, Multilines, Father Ronald Murphy of Georgetown University, Professor Doctor Ludwig Narziss of Weihenstephan, Hans Nordlov, Ryouji Oda, Barrie Pepper, Chris Pietruski, Portugalia Wines (UK), Bernard Rotman, John Rowling, Rüdiger Ruoss, Silvano Rusmini, Margarita Sahm, the late Dr Hans Schultze-Berndt, Frau Schultze-Engels, Professor Paul Schwarz of North Dakota State University, Todd Selbert, Conrad Seidl, Willie Simpson, Simpson's Malt, Ritchie Stolarz, Peter Terhune, Unto Tikkanen, Anastasy and Jo Tynan, Mike Urseth, Derek Walsh, De Wolff Cosijns Malt, Sabina Weyerman, Przemyslaw Wisniewski, Kari Ylane...

...and everyone else who has helped me or shared a beer on the road.

Michael Jackson's necktie by Cynthia Soboti.

Bibliography
BOOKS CONSULTED
Additives in Beer Jeffrey Patton (self-published)
On Food and Cooking Harold McGee (Scribners)

FURTHER READING
Michael Jackson's Beer Companion (Running Press/Mitchell Beazley)
Simon and Schuster Pocket Guide to Beer/Michael Jackson's Pocket Beer Book (Mitchell Beazley)
The Great Beers of Belgium Michael Jackson (Running Press/Prion)
Everybody Eats Well in Belgium Ruth Van Waerebeek (Workman)
American Brasserie Rick Tramonto and Gale Gand (Macmillan USA)
Cooking with Beer Lucy Saunders (Time-Life)
Designing Great Beers Ray Daniels (Brewers' Publications)

Publisher's Acknowledgments
Photography: Steve Gorton, Ian O'Leary, Sarah Ashun
Additional photography: Philip Dowell, Neil Fletcher, Dave King, David Murray, Martin Norris, Roger Phillips, Jules Selmes, Matthew Ward.
Thanks to Harveys brewery at Lewes, East Sussex, for kind permission to take photographs.
Home economist: Ricky Turner
Artwork: Ruth Hall 9, 15; Janos Marffy 11
Design assistance: Simon Oon, Fay Singer
Editorial assistance: Edward Bunting
Index: Margaret McCormack

Picture Credits
The publisher would like to thank the following for their kind permission to reproduce their photographs:

a=above; c=centre; b=bottom; l=left; r=right; t=top

AKG London: 52 br, 96 br, 118 br; Bass PLC: 18 tc, 18 c; Bières de Chimay S.A.: 165 tr; Boston Beer Company: 16bl; Brasserie Friart S.A.: 20 bl; Brasserie d'Orval S.A.: 128br; Brouwerij Palm: 56tr; Brouwerij Rodenbach: 94tr, 147 tl; Brouwerij Verhaege: 76tr; Budweiser Budvar: 153 tr; Pierre Celis: 78 tr; Christie's Images: 98 br; Colorphoto Hans Hinz: © Jasper Johns/VAGA, NY and DACS, London 1998, 66 br; Corbis UK Ltd: 162 tr; Antoine Denooze: 130 tr; E.T. Archive: 70 br; Teri Fahrendorf: 132 tr; Charles Finkel: 28 br; Guinness: 18 cr; Robert Harding Picture Library: Adam Woolfitt 58 tr; R. Richardson 32 tr; Heather Ale Ltd: 16 br; Hans Hennebach: 141 tr; Ian Howes: 21br; Illustrated London News Picture Library: 40 tr; Images Colour Library: 70 tr; Michael Jackson: 14 bl, 18 bl, 19 bl, 20 bc, 66tr, 74 tr, 90 tr, 92 br, 94 br, 114tr, 114br, 136 tr, 150tr, 151 tr; Klosterbrauerei Weltenburg GmbH: 148 tl; Hank Kosollek: 167 tl; Franz Mather: 48 br; National Maritime Museum Picture Library: 132 br; Pilsner Urquell: 124 br; © Retrograph Archive Ltd: 46 tr; Royal Horticultural Society, Lindley Library: 78 br; St Peter's Brewery: 108 br; Schlossbrauerei Kaltenberg: 28 tr; Frau Schulze-Engels: 46br; Claus Schunk: 86 br; Staatliches Hofbräuhaus München: 44 tr; Still Moving Picture Company: Doug Corrance 62 tr; Tony Stone Images: John Lawrence 145 tr; Stephen Studd 36 tr; T & R Theakston: 110 br; United Distillers & Vintners: 10; University of Pennsylvania Museum: (negs #B16688 & #B17694) 11 bl; Bethany Versoy: 173tr; Yakima Brewing & Malting Co.: 179tr.